TEAMPOWER

Lessons from America's Top Companies on Putting Teampower to Work

Clay Carr

PRENTICE HALL
Englewood Cliffs, New Jersey 07632

Prentice-Hall International (UK) Limited, *London*
Prentice-Hall of Australia Pty. Limited, *Sydney*
Prentice-Hall Canada, Inc., *Toronto*
Prentice-Hall Hispanoamericana, S.A., *Mexico*
Prentice-Hall of India Private Limited, *New Delhi*
Prentice-Hall of Japan, Inc., *Tokyo*
Simon & Schuster Asia Pte. Ltd., *Singapore*
Editora Prentice-Hall do Brasil, Ltda., *Rio de Janeiro*

© 1992 *by*

PRENTICE-HALL, Inc.

Englewood Cliffs, NJ

10 9 8 7 6 5 4 3 2 1

Library of Congress Cataloging-in-Publication Data

Carr, Clay,
  Teampower : Lessons from America's top companies on putting
teampower to work / by Clay Carr

    p. cm.
  Includes bibliographical references and index.
  ISBN 0-13-892761-8
  1. Work groups. I. title.
HD66.C37   1992
658.4′03—dc20   91-35726
                                                     CIP

ISBN 0-13-892761-8

PRENTICE HALL
Business Information & Publishing Division
Englewood Cliffs, NJ 07632
Simon & Schuster, A Paramount Communications Company

PRINTED IN THE UNITED STATES OF AMERICA

*I affectionately dedicate this book to
Houston Carr (who got the family doctorate) and
Suzanne Fitzgerald (who became the world traveller),
my brother and sister.*

Acknowledgments

I could not have provided the factual and current examples of teampower used in this book without the personal contributions of:

- John Helmsdoerfer, formerly Vice-President for Financial Operations, Litel Telecommunications

- Robert Rose, Manager of Customer Service, the Word-Perfect Corporation

- The "Fixit Four" of GE Superabrasives: Rob Harris, Mike Mowery, Bill Slavens, and Harold Sullivan, and their sponsor, J. R. Widders, Manager of Quality Services

- Norman Burgess, Manager, Operation EXACT, Domtar Corrugated Container Division

- Richard Quillin, Manager, Information Systems Division, Department of Finance & Management, City of Alburquerque, NM, and Mrs. Suzanne Maxwell of Maxwell and Associates

- Steve Jacobs, Manager, Quality Improvement, AT&T American Transtech

- Todd Peterson and Barbara Hershkowitz of New Society Publishers.

My heartfelt thanks to each and every one of you.

I must also acknowledge the invaluable assistance of my agent, Mike Snell, in shaping this and all of my books. I'm grateful to Tom Power, my editor at Prentice Hall, for his suggestions.

I remain indebted to the public libraries of Columbus, Westerville and Worthington, Ohio, and the library of Franklin University. They're a constant reminder to me of just how great an asset the libraries of this country are.

Finally, Tim Peterson of the University of Tulsa School of Management took time in an extraordinarily hectic summer to write the fine foreword. Thanks, Tim.

Foreword

We all know what a team is and can give several examples—a football team, a drill team, or a debate team. Most of us have even played on a team at least once in our lives. For example, I played on my high school football team. I still can remember the exhilaration we felt when it all clicked and we scored. In fact, most of us understand the potency of a successful team effort. However, most of us would be hard pressed to explain how to create and manage a successful team. Yet today that is the challenge being thrust upon American managers.

American businesses are undergoing sweeping changes in an effort to stay competitive in a global marketplace. One of the changes is the creation of self-managing work teams. Organizations such as General Foods, American University, New Society Publishers, and the City of Albuquerque have all redefined their work around the self-managing work team concept. Each of these organizations has had remarkable success with this new work environment. But what practicing managers need more than anecdotes about past successes is a clear set of techniques for implementing self-managing work teams.

I believe Clay Carr's book, *Teampower*, takes a giant step in that direction. Clay provides a clear set of skills that a manager needs to establish and maintain a self-managing work team environment. While this could be another dull management treatise, Clay's writing style keeps it both interesting and on target.

It has been said that "knowledge is power" and that "the value of knowledge increases as it is shared." In his book, Clay has provided both power and value to all managers facing the challenge of self-managing work teams.

Tim O. Peterson, Ph.D.
Professor of Management
University of Tulsa

Introduction ═══════════════

LITEL TELECOMMUNICATIONS DISCOVERS TEAMS _____

Fourteen days to process an order for service! A 40% error rate on service orders! John Helmsdoerfer, Litel Telecommunication's Vice-President for Financial Operations, was frustrated. The just-completed reorganization was supposed to have helped the order processing problem—but it hadn't. Something had to be done! Litel was a small, fast-growing carrier in the highly competitive long-distance business. The firm couldn't stand its current processing time and error rate. But what could it do?

Stop and ask yourself: What would you do? Try to motivate workers to do better? Counsel and discipline the people who made the errors? Set a shorter processing time and insist that the different functions cooperate to achieve it?

John and Litel did none of these. Instead, with the help of Andersen Consulting, they looked carefully at the problem they had. When they charted out the way that orders were processed they found, in John's words, a "serial and snakelike process." Orders came into the mailing and sorting function. From there they moved to a group that screened orders for proper information, then to another group that screened them for credit information. After that, yet another group keyed the orders into the computer system and a final group set the new customers up in the billing system.

Even though handling orders was essentially one process, each group specialized in one small piece of the total pie. Everyone concentrated on their little bit of the action, and no one looked out for the customer. There had to be a better way. There was.

In March of 1989, Litel began to review its order processing in detail. It found orders passing back and forth among groups unnecessarily. Even worse, an order could get into the process, move along for several days, and then have to be sidetracked because it lacked necessary information.

If there was ever a place for teampower, this was it. By July 1, 1989 the separate functions had been reorganized into three teams of five to six workers each. Each team performed the full range of order processing functions for a specific geographic area. Each member of the team was cross-trained in all of its functions. Supervisors became team leaders.

Before, when someone from Cleveland called in to check on an order he might have to talk to three or four different people to get an answer. And the people might be different each time he called. Now, he talked to one team about any problem. And it was always the same team, no matter when he called.

Suddenly, though, there weren't as many problems to talk about. Litel thoroughly trained everyone involved in the process. Individuals both in field sales locations and in corporate headquarters understood the whole process. Orders with missing information didn't slip into the flow; the team caught them right away and got the information before processing began. Dozens of non-value-added tasks—such as logging orders in and making duplicate copies of them—were eliminated.

This sounds good, of course, but what did reorganizing into teams really accomplish for John Helmsdoerfer and Litel Telecommunications? Well, the morale of the team members went up sharply. The people in the field were happier with headquarters. Oh, yes, there were two other benefits, too. By August 1989,

- order processing time dropped form 14 days to *one* day, and
- the error rate dropped from 40% to *less than 5%*.

Did you notice the time period? All this happened in just over 30 days. That's teampower!

Impressive as these figures were, there was more. Another benefit took a little longer to surface. Just before teams were created, Litel was generating $147,000,000 a year in annualized revenues and fighting a constant backlog in order processing. One year after the teams were started, revenues had risen to

$260,000,000 a year on an annualized basis. There were still only three teams, they each still had only five to six members—but they were processing the higher volume of orders quickly and with few errors. And they were doing it *without a backlog.*

That's impressive, isn't it? Litel isn't alone, though. All over the U.S., firms are using teampower to increase their competitiveness, improve their quality, and shorten their cycle times. This book will show you how they do it. More important, it will show you how *you* can do it.

SHOULD YOU READ THIS BOOK? _____

This book is written specifically for managers. If you are a manager or executive at any level, you can profit from it, particularly if

- someone higher up in the organization (perhaps even the CEO) has made it clear he expects managers like yourself to use teams, or

- you would like to try using teams, but you need to know whether they would work for you and how to go about it, or (most important of all)

- you need to improve the quality and productivity of your organization and are looking for an effective way to do it.

You'll derive the greatest benefit from this book if you're a manager at the first or second level. As much as I hate to say it, managers at your level are largely the forgotten players in the teampower game. Typically, higher-level executives decide that the firm needs to use empowered teams. Consultants, internal or external, are called in, and the process gets under way. Managers close to the action often aren't considered or, worst of all, are considered part of the problem rather than the solution.

This doesn't have to be, so I'm writing this specifically for you. If your organization is implementing empowered teams, this book will enable you to get out in front of the parade and stay there. It will give you the tools you need to implement empowered teams in your part of the world—and to do it before someone else tries to impose them on you.

Suppose your organization hasn't committed itself to empowered teams? That doesn't mean you can't use them. They *work*, and you want them to work for you whether higher levels are doing business that way or not. This book will show you how.

Are you a higher-level manager or executive? This paragraph is just for you. Learn from others' mistakes—don't treat your first- and second-level managers as part of the problem. Empowered teams change the jobs of these managers, but there are still challenging and satisfying roles for them to play. Get them on the team from the beginning by making these roles clear to them. This book can help you do just that.

HOW IS THE BOOK DIFFERENT?

The shelves of bookstores and libraries are sagging under the weight of books on teams and teamwork. Some of these books describe how to create teams using something called Socio-Technical Theory. Others explain how to use teams in a Total Quality context. Yet others talk about group dynamics, or team problem-solving methods.

This book mentions all of these, but it isn't about any of them. Instead, it's written specifically for managers who want to find how teampower can benefit them. If you read it, you will learn

- the different kinds of teams, how each works and where each works best, and

- the five key managing functions that must be performed in an organization that uses empowered teams— functions quite different from the traditional functions of supervisors and managers, and

- the skills you need to perform these functions effectively and succeed with empowered teams.

HOW THE BOOK IS ORGANIZED

Chapter 1 explains how and why teampower unlocks the competence and commitment that you and I as managers are looking for.

Chapter 2 will help you decide what kind of teamower will work best in the real world of your organization. It also discusses the eight absolutely necessary characteristics of all successful teams.

Chapter 3 describes the basic types of teams, from quality teams to full self-managing teams.

Chapter 4 describes how a wide variety of organizations have successfully implemented teampower. These aren't the old "war horses" you find in so many books on teams, taken from second- or third-hand accounts. The information on every organization was furnished by the individuals involved. In other words, each account is real, accurate, and up to date.

When you finish the first four chapters, you'll have a good understanding of what teams can accomplish for you. *Chapters 5 through 9* take the next step. They explain the five basic management functions required for effective teampower. These chapters also show you *how to develop the skills you need* to perform these functions.

The last two chapters get down to the nitty-gritty of implementing teampower. *Chapter 10* helps you prepare to empowered teams by describing some of the basic issues you confront when you decide to implement teams.

Finally, *Chapter 11* shows you how to prepare for teams, and how to move from limited self-managing teams to fully self-managing teams to truly entrepreneurial teams.

LET'S GO

I hope I've whetted your appetite. Teampower is exciting and challenging. Done well, it will make your organization significantly more competitive. It will also make life and work in the organization more satisfying. It is one of the true win-win prescriptions for organizational success available today.

Won't you join me as we explore how teampower can make *your* organization more effective?

Table of Contents ════

Chapter 1

The Power
in Teampower

The introduction had an example of what empowered teams can accomplish. Here are a few others:

- Xerox and Harley-Davidson are two of the very few firms that lost significant market share to the Japanese and then actually took it back. Both of them used empowered employees and teampower as a cornerstone of their success.

- In 1971, the Gaines Dog Food plant in Topeka, Kansas was opened, organized around self-managing teams. Since then, for more than 20 years, it has consistently outproduced similar traditional plants by 20% to 30%.

- Procter and Gamble experimented with self-managed teams in their Paper Products Division in the early 70s. When they compared results from these plants with more traditional plants in 1975, the plants based on self-managed teams clearly outproduced the others. From then on, self-managed teams became the standard way of organizing in that division. Now they're spreading throughout the entire corporation.

- Another company that believes in teams is Digital Equipment. Their Enfield, Connecticut plant, built in the early 80s, is organized around 18-person teams. Each person on a team knows how to do all of the 20 or so jobs that the team performs. The results? The teams complete a circuit board in 40% less time than a traditional organization, with half the industry-average amount of scrap.[1]

- Roger Smith called the Saturn plant "the future of GM." This plant radically empowers workers individually and (especially) in teams. Ford led the way with the use of teams in the American automotive industry; the creation of the highly successful Taurus and Sable used teams in a way never before seen in American carmaking companies.

- The new Corning plant in Blacksburg, Virginia is organized around self-managed teams—with only three managers for the 150-person plant. The company thought the plant would lose $2.3 million during the startup period; that kind of loss is normal when a plant is just getting going. Instead, the plant turned a $2 million profit during the first eight months of operation. Wow![2]

As you go through the book, you'll find more detail on these and other companies, large and small, in many different industries, in many different locations. In short, teampower has the potential to work anywhere—*anywhere!*

THE KEYS TO TEAMPOWER

Converting from a traditional organization to a teampower organization takes time and effort. The essence of it, though, is quite simple. As a manager, what you want and need from your workforce is timely, high-quality production at minimum cost. That's what I want, certainly—and this is how I look at it:

You and I get timely, high-quality production at minimum cost when workers are Competent and Committed in support of our (and their) Customers.

That answer raises another question, though. Of course we want competent and committed workers who focus on customer satisfaction—but how do you and I get them? That takes us closer to the heart of this book, which is this:

Workers become Competent and Committed to the extent that their work Challenges them, lets them Control it, and provides them the opportunity to Cooperate with each other.

This still isn't quite enough. At the very core of teampower (and any form of employee empowerment) is one more characteristic: The rest of it only works when everyone is *Self-Managing*. This is the basic skill. With it, almost anything is possible. Without it? Well, if the hill is steep enough you can go sledriding on grass— but it isn't really exciting to most of us. Neither is trying to run a firm based on worker empowerment unless those workers are skilled at self-management.

Here's a simple diagram of these points:

CUSTOMERS
benefit from
COMPETENCE & COMMITMENT
based on
CHALLENGE, CONTROL & COOPERATION
resulting from skillful
SELF-MANAGEMENT

It's impossible to show all of the interrelationships among these factors; each one is closely connected to every other. You won't have any real competence unless the job is challenging and the individual can control his work. You certainly won't have a strong customer focus without commitment. If the work isn't challenging, it's not worth controlling and there won't be any commitment. Cooperation doesn't work unless the individuals cooperating are competent, challenged by the work, and committed to it. Etc., etc. In other words, it's a package deal.

Since self-management is the basis for all of the rest, let's begin by looking at it.

WHERE IT ALL BEGINS: SELF-MANAGEMENT _____

In the summer of 1990, the National Center on Education and the Economy released a farreaching critique of America's technical education system. The Center gathered information for the study by interviewing employers all over the U.S. When asked if they foresaw a problem in getting the skills they needed, only 5% of the employers answered "Yes." More than 80%, though, said that they had difficulty getting workers with "a good work ethic and appropriate social behavior."[3] In other words, firms are having trouble finding workers with both the desire and the skill to become competent, committed workers.

One way to look at this is to say that the quality of our workforce is deteriorating. If you believe that, you're in good company; that's a favorite topic whenever managers get together. There's another approach, though. The MacFletcher Company of Scottsdale, Arizona, has systematically collected statistics over the past decade that show that workers increasingly do not want to be supervised. That doesn't mean that they all have highly developed skills at managing themselves; it does mean that they aren't apt to commit themselves to any organization that doesn't provide them a reasonable opportunity for self-management.

In short, modern American workers are increasingly willing to put out for employers only when they have the opportunity to manage how they will do their jobs. This trend isn't new, but it has been gathering steam for the last decade. Just as managers are discovering the power in employee empowerment, we're confronted with a workforce that wants to exercise this power.

This isn't a simple matter. Firms in many areas are having serious problems finding individuals who are ready to manage themselves. In fact, the Center study emphasizes the basic point that schools aren't equipping workers with the skills they need to perform in a self-managing environment. The study also points out that most noncollege students see little point in getting these skills; they just don't seem to matter once you get to work.

Let me give you an example. In my salad days, I played first the trumpet and then the saxophone in small jazz bands. When I could find the time, I practiced two and three hours a day—everyday. This was a lot of time, but I spent it willingly—because I took great satisfaction in playing expertly.

Suppose, though, that all I was allowed to do when I was on stage was play scales. And not just scales, but only the B-flat scale. Just how "motivated" and "committed" do you think I would have been? Just how often do you suppose I would have practiced two hours or more a day for the joy of playing that one scale over and over?

This is almost exactly the situation we put many of our noncollege-educated workers in. Why should they learn skills, especially self-management skills, when the job they'll get is boring, routine and deeply unsatisfying? What kinds of skills do you need to work on an assembly line, cook Big Macs, or punch data into a computer? And how does doing well in school increase your all-too-poor chances of getting training for a skilled job?

(There's a clear illustration of the last point in a statement from David Merchant, Vice-President of Personnel for the Mazda plant in Flat Rock, Michigan. Mazda, like most Japanese plants, looks for individuals who "will work well in teams, are flexible of mind, who adapt well to change." When someone asked Merchant about the educational level of the thousand workers they hired, though, Merchant said "We don't track that."[4] In short, To get the workforce it wanted, Mazda didn't find it useful to ask how educated the candidates for their workforce were.)

You've heard a lot about "empowering" employees, I'm sure. It's one of the big buzzwords. Sometimes it's hard to tell just what this person or that one means by it. I can tell you very simply what I mean:

Empowerment means enabling employees to manage themselves in pursuit of organizational goals.

I chose this definition because it emphasizes four key points about empowerment:

1. *No one can give power to another person.* Neither you nor I can walk into the factory or office one Monday morning and say to our workgroup: "I've decided to empower you. Now that you're empowered, go do great things!" Yes, that sounds silly—but it's not that different from saying "Starting Monday morning, everyone is going to be responsible for the quality of all of their own work," when they're used to having it inspected and reworked routinely. Only an individual can truly empower himself. The most a manager can do is to enable workers to empower themselves.

2. Then there's the other side: *no one can be empowered to do something unless they're permitted to do it.* This is what most books on "empowerment" concentrate on. And it's a necessity; the silliness in the paragraph above is nothing compared to saying "You're all responsible for the quality of your own work, and I'm going to do a 100% inspection to see that

you get it right." As a manager, I cannot empower you; only you can do that. But I must give you the opportunity to empower yourself.

3. And that leads to the next point. *Self-management requires both skill and motivation.* It took you and me quite a few years to learn how to manage our lives—and we only learned to do it because we saw real benefits in doing it (such as getting to use the family car, for instance). So when we speak of enabling employees to manage themselves we must mean seeing that (1) they have the *ability* to do so and (2) they will *benefit* from doing it.

4. Finally, empowerment is useless, and possibly even harmful, unless it is devoted to *achieving organizational goals.* That goes without saying, of course—but it still helps to say it clearly every once in a while.

The book will talk about employee empowerment, primarily in empowered teams, again and again. For now, though, just keep in mind whenever you hear or read about empowering employees that it means enabling them to manage themselves in pursuit of organizational goals. That's the critical point.

You may already be shuddering. Self-management is a real change in how most organizations do business—because it lets workers take real control of their work. The result is that management doesn't have the same kind of control it had before. The first reaction of many managers to this situation is: CHAOS! It's not, though before it's over you may think that you and your workers have to go through chaos to get to real self-management. One of the purposes of this book is to help you keep that chaos at the lowest possible level. And to understand that any chaos is just transition; a self-managed team is far more controlled and disciplined than any manager-managed work can ever be.

HOW TO DEVELOP COMPETENCE, COMMITMENT & CUSTOMER FOCUS _____

Let's jump from the bottom of the diagram to the top. This is where, as the saying goes, the rubber meets the road. Productivity, quality, timeliness—none of these matter unless they're creating value for an internal or external customer. I'm going to assume that you intend to create value for your customers—and that you know just what value your organization adds and just who its customers are.

Unfortunately, most firstline work is terribly fragmented. When this happens, when complete processes are organized into simple, repetitive tasks, workers lose all feel for their customers. They don't seem to be part of the total effort, they can't see how what they do matters to the customer. They concentrate on the fragment in front of them and ignore the purpose of what they do. ("I'm sorry, but that's not in my department.")

When workers are empowered to control their own work and to perform as much of the whole task as possible, their focus changes sharply. They understand how what they do fits in, they understand what the whole product is. You've heard over and over about the customer focus of Federal Express and SAS airlines—two other firms well known for empowering their frontline people. You may not know that in many firms that use empowered workers—such as Worthington Steel and Kingsport (Tenn) Foundry and Manufacturing—workers actually go out and talk with customers about their needs. (Kingsport Foundry has been known to take teams as far away as Chicago to see problems customers were having with their castings. These workers come back and tell others "Hey, here's what we really do for this company up there.")[5] Rosabeth Kanter, Editor of the *Harvard Business Review*, identified "making customers real to all employees" as one of the five major challenges facing firms that want to get close to their customers.[6]

When workers focus on their customers, what each customer sees—and what you should see—is competent, committed people working to meet the customer's needs. That may not be what the customer sees now; in fact, it's my impression that this isn't what most customers of most firms see. But you and I aren't in most firms. Our goal is workers who demonstrate competence and commitment daily to our customers.

If you want to know more about empowerment for customer service, look at my earlier book, *Front-Line Customer Service* (listed in the bibliography), or one of the other works that explain how to create it. Right now we need to look at the two primary factors that directly support customer focus: competence and commitment.

Competence

In a traditional organization, competence usually means that a worker can do her individual, specialized job satisfactorily. Once she learns how to be a voucher examiner or claims examiner or assembler, she keeps doing it indefinitely. Perhaps there will be a little update training now and then, when a new system is installed, but that's the exception. Other than that, it's learn relatively simple skills, repeat them day after weary day, and wait for promotion, retirement or a big lottery win.

If you intend to use teampower, forget that understanding of competence. As you read through this book, you'll see just how much competence members of teams develop and use; it's really remarkable how competent they become, and how strongly they seek even more competence. Company after company has been amazed at what their workers can and will do when given the chance. For now, though, here's a brief summary of what real competence means:

1. Typically, it means knowing how to do a much more complete and challenging job. In firms that process documents sequentially, the document goes from one desk to another to another. Each worker performs his or her little bit of the action: logging it in or doing a set of computations or contacting the customer for information or whatever. All the worker has to know is that one little fragment of the job. No one has to know much, and it doesn't take long to learn how to do the job—but then the system doesn't work very well, either.

    This isn't how it works when you use teampower. If jobs are simple, team members typically learn how to do most or all of the jobs on the team. If the jobs are more complex—such as those needed to select a contractor and let the contract— team members develop an understanding of the basics of the other jobs and an appreciation of what they contribute.

    For instance, in more and more companies, documents are processed by teams that are responsible for everything about that document. We saw how that change paid off for Litel Telecommunications. Another example is a major bank that used to process mortgage applications through several departments. It replaced this linear flow with teams, each of which does all of the mortgage processing for its customers. The team does whatever is required to process the mortgage from beginning to end. It does any research necessary, contacts the customer if necessary—any and everything necessary to serve that customer. That's competence. And using teams this way cut the bank's processing time from 21 days to 9 days, and cut costs by 33%.[7]

2. Truly effective teampower also means constantly coming up with ideas to improve the process. We associate this with Total Quality Control and Continuous Process Improvement—but it doesn't have to be limited to these. Wherever organizations truly enable their teams to manage themselves and encourage constant improvement, teams deliver just that.

3. The last point brings us to one of the most important characteristics of competence in a teampower environment: it's a neverending process. Teams almost never say "Well, we've learned all about this we need to know; we'll rest on our laurels." Instead, once they're given the opportunity to do challenging work, it becomes habit-forming and they look for even more challenging work to do. As you'll see in a later chapter, learning becomes a major activity of the team. (It's no coincidence that the idea of the "learning organization," has become popular at the same time that employees empowerment has begun to catch on.)

Commitment

Competence without commitment is like the proverbial loose cannon on deck; you never know what's going to happen, but you'll probably wish that it didn't. Commitment is the focus that makes competence and self-mastery effective.

Let's tackle one important issue right now. It's the whole question of "ownership." In a traditional organization, the supervisor usually owns whatever his unit produces. He tells workers what to do and how to do it, then checks their work (or has it checked) to see that they did what he told them. If something goes wrong, it's his responsibility to fix it—and to fix the worker in the process. If things go right, he gets the credit.

If you intend to have self-managing, empowered workers, you have to give up ownership. The product can't be yours any more—it must be theirs. That's what commitment means. If you try to look over their shoulders, to give advice when it's not asked for, to tell someone how to do it better, to criticize honest mistakes—or, heaven forbid!, have someone else inspect their work—you'll turn that commitment off. As you'll see throughout the book, your job is to support them as they do *their* job. If you want commitment, there's no other way.

Does that sound very, very different from the way you've managed in the past? If you're a traditional manager in a traditional organization, this new way of managing *is* different. It really does mean supporting your workers, not bossing or directing or forcing them to perform. If that seems unrealistic, it's not—at least not if you really mean to empower your people. Surprising as it may sound, empowered employees in teams will often set higher performance standards and meet them more constantly than you would believe. As you read through the book, you'll find out why that is and how you can facilitate it.

WHY THE TRADITIONAL APPROACH ISN'T ENOUGH _____

To understand what creates challenge, control and cooperation, we have to understand what doesn't. And what doesn't is work that's simplified to the point of boredom and repeated over and over again. This is how "low-level" work is organized in most firms. These are the basic principles:

1. *Work should be subdivided into simple, specific groups of tasks that can be learned quickly.*

2. *Management should determine the most efficient method of performing each task and teach that method to each worker.*

3. *The individual does it that way, at a set rate, until told to do otherwise. Where possible, he should get a piece rate based on his production rate.*

4. *Insofar as possible, work is broken down into separate jobs with minimal interaction.*

5. *The result is isolated jobs with a very low skill demand and low pay (and high turnover, high absenteeism, and high grievances).*

You can't argue with the consistency of this approach. Nor, until the Japanese began eating our lunch before breakfast, could you argue with its effectiveness. Now it doesn't look quite so effective—and the immediate reason is a sixth characteristic of work organized this way:

6. *When work is organized in this simplified, isolated way, it is extremely difficult to produce a quality product—and impossible to produce a quality product cheaply.*[8]

This fact is the major reason why any company that attempts to compete globally (or against the Japanese anywhere) by using these principles is at a major disadvantage. In the words of Richard E. Walton,

> an intensified challenge from abroad has made the competitive obsolescence of this strategy clear. A model that assumes low employee commitment and that is designed to produce reliable if not outstanding performance simply cannot match the standards of excellence set by worldclass competitors. Especially in a highwage country like the United States, market success depends on a superior level of performance, a level that, in turn, requires the deep commitment, not merely the obedience—if you could obtain it—of workers.[9]

Why should all this be true?

There are a variety of answers, but one seems more fundamental to me than any of the others:

> *This approach treats workers as though they were purely physical—as machines. It literally organizes work mechanically. Unfortunately, human beings make relatively poor machines. And they simply don't like being treated as machines (do we?).*

If you look at the principles above, they all make very effective machine design principles. While machines may be very complicated, you still want them to be as simple as possible, and you want them to function the same way every time. It works fine if you have one machine do one part of the process, then pass its output to the next machine. Above all, machines don't need to think or talk to one another—they simply need to perform their programmed function over and over and over without deviation or disruption.

Most people don't operate like this. If you organize work on these principles, you are guaranteeing yourself that your workers will be neither committed nor significantly competent—because they will have no satisfaction from serving customers, no challenge, no control and no opportunity to cooperate. You are also guaranteeing that you will have to choose between productivity and quality.

That statement may sound strong, and it is. I know of no company in a seriously competitive market that has found an exception to the statement.

THE TEAMPOWER ALTERNATIVE _____

That's the traditional approach—the mechanical approach most of us identify automatically as the way to organize work efficiently. Before we look at the alternative—organizing for worker control, challenge and cooperation—let's face one critical fact together:

The more you want to use teampower—or any form of operation that empowers workers—the more you have to learn new ways of organizing and managing. You cannot simply paste teampower on top of an existing traditional operation and expect it to work.

That's just a "heads up!" for you. Before long, you'll understand in much more detail just how great the change is. Then you can decide whether you want to make that change. (If you do, the rest of the book will show you the key functions and skills you need to manage teampower successfully. It will also explain how to implement empowered teams in your organization.)

The mechanical organization of jobs cannot develop workers with competence or commitment. What can?

Look back at the diagram on page 3. It shows that competence and commitment come from work that is challenging, is controlled by the workers that perform it, and is performed cooperatively. Now it's time to look at each of these factors in detail.[10]

CHALLENGING WORK _____

Have you ever watched a small child try to learn a new skill— say, tie his shoes? He tries, makes mistakes, perhaps quits for a while in frustration. With a little encouragement, though, he's back at it again. Eventually, he gets it right, and then shows off his new skill to every relative and friend around, untying the shoes and then tying them again.

The satisfaction from learning a new skill doesn't go away just because we grow up. An angler grins broadly as he finishes tying a new and demanding fly; his wife smiles (probably a bit more demurely) when her new casserole is a hit; and their retired next-door neighbor admires the Japanese garden he slowly and carefully created. Anywhere you look, you see people of all ages learning new skills and taking pride in using them.

Anywhere, that is, except in the average American company. Bored kids cook and serve hamburgers; bored clerks enter data into computer terminals and handle turn-ins for discount stores; bored assemblyline workers do the same ten-minute task hour after hour, day after day; bored supervisors and stewards wrangle over who has to work overtime this weekend.

Of course there are exceptions: the housewife-turned-entrepreneur who bustles around preparing hors d'oeuvres for a dinner she's catering; the analyst who's just found the root cause of the cost overruns; the customer-service rep who's just turned an irate buyer into a satisfied customer. You or I may not think what they're doing is all that great, but they do.

They do because, whatever someone else might think, their work is challenging to each of them. Part of it is matching the person to the job; the cook would probably be as bored with the spreadsheet as the analyst with the hors d'oeuvres. Beyond this, there are three characteristics that make jobs challenging:

1. *Variety.* For most of us, variety is truly the spice of life. The jobs that involve doing exactly the same thing day after day, week after week are the boring ones. The ones that challenge us are those that *aren't* the same time after time. Just as traditional organization simplifies the work to do away with any complexity (variety), effective teampower requires that the work be interesting.

2. *Completeness:* Traditional organization doesn't just make jobs boring; far more seriously, it divorces the worker from the final product. If all you do is a small part of the total job, and if all you ever see is the little bit you do, you lose the satisfaction of actually completing something. You also lose the satisfaction of creating something for a customer. Even more than variety, participating in making a complete product is a critical component of a challenging job.

3. *Problem-Solving.* Variety and completeness are important, and sometimes they're enough. Most of the time, though, each of us wants one more challenge: problem solving. Being able to do one's assigned work well is good, but solving (or helping solve) the sticky problems is even better. To anticipate something you'll read in detail later in the book, one reason workers like quality teams so much is that they involve them in problem solving.

The first support for competence and commitment, then, is work that is challenging to the individual—work that provides him or her variety, a sense of completeness, and the opportunity to solve problems. Challenging work is also a necessity if you want truly empowered workers. It makes no sense at all to call a worker "empowered" when all she does is repeat the same, simple task over and over—and particularly if she never sees or feels a part of the whole process. Empowered workers require empowering, challenging work.

If you watched the Saturn commercials when GM first introduced the car, you heard a worker describe just this; he felt differently about working for Saturn because he really felt a part of it. This was no accident—the Saturn plant is based on highly independent, empowered teams, the most effective form of teampower.

Here's another example. Don Wilson, a member of the team that developed the personal computer at IBM, said this of the way the organization worked:

> Don [Estridge] would give us an assignment, or our assignments would require us to take some action and so we would just go and do it. We didn't have to wade through the layers of the corporation's bureaucracy. We knew what counted and we could see the results. It was like the brass ring. You could see it, it was right there, and you could touch it and you could quickly reach out and get feedback on it. . . .

> Before I went to work on the team, I helped develop a printer at IBM. That printer was in development for seven years! . . . No individual, or any group, has a clear, visible identity—not even an opportunity to see what I call 'the whole pie' of a product. . . .

> But with the pc project, I saw the whole pie for the first time. We saw the costs, we solved the problems ourselves, we lived with the good and the bad. It's no exaggeration to say that I made more decisions in my first 30 days with that group than I made during my first 14 years with IBM. I mean, these were real decisions![11]

WORKER CONTROL

Challenging work is a good start, but it's not enough. If the work is challenging but the worker has no control over it, what you'll get is a frustrated worker.

The traditional organization of work deliberately takes control of the work process away from the worker. He's told the tools he will use and the way to use them—whether he works in a factory or an office. To make matters worse, the pace and content of the work is often controlled by a machine; this is as true for the claims clerk using a computer system as for the worker adapting his pace to that of the assembly line. Peter Drucker once described the place of humans in such systems as "the missing part of the machine." Certainly that's how workers often feel.

You cannot tap the power of workers either individually or in teams if they don't have control over their work processes. Period.

Psychologists confirmed during the 80s that one of the most important components of mental health and self-esteem—perhaps the most important one—is the belief that I am in control of my own life. It doesn't just apply in the big choices—whom to marry, what occupation to follow, where to live. It's just as important in the daily decisions and activities that make up your life and mine.[12]

Sometimes this is hard to see on the job. Perhaps you've thought about giving your workers more freedom and responsibility, then been put off because you didn't think they could handle it. You may even have thought that they didn't want it. Many organizations have considered, perhaps even started programs to make workers more responsible—only to have them fail because the workers themselves wouldn't buy into them.

The truth of the matter is that most of these same workers are amazingly good at handling freedom and responsibility off the job. They raise families—which is more challenging than most jobs. They run PTAs, VFWs and Little League teams. They serve as mayors, city councilmen and trustees of homeowner's associations. And many of them operate their own businesses. It's only on their jobs—because they've been conditioned so well to over-organized and overcontrolled jobs—that they would even think of being passive.[13]

Even here, workers may not be quite so passive and routinized as we might think. In 1979, Lucy Suchman, on the staff of the Xerox Palo Alto Research Center, studied the jobs of accounting clerks performing "routine" work. This is what she found:

> When Suchman asked the clerks how they did their jobs, their descriptions corresponded more or less to the formal procedures of the job manual. But when she observed them at work, she discovered that the clerks weren't really following those procedures at all. Instead, they relied on a rich variety of informal practices that weren't in any manual but turned out to be crucial to getting the work done. In fact, the clerks were constantly improvising, inventing new methods to deal with unexpected difficulties and to solve immediate problems. Without being aware of it, they were far more innovative and creative than anybody who heard them describe their "routine" jobs ever would have thought.[14]

Wow! However, no matter how inventive your people who perform routine jobs are, we're talking about a significant change from the kind of work organization that they—and you—are used to. It took time and effort for workers to adjust to a situation where they're expected to be passive, do what they're told, not rock the boat. It takes time and effort for them to adjust to a new situation where they have freedom and responsibility. One of the main purposes of this book is to help you pick the kind of teams that are most apt to succeed in your current situation. If you've given your workers little control over their work before, you want to start slowly. On the other hand, if your workers are used to exercising responsibility for their jobs you can hit the ground running with empowered teams.

Control of their work, then, is the second key characteristic of empowered workers. Studies have shown that workers who perform potentially challenging work but have little control over it experience not challenge but stress.[15] As long as the work is proceeding routinely, the issue of control isn't important. What happens, though, when a problem comes up? A customer has an unusual request? An essential machine suddenly performs erratically? An insurance claim doesn't fit any of the guidelines? Workers will be committed to finding the solutions only when they have the freedom and power to do so. (After all, how challenging is it to call someone else to solve the problem and then sit and wait for the answer to arrive?)

Remember that we're talking here about the necessary basis for competence and commitment. Challenging work allows (and requires) a worker to develop significant competence; when he has a hand in the complete process, the work also calls forth his commitment. Controlling the process is at least as much a key to commitment. Neither you nor I would commit ourselves to a job we couldn't control; neither will our workers. None of us will commit ourselves to a project knowing that someone else—whose judgment we might or might not trust—will make the key decisions.

Control of work is a necessity for empowered workers. It may be something so simple as the power of any worker at the Coulter Electronics Corporation to shut down the line when something is going wrong. It may be as complex as the responsibility of Saturn teams to interview and hire the members of their teams. But it must exist if you want competence and commitment.

COOPERATION _____

You don't have to use teams to benefit from empowered workers. Both Federal Express and SAS, for instance, are famous for empowering their frontline workers—but they're not fundamentally organized into teams. Empowerment in any form, done thoughtfully and sensibly, will increase quality, productivity, and customer service in almost every situation.

True as that is, only an empowered team can tap the full measure of worker resources. Let's spend a minute investigating why working cooperatively makes such a difference.

The fact is that most of us prefer to work with others instead of alone. True, working in groups does create problems: power struggles, feuds, jealousies, wasted time, and all the rest. And nothing is more unproductive than a team created for its own sake, without a clear need. Remember, a camel is a horse designed by a committee. Work done by groups multiplies communication problems and can diffuse responsibility.

These are real factors, ones we'll revisit later in the book, but they don't change the reality that most of us would rather work in groups. In fact, one of the problems with teams is that they sometimes prolong themselves longer than necessary simply because the people on them like working together. We're inherently social beings, and we enjoy the stimulation and satisfaction of working together. When a team is appropriate, this turns into motivation and commitment.

There's a major business side to this, too. Most activities in organizations require more than one person to complete. Whether it's responding to a customer complaint, designing a new product, or redesigning the workflow, one person can't do it. In some way or another, people with different skills have to get together and pool their skills.

This doesn't mean that they have to form a team; individuals can work on them serially. Seven people can work on the customer complaint in turn, with number seven finally responding to the customer. The problem is, as many organizations are finding all too painfully, that this organization of work is neither very productive nor very effective. Because it fragments the work and the responsibility, no one really takes responsibility for the final product. And every time a product moves from one station to another, it gets delayed. Remember the mortgage-processing operation of the major bank we looked at a few pages back? At least half of the 21 days it took to process a mortgage through different departments was caused by this fragmentation and delay.

We've been talking about effective teams as though we knew what they were. Perhaps we do; perhaps we don't. It's time to find out. According to Arie de Geus, former coordinator of Group Planning at Royal Dutch Shell, teams are "people who need one another to act."[16] In its simplest form, this says that teams are appropriate when the problem or project requires the combined abilities or points of view of several people.

In general, teams are effective when the team is focused on one process, one project, one or a single group of customers, or one product or service. As we go through the book, you'll get a clearer view of what this means. For now, though, keep in mind that cooperation only works when it's needed; if you use a team where one or more people working individually could do the task well, you'll increase time and decrease results. Like any other solution, teams only work when you've found the right problem.

When a team of some kind is the right solution, our human desire to cooperate becomes a tremendous resource. In fact, a properly structured and operating team will take over many of the functions we've associated with supervision in the past. The team itself will keep its members producing and contributing, even to the point of informally disciplining individuals who don't contribute. More on that later. (If you'd like more information on how powerful our urge to cooperate is, I suggest Alfie Kohn's book, *No Contest*. It summarizes most of the research on cooperation done by the middle 80s. Stephen Covey's very popular *The 7 Habits of Highly Effective People* also has some interesting thoughts on cooperation. Both books are listed in the bibliography.)

HOW SATURN FITS IT ALL TOGETHER

We've looked at Competence and Commitment focused on the Customer and supported by Challenging work, worker Control over work and Cooperation—individually. Now it's time to put them together. This is *Time*'s description of GM's new Saturn plant:

[T]he labor agreement established some 165 work teams, which have been given more power than assembly-line workers anywhere else in GM or at any Japanese plant. They are allowed to interview and approve new hires for their teams (average size: 10 workers). They are given wide responsibility to decide how to run their own areas; when workers see a problem on the assembly line, they can pull on a blue handle and shut down the entire line. They are even given budget responsibility. . . .

Not all of Saturn's progressive ideas sprang up in Tennessee. Many were borrowed from around the world by the Group of 99, a team of Saturn workers who traveled 2 million miles in 1984 and looked into some 160 pioneering enterprises. . . . Their main conclusions: that most successful companies provide employees with a sense of ownership, have few and flexible guidelines and impose virtually no job-defining shop rules.

From that blue print grew the most radical twist in Saturn's labor agreement. . . : the provision for consensus decision making. The Saturn philosophy is that all teams must be committed to decisions affecting them before those changes are put into place, from choosing an ad agency to selecting an outside supplier.[17]

Even in so short a description, you can see each key element of the 6C model:

- The entire structure assumes *commitment*. Can you even imagine the shambles such a system would fall into without this commitment at every point? Further, the commitment is customer focused; early Saturn ads made clear how important the final product is to the Saturn workers.

- It also assumes a degree of *competence* far above that of the typical production worker. Not only do the individuals on the teams have to know how to build cars, they have to find the best ways to do their jobs, understand personnel management and budgeting, and practice effective consensus decision making.

- Do I even need to mention how *challenging* this work is, or the obvious *control* that the teams have over their work processes?

- Finally, the amount of *cooperation* is staggering, particularly when compared with the operation of most organizations (like yours?). Remember, in the Saturn plant individual teams not only reach decision by consensus but the entire plant depends on consensus for decisions.

Perhaps more important than the individual factors themselves, the Saturn plant illustrates how closely interconnected the factors are. Take away any one factor, and the system would be crippled—possibly fatally so. Put them all together, and they support each other synergistically.

If you have your crap detector up and working, there are at least two questions that you have: Just where did they get their workers? and How well does it work?

We're not talking about naive youths straight off the impoverished family farm here; Saturn workers were recruited from U.A.W. locals throughout the country. Sure there was a high degree of selectivity on the part of both the company and the people; Saturn workers are younger, more entrepreneurial and more interested in results than the average GM workers. But they are union workers, and Saturn is a union plant.

When you read this page, you'll know more about how well Saturn's teams work than I do now. I can tell you, this, though: GM has been able to price the Saturn about $1000 below its main competitors. Unless the company has a philanthropic streak that hasn't been clear until now, that seems to suggest that something is going very right.

ARE YOU READY FOR IT? _____

The secret of empowered teams is Challenge, Control and Cooperation, built on Self-Management, creating Competence and Commitment to Customer satisfaction. In the next chapter, we'll put the final blocks in place. I'll help you look at whether your organization is ready for teampower. Then I'll suggest what you, the manager, must provide to teams to make them work.

Chapter 2

Making Teampower
Work for You

The General Motors powertrain plant in Bay City, Michigan wasn't your sterling example of American profitability in the middle 80s. Estimates were that it would lose some $3.5 million a year through 1987. But the estimates didn't take account of Pat Carrigan. As the first woman in GM's history to manage an assembly plant, she'd turned a poor situation at Lakewood, Georgia around between 1981 and 1985. Well, there wasn't anything to lose—so she took over the Bay City plant.

She used the same tactics there she'd used at Lakewood: Be open with people and see that they communicate with each other. Train everyone, then train them some more. *Use teampower*. She created some 43 teams, and 13 of them evolved into fully self-managing teams. They set their own goals and schedules, as well as their own objectives for quality, quantity and delivery.

Did it work? Well, the plant stopped losing money and started making it. Grievances dropped to almost nothing. Lost time dropped to 35% less than the GM average. Productivity rose 24 percent in 18 months, while factory rejects dropped by 10%. Perhaps most interesting of all was the cost-reduction team, made up of people who eliminated their previous jobs. By the late 80s, the team had saved the plant more than $2 million.[18]

Both partially and fully self-managing teams work tremendously well for Pat Carrigan; the question, though, is what kind of team is going to work best for you. That's what this chapter is about. When you finish it, you'll know where you can begin with teams and what teams must have from you in order to succeed.

23

HOW TO DECIDE WHERE TO START _____

Let's get right to the bottom line:

How can you use teampower in your organization?

The first two critical elements we looked at were Competence and Commitment, focused on the needs of the Customer. I know your organization would like to have more of both. How much it wants them, though, is a secondary issue. The gut-level question is this: Where does it stand on work that is challenging, controlled by workers, and performed cooperatively?

Before we answer this question, we need a quick look at why organizations do what they do and at the levels of organization that are most important to you.

FORCES THAT HELP AND FORCES
THAT HINDER TEAMPOWER _____

Each organization performs as it does because of the balance of forces pressing on it.[19] For instance, the quality of its products depends on the forces (such as competitive pressure, the power of the Quality Control Department, etc.) pushing high quality forward against the forces (pressure for quick results, cynicism, etc.) pushing back against it. Things are as they are now in every organization because of its balance between the forces pushing forward and those pushing back; change that balance, and you change how the organization performs.

This is true at every level in the organization. Robert W. Galvin transformed Motorola during the 80s from a so-so electronics producer to a world leader—because he radically changed the factors pushing high quality forward. (Even then, the strength of the existing forces pushing back handicapped progress for years.) The same process happens at the first and second levels. I've transformed several units into much more participative operations by pushing forward for participation—and it took me months to do it because of the existing forces pushing back against me.

The balance of forces pushing forward for empowered teams

with those pushing back against them will determine what kind of teams you can use and how successful they will be. You can add your push to the forces pushing for them and you can neutralize some of the forces pushing back—but not all of them. To succeed with teams, you must understand the situation clearly and act realistically.

THE THREE CRITICAL SUCCESS LEVELS _____

There are three levels in the organization that will make or break your attempt to use teampower; you need to understand what's happening in each one and use this understanding to create success. These are the critical levels:

- You know that *the organization as a whole* has a certain style or "culture." How you can use teampower depends on how well teampower fits this overall style.

- As you also know so well, *the two management levels above you* will heavily influence your success or failure with teampower. If your boss and your boss's boss support you, they can insulate you from adverse pressures further up the line. Conversely, no matter what the CEO wants, if your boss and his boss don't want it you'll have a devil of a time trying make it work.

- *Your immediate organization*, the people who report to you, will ultimately determine your success or failure.

HOW TO PUT IT TOGETHER _____

You must deal with the forces pushing teampower forward and those pushing back against it, and you must deal with them at three levels. Here are some examples of major supports and blocks that affect each of the three critical C factors (challenge, control and cooperation) in the organization as a whole, in the organizations of your boss and boss's boss, and in your own organization:

	Forces Pushing Forward	Forces Pushing Back
Job Challenge	The organization tries to make jobs as interesting and challenging as possible.	The organization tries to simplify jobs as much as possible.
	The organization tries to hire intelligent workers who learn fast and like to be challenged.	The organization tries to hire minimally skilled workers who will be dependable and do as they are told.
	The organization expects workers to identify where work processes can be improved and to suggest improvements.	Management is expected to identify any need for work process improvement and to make the improvement.
	The organization actively solicits ideas from workers.	Managers or staff specialists are expected to come up with all of the new ideas.
Worker Control of Work	The organization gives workers broad latitude to choose how to do the job.	The organization expects workers to perform the job exactly as they are taught it.
	The organization encourages workers to display considerable initiative in doing their work and solving any problems that arise.	The organization discourages any worker initiative. When problems come up, managers or specialists solve them.
	The organization has an effective suggestion program that is supported by supervisors.	The organization either has no suggestion program or it is simply given lip service.
	The organization has an active quality program based on quality circles or similar worker participation.	The organization's quality program is based primarily on inspection of workers' outputs.
Cooperation	The organization values internal cooperation between individuals and departments.	The organization expects individuals and departments to work independently (or even competitively).

(cont'd.)

The organization specifically appraises workers and managers on cooperation with others as well as on individual accomplishment.	The organization appraises members on their individual results only.
The organization has effective management teams at one or more levels.	The organization does not use management teams
The organization occasionally uses teams for important purposes.	The organization uses few if any teams; when teams are used, they deal primarily with less important matters (United Fund Drive, Company picnic, etc.).
The organization has effective, productive union-management relations.	The organization has adversarial union-management relations.

Clearly enough, the more forces in the organization pushing for work that is challenging, worker controlled and cooperative at every level, the easier it will be to use empowered teams. But don't miss another aspect of the chart that's just as important. It's this: the more blocks there are to effective teampower, the harder it will be to implement—but the greater the quality and productivity improvement the organization can realize from it. Organizations that confine their workers to simplified individual jobs under close control waste most of the contribution their workers could make. It's very difficult for them to change—and it normally happens only when their survival is at stake—but when they do the gain can be enormous.[20]

Look realistically at the balance of forces pushing for empowered teams and those pushing back against them at each of the three organization levels mentioned on page 25. Remember that support in your own workgroup and from your boss and boss's boss is more important than the overall style of the company—in the short run. If your workgroup and the next two levels are strongly supportive but the organization isn't, there will certainly be real problems in the long run getting teampower accepted—even if it's successful. Don't let that stop you. At worst, you'll be prepared for the challenge; at best, the organization will start to change in a supportive way (and you'll be out in front of the parade).

Your best strategy is to begin where there's the strongest support. Based on this strategy, here are some suggestions:

1. If the forces pushing back dominate the organization at all levels, begin with careful empowering of individuals and carefully controlled and limited team projects.

2. If there are forces pushing for challenging work and worker control but the corporate style is highly competitive and individualistic, go for really strong individual empowerment and try gradually to shift toward teams. Look at the first part of Chapter 3 for ideas on empowering individuals. Then start to use some of the worker teams described in the last part of that chapter.

3. Has the organization been trying to create challenging and worker controlled jobs, along with opportunities for cooperation? You're ready to use one or more of the forms of teampower described in Chapter 3. Once the groundwork is laid, by the way, there's no limit on how many different forms of empowered teams you can use in an organization.

4. If the tradition of challenging work, worker control, and cooperation is strong, get ready to take the jump to self-managing work teams. Where work permits this kind of organization, there simply is no more productive way to organize —and no way that produces consistently higher quality output.

5. Finally, if everything's pushing against teampower, but the company's in lots and lots of pain, *and* you have strong support from your boss and boss's boss—consider taking the plunge all the way to self-managed teams right now. It's risky. It may not be worth the risk. If it succeeds, though, you may find yourself at the head of a very large parade. (Remember, real innovation in organizations doesn't begin at the top; it begins with individuals like yourself who take risks and succeed.)

OK—now you have an idea of how teampower can work for you. It's time for the next step: what teams have to have *from you* in order to succeed.

THE EIGHT CHARACTERISTICS OF SUCCESSFUL TEAMS _____

Effective teams don't just happen; their members have to learn and use a variety of skills. Most books on teams concentrate on these skills. There are dozens of these books, and the bibliography lists many of them. This book isn't about team skills, though; it's about what you, the manager, must do to create and maintain successful teams.

No matter how skilled you or the team members may be, though, there are certain characteristics that all teams must have before they can successfully exercise these skills. Fully functioning teams can maintain and enhance the characteristics, but in the beginning it's up to you—the manager—to develop these characteristics in the team. In fact, you must insist that any team have them before you allow it to function.

Why are they so important? Because

If the team is lacking even one of these eight characteristics, it will have a more difficult time than it needs to. If it lacks two or three of the characteristics, it is probably set up for failure—no matter how skillful its members are and no matter how motivated they are.

Let's look at these critical characteristics.

1. Shared Values That Support Teamwork

This is where it all begins. Influence, trust, commitment—all of these originate in shared values. Values are what we believe in, what we are willing to work for. Goals, when they mean anything, are the end results that will embody our values.

We've already looked at some of the basic values required for teampower. It depends on managers and workers who value competence and commitment, work that's challenging and worker controlled, and cooperation wherever possible. These are real, concrete values. Some organizations have them, many don't. Many organizations state them in decorative vision statements, fewer follow them.

There are other values that teams need. Commitment to the company and its customers, and to the idea that good ideas can come from everywhere. Respect for everyone and for all opinions—even when we disagree strongly with them. The willingness to take risks to develop trust in each other. The commitment that we will do what we say, when we say we'll do it. Dedication to doing things right, and doing them better and better.

How do you tell if your organization has these values? There's a simple way, if you want to try it. Just do something that clearly violates them. Tell your boss that you don't care whether your workers are committed or not, that you're going to tell them what to do and how to do it. If your boss smiles and starts talking about something else, the noble statements are just decorative wallpaper. If he pulls you up short and gives you a pep talk about how that's not the way that things are done around here—well, you've found some real values.

You've probably learned this already, but it's important that you keep your crap detector set on high when you look for your company's values and goals. What's posted on the wall may really be it; IBM really does expect many of its people to THINK. More often, the real values and goals are buried in the everyday life of the organization. The poster says that people are the firm's most important asset, but when business falls off the personnel department hands out the pink slips. The gilt-edged plaque says that the firm wants the maximum contribution from everyone, but the word on the floor is that to get ahead you do your work and keep your mouth shut.

Read the posters and plaques, but read them with your eyes open. You're looking for the firm's real values. If you want to use empowered teams, they must be supported by what the company really does, not just by what it says.

2. Clear, Worthwhile Goals

A few years ago, Carl Larson and Frank LaFasto set out to find what made teams of all kinds successful. When they had finished their search, one requirement was crystal clear. It is that

> high performance teams have both a clear understanding of the goal to be achieved and a belief that the goal embodies a worthwhile or important result.[21]

Notice, first of all, that only *management* can do this. You can send your workers to team-building and small-group skills courses until they and you turn blue in the face (and perhaps the rear end), and it won't make a team of them. You create a team when you provide them a goal they can believe in and then are completely clear about what this goal is.

Now you see why the entire process has to begin with shared values: values and goals are simply two sides of the same coin. What we value we will try to attain; we will do the work to attain only what we value. People are made that way, and so are organizations. If you want to succeed with empowered teams, the first requirement is for you and the team members to be very clear about what you value, and to value the right things.

Then, when everyone is clear on what they value, you can set goals consistent with these values—and the team will believe that the goals are worthwhile and important. That's not all there is to it, of course. Among other things, people must believe that the goals are attainable and that they have the resources required to attain them. None of these will matter, though, unless the goals are consistent with the basic values that your firm, your people and you hold. Let me give you an example of this:

Workstations are the hottest thing in computers these days (at least at the time I'm writing this). They're small computers, about the size of a personal computer, but with immense power. Not long ago, Sony decided to enter the Japanese market with a workstation of their own. Traditional Japanese management would have dictated a slow, orderly, consensual process—but Akio Morita, Sony's CEO, has never been a traditional Japanese manager. In the best tradition of the American "skunk works," he got a small team of highly talented engineers together, isolated them from the rest of the company, and told them to design the machine. They did, and the workstation proved a rousing success—but only because both the team and Morita shared a strong set of innovative values, the values were translated into very specific goals, and the team was isolated from those in the company (which was most of the rest of the company) who didn't share these values. Of course, they had a good model; this was how IBM got its first personal computer to market in record time.

When teams have goals that are aligned with their real values, they commit themselves to them. Alignment isn't enough, though—the goals must be very, very *clear*. This isn't unique to teams, of course; all of us perform more effectively when we have very clear goals to pursue. Clear goals are even more important for teams, since the goals are the source of unity and teamwork for different individuals with differing personalities, points of view, interests and talents.

Look at a simple situation: a team set up to determine whether to keep a new product on the market. One of the representatives from marketing was responsible for the product idea in the first place; the other marketing representative opposed it. The manufacturing representative thinks that the specifications for the product were unrealistic, which led to unsatisfactory quality. The engineering representative believes that dropping two of her key design features was a basic cause of the sales problem. The sales representative, on the other hand, knows that he could make a go of it if the price were cut and the warranty extended.

Unless the team is completely clear about its goals, its work will quickly degenerate into individual members wrangling with each other, building alliances and attempting to subvert the whole process by making end runs to higher management. There will be problems even if the goal is clear, but the team leader at least has a way to direct the members' attention away from their personal agendas.

Look at Sony in the example above. The individuals on that team knew exactly what their goals were: create a competitive workstation. (IBM's case was similar—create a personal computer). We can bet that there was considerable wrangling and disagreement, but the team was successful—because its goals were aligned with its values and were clear. As a member of an American software development team put it,

> a clear description of our purpose and who we serve . . . was helpful in two ways. Unlike many teams, we have all agreed on a common purpose. Further, we have a nice guideline for deciding between conflicting demands: "which alternative most clearly relates to the group's mission?"[22]

There's one final, crucial point about goals. It may not be more important than any of the others, but it's certainly no less important. The point is this:

Establishing a functioning team is never, ever itself a primary goal.

Now, this may sound a little silly to you. Let me assure you that it is not. Even as I write this, an executive somewhere is saying to his management team, "We're not as competitive as we ought to be. We need to establish teams in this organization!" So managers have a mandate to establish teams—and they rush around trying to get them set up and find something for them to do. (Don't kid yourself that this is overstated. I led a workshop recently attended by a department manager of a major company. He'd been told by his company to establish empowered teams in his department and then spread them to other departments. And that's all he was told. He was in the workshop to find out what empowered teams were and how to go about setting them up.)

This makes the establishment of teams the goal, and virtually assures failure. In other words, a team will be successful *only* when it exists to accomplish a worthwhile goal outside itself. Further, as de Geus's definition (teams are "people who need one another to act") makes clear, teams only work when the goal requires the coordinated efforts of several people. It's the goal that creates the team, not the other way around. And this leads to the third characteristic of successful teams.

3. Genuine Need for Each Member of the Team

The fact that values are shared and a worthwhile goal is set doesn't add up to a successful team. There must be a genuine need for the combination of skills and/or stakeholders that the team represents. A team is a team only if the members really need each other to accomplish its goals; otherwise, it's a collection of individuals doing together what one or a few of them could do more effectively on his or their own.

This point can't be emphasized too strongly: there should be a definite need for *every* member of the team. Each individual should contribute an important skill, a useful point of view, or a clear interest in the outcome of the team's work:

- One of the best foundations for a team is a goal that requires *different skills* to accomplish. The team that created the Sony workstation required several different kinds of engineering skills; the work teams at GM's Saturn plant and Corning's Blacksburg plant combine different skills to produce a product. This doesn't mean that everyone has to have a different skill; it may take more than one individual with the same skill to accomplish work. Nor does it mean that skills can't be shared; members of self-managed teams often learn each other's jobs and trade off jobs among themselves. But there must be a clear need for the skill of each individual.

- The same type of contribution can be made by combining individuals with *different points of view*. A classic example of this is the team that combines individuals from product development, engineering and manufacturing. Two thirds of the team may be engineers, but the process engineers from manufacturing will look at the task very differently from the design engineers in product development. The more the team is able to combine and synthesize these different points of view, the stronger the final product will be.

- A team can also profit from *different stakes* held by different members. It may include the supervisor from a manufacturing unit and the steward for that unit. They may share similar points of view on what's important in a product, but their stakes in the final decisions are apt to be far different. (The supervisor may want to manufacture the product with minimal changeover from her current operation, while the steward is pushing for several line changes that are important to workgroup members.)

While it may not kill a team to add an individual who doesn't make one of these contributions, it will weaken it. Add very many individuals without a real contribution, and the team is doomed. Here are some of the *wrong* reasons to add members:

- "Well, Charlie's work is kinda slack right now, and he needs something to do. Let's put him on the product-development team."

- "Edna just doesn't want to change. Let's put her on the committee to design the new work teams and see if some of the others won't rub off on her."

- "Marilyn knows everything there is to know about our automated system. Let's slip her onto the team just to make sure they make the right decisions."

- "Angel is a real loner. Let's add him to the process correction team and get him participating."

Successful teams exist to accomplish clear, meaningful goals. Every member should be needed to accomplish that goal and should have a distinct contribution to make. Each team member that fails to meet these two criteria will handicap the team.

4. Genuine Commitment to the Goals

As Larson and LaFasto found out,

> in the descriptions of ineffectively functioning teams the factor that occurred far more frequently than any other was very simple: The team had raised—or had allowed to become raised—some other issue or focus above the team's performance objective.[23]

What were these issues? A "personality conflict" between two members? A power struggle between two departments? A side issue that seemed interesting? It doesn't matter—the point is that some or all of the team spent time and energy working agendas unrelated to the goal of the team. With its focus lost, the team failed.

Wait a minute—this isn't a management issue! Only members of the team can commit themselves to the goals of the team; neither you nor I can do it for them. That's true, but what a manager can do is

1. see that individuals are put on the team only if they can contribute to or have a stake in the outcome,

2. make it crystal clear that he or she expects complete commitment to the team's goals,

3. make it equally clear that anyone who cannot make this commitment should leave the team,

4. and then keep abreast of the team's progress, confront any member who is not demonstrating commitment day-in-and-day-out, and replace that member if necessary.

This item is no less important than the others, and it shouldn't be left to chance. Keeping a team focused on its objective is a demanding job. The team leader picks up the responsibility for commitment—but if you're the one who sets up the team you have to require this commitment up front, and then make it stick. And you don't every really give up the responsibility. In fact, one of the basic jobs of a manager in a team-oriented environment is to check constantly to see that each team is committed to its goals and to see that those who are not so committed correct their courses at once.

Shared values, clear and worthwhile goals, the need for all team members, and commitment to the team's goals are the broad underpinnings of any successful team. These must be supplemented by four more, very positive management actions: specific, measurable objectives, useful feedback, team-based rewards, and assured team competence.

5. Specific, Measurable Objectives

How do you eat an elephant? One bite at a time. How do you accomplish a demanding goal? One step at a time.

That's how we think, and that's how we live our lives. The most extreme example of this is the "one day at a time" philosophy of AA, but the approach pervades every large endeavor we complete successfully. A football team in pursuit of a bowl bid must focus its attention and energy on this Saturday's game; once the game has started, it must focus on this drive, this play, this block. A would-be doctor must first pass organic chemistry this semester, which means getting this experiment right.

If a team is established for a clear, short-term goal, the goal can be the measurable objective. For teams with a longer life or more complex goals, intermediate objectives are critical. Equally critically, these objectives must be meaningful. If possible, and it often is, they should be measurable. At the least, they should be *observable* to an outside, disinterested observer. Here are some examples:

1. If you're creating a team to handle a routine process—say responding to customer complaints—it should have performance objectives with very specific measurements. You might use the percentage of complaints responded to within a given time, the percentage resolved by the first contact, or similar measures. If the goal of the team is to respond effectively to customer complaints, they can only know how they're doing if the goal is reduced to specific, measurable objectives.

2. If the team is on a one-time project—say designing a management development curriculum—the objectives can be stated as milestones. By this date, analysis should be complete; by this one, the curriculum should be ready for initial field review. Nothing is really being measured, but checkpoints are established to see that the process is moving as it should. If the checkpoints are properly described, everyone can observe whether they've really been met or not.

3. The situation really gets sticky when the team is chartered to come up with a major innovation. At least in the first stages, it's almost impossible to reduce this to something measurable or even observable. Instead, it often takes the informed judgment of an expert in the field to assess the team's progress. If that is all there is, use it. Establish clear points in time where the team must present its current progress to that expert. Never leave a team wandering for long periods of time without checkpoints of some kind.

To avoid a certain amount of awkwardness, I'm just going to talk of *measurable* objectives from here on—as long as we both understand that sometimes "measurable" will have to mean "observable." The key point is that the objectives are specific, with an agreed-on way to tell whether they've been met.

Why this emphasis on specific, measurable objectives? One reason, mentioned just above, is that without them the team doesn't have a clear idea of how it's doing. They're also important so that the team can see whether it's really accomplishing something; when it meets an objective, its success helps it attack the next objective enthusiastically. In addition, observable objectives provide an effective way for the team and management to communicate with each other—and give managers a way of evaluating their comfort level with the team.

The team must be committed to these objectives, just as they are to the ultimate goals. (It doesn't make a lot of sense to say "Oh, yes—I believe in what we're really after but I don't think I want to take this next step to get there.") Since people often commit themselves more readily to objectives they have participated in developing, the team should have a hand in creating both the objectives and the way they will be measured or observed.

There's another reason for involving team members in setting objectives and measurements. As I can tell you from my own experience, with each step you move up the management ladder, you forget more of the detail of what's happening below you. This has its advantages, because it helps you see and deal with "the big picture." But when you overlook the details you start to distort and simplify what's happening—because life in the real world is lived in the details. If the team participates in setting its objectives and measurements, reality gets brought back into the picture. The results will almost always be superior to objectives set two or three levels above the team. (Note, by the way, that this is true of objectives, but not of goals. Often, especially in the beginning stages, goals are best set a level or two above the team.)

I also can't stress too much how important it is to measure the team's progress—however you can. How many times have you been part of a bright, new organizational program that ended with a final evaluation of "Well, we can't really point to any specifics, but we're a lot more motivated now and we're sure this has really helped us."? That's orgspeak for "That's another program that didn't fulfil its promise, so let's put it away and go look for the next one." It can get even worse. Suppose a rarity happens and a program gets implemented that appears really to work. But there aren't any specific objectives, and no measures. How in the world do you demonstrate to anyone—particularly all those anyones who've been fighting it all along—that it's a success? The answer is: You don't.

In short, the objectives and their measures should make it clear whether or not the team is achieving its goal. They should also make it clear whether it *achieved* its goal. Did productivity and quality go up? As much as we expected? If not, was the improvement worthwhile enough to justify the time and effort? Will the design really be easier to manufacture, or the new system meet the needs of customers better than the old one? Is the new organization really an improvement on the old one? Why? Unless the team's goals are specific and measurable, you'll never know.

6. Direct, Prompt, Dependable, and Usable Feedback to the Team

If you read the section on objectives carefully, you know that feedback is critical. After all, what good are objectives if the team doesn't know how they're doing on them? The feedback serves its purpose, though, only when it possesses all of these four characteristics:

1. It goes *direct* to the team, not through intermediaries. In traditional organizations, feedback often goes to higher levels of management, then works its way down—perhaps—to the working level. That won't cut it with empowered teams. The feedback needs to go directly to them. If managers need it, send them copies.

2. It is *prompt*. What does prompt mean? It means that the team gets the feedback in time for them to make any corrections they need. That may be the same month, the same week, the same or next day, the same hour. It all depends on what the feedback is and how they need to use it. A project team, for example, will usually operate with much less frequent feedback than a self-directing work team.

3. It is *dependable*. This means, of course, that it's accurate. It also means that it's always available at the time it's supposed to be available, in the form that the team expects. And it's complete.

4. Finally, it's *usable*. It must be specific and detailed enough for the team's purposes. It must not be in jargon or use codes that are hard for the team to understand or time consuming for them to translate. When the team looks at the feedback, and there's something wrong, the information itself should help them find the problem.

One other point is important: the team must know how to use the feedback. This sounds simple and obvious. It's not—because the fact that an individual or team has feedback doesn't mean that they have the know-how to use it effectively for planning or scheduling. They may need formal training in how to use the feedback, or perhaps just informal coaching. But the manager responsible must see that they develop the skills they need to make the feedback useful.

7. Rewards for the Team, Not Just for Individuals

This is probably the single most often violated requirement for effective teams. Organizations typically have compensation plans based primarily on individual performance; you and I sink or swim on how we do in our specific jobs, and only secondarily on how we work with others. If this carries over to the team—if you try to determine each individual's performance and reward him or her for it—you will surely kill the team.

Let me give you an example that doesn't even involve a team. In the late 1970's, the Federal government adopted a performance-based pay plan for managers known as Merit Pay. At one activity, characterized by complex operations that required careful coordination among different organizations, pay for performance was implemented on a purely individual basis. Each manager answered only for the performance of his organization. Because of the complexity, cooperation among managers had never been outstanding; once individualized pay for performance was implemented, cooperation simply ceased to exist. Each manager looked out for himself, period. The impact on the organization was devastating. Performance standards were changed the next year to incorporate mutual support and coordination, but the after-effect of the individual standards continued to handicap operations for several years.

Think how much more harmful individual rewards are when what you want is effective *team* action. Each individual is looking over his shoulder at his boss—and simultaneously looking for ways to be a "star" on the team. A group of independent stars may make a beautiful constellation, but they make a lousy team.

If you really want a team, you must commit yourself to the team, period. You evaluate the *team's* performance, not that of the individuals who make it up. What if different individuals make very different contributions? That's a matter for the team. If it accepts less than the best from each member, it has already compromised its goals and is well on its way to a mediocre product.

A final note where incentives and rewards are concerned. As best I can tell, almost every individual and almost every team believes that their efforts are not adequately recognized and rewarded. This seems to be almost universal. Make it a continuing priority to see that the team is not only rewarded as a team, but that its successes *are* rewarded and recognized—over and over and over again.

8. Solid Individual and Group Competence

For the team to succeed, its members must be competent—and you're the one who has to see that they are. If you're not effective at this, the first seven characteristics won't be enough. It takes real competence to work effectively as part of a team—and you don't develop this competence just by deciding you're going to work in the team.

The first competence the team needs, of course, is subject-matter competence. Each member of the team needs to be good at what he or she does, and the team must have the cumulative competence in its members to accomplish its goal. But that's not enough. The team also needs to be competent at being a team— and that requires a completely different set of skills.

Let's be clear what we're talking about. Team competence doesn't mean "groupthink," or the kind of nicey-nicey behavior you see in groups whose members are trying not to offend each other. In fact, when you see groupthink or nicey-niceyness, you can be relatively sure that the team has not yet developed the basic competence it needs.

At least initially, it's up to you to see that the team gets any training it needs to have basic team competence. You don't want to bet the success of a team project on the members somehow muddling through and doing the right thing together. Quality circles and their successors in the quality movement provide an excellent model of how to do this right. If quality circles are organized as they should be, their members get training not only in specific problem-solving techniques but in group processes as well. Then they have a facilitator who works with them to see that they use this training effectively.

As we go through the book, you'll develop a more complete idea of the kinds of competence that teams must have. For right now, the important point is this: When you decide to set up a team, allow whatever time is necessary for them to develop their competence as a team. For heaven's sake, though, don't think of this as just something for first-level workers. It may be much more difficult to get managers to work on group skills—but they may need to work on them even more than first-level people do.

ASK THE EIGHT KEY QUESTIONS

Now you have the basic requirements to move out with teams in your own organization. You know how to evaluate the organization as a whole, the two layers of management above you, and your own organization to find their readiness for teampower. And you know the eight characteristics of successful teams.

To end the chapter, let me suggest that you convert these eight characteristics into eight questions—and ask them each time you're thinking of establishing a team:

1. What are the important values shared among the team players, and between the team and myself, that will support teamwork?

2. What are the clear, worthwhile goals the team is to accomplish?

3. Why do the team members need each other to accomplish these goals?

4. What will create genuine commitment to the team's goals?

5. What are the specific objectives by which the team's success will be measured?

6. How is the team going to get direct, prompt, dependable, usable feedback on its performance?

7. What rewards are there for team, rather than just individual success?

8. How competent is the team, both as individuals and as a team?

If you ask these eight questions each time you start to create a team, they'll help you identify in a hurry the major problems you need to solve for team success. Asking the questions will also sharpen your sense of how very easy it is to misuse teams and end up with wasted time and disappointed members. In short, you will save yourself an immense amount of grief if you make sure you have the answers to the seven questions *before* the team begins to function.

Of course, you can't relax and forget these points once the team is set up. As we go through the book, you'll see one or another of them come up again and again as part of the process of managing empowered teams.

Chapter 3

The Many Different Kinds of Teams

This chapter describes several ways you can start using teampower. It focuses on quality teams, project teams, multiskilled/multifunctional teams and fully self-managing teams. Before we look at them, though, we need to detour quickly through two other topics: what to call people who work in teampower environments, and the fundamentals of empowering individuals—whether they work independently or as members of teams.

WHERE TO START: EVERYBODY'S A PLAYER

I hope this section title caught your eye, because right here we change our vocabulary. One way that you can tell an organization that makes full use of teampower is that you don't hear the words "manager" and "employee." In a real team-based organization, everyone—*everyone*—is a player.

You may not be able to move all of the way to fully self-managing teams for years, but you might as well make this mental shift now. No matter what form of teams you use, you'll have the greatest success if you think of yourself and every other person involved as a full-fledged player.

Does the word seem a little forced to you? Frankly, it does to me. But I can' find another word that comes as close. J. C. Penney Co. and many who follow them call employees (but not managers) "associates." That doesn't seem to accomplish much. The military refer to everyone, enlisted and officer alike, as "members"; no military service has military "employees." Certainly that's better than "manager" and "employee," and it makes sense to talk of members of teams. All in all, though, I prefer to talk about players—because what teams must have to succeed is not members but *players*.

Pick your own vocabulary—but make sure you understand why the change. An organization that uses empowered teams, and empowered players in any form, doesn't have the nice, neat division between people who manage and people who are simply employed. In these organizations, everyone has a role to play—and no one's role is more important than anyone else's.

You can see the analogy with a sports team (which has been made many times). The quarterback may call the plays, but he's in deep peanut butter if his line doesn't play as well as he does. The inside linebacker may be a "star," but on a critical play it may be one of the outside linebackers who makes a saving tackle. The same is true in all team sports: everyone has a crucial part to play, if one person fails the whole team fails.

The idea of "players" is much wider than this, though. Whether you like golf, tennis, bridge or poker, you're a player. If you speculate on the stock market, you're a player. And even the people around Las Vegas' tables are players. The point, of course, is that players are involved, trying to accomplish something, committing themselves to an outcome they believe is valuable.

We decided many pages ago that you want individuals who are competent and committed—and what's that but to say that you want individuals who are all first-string players in your organization. Not employees who are both less competent and less committed than you, but players who are focusing their energies on the same goal you are.

You're a player, too. Just as the others are players, not "employees," you are a player, not a "manager." Your roles may be different from theirs, but yours are no more and no less important than theirs. If you want effectively empowered individuals—and especially if you want them producing high-quality work in empowered teams—then you all need to understand that you're in it together. Every one of you is a player.

HOW TO EMPOWER PLAYERS AS INDIVIDUALS _____

This is the last detour before we get to empowered teams. It's based on a simple fact: you can't really empower a team. What you can do is empower individuals, and then they create an empowered team. This brief section hits the high spots of what you need to do to empower individuals.

In traditional management books, empowering individual players is called "delegation." That's accurate, at least as far as it goes—and that's where you have to start. If you're not comfortable with delegation, you might want to look at my *The New Manager's Survival Manual* or William Oncken's *Managing Management Time* (both are listed in the bibliography).

DO MORE THAN JUST DELEGATE _____

To really empower players so they can create empowered teams means going beyond the basics of delegation, though. For instance, it means creating a structure for individuals much like the structure you create for teams. In particular, four of the requirements for effective teams are just as applicable to effective individual empowerment:

1. *Clear, Worthwhile Goals.* This is just as important for empowered individuals as it is for empowered teams. If individuals are to take responsibility for their work, it must be clear what they are to accomplish. It must also be worth accomplishing. This sounds so obvious as to be repetitious—except that higher-level players are sometime tempted to keep the interesting work for themselves and delegate the routine, boring work to other players. You may need to spread the dull work around; no law says you or any other individual has to do it all. But don't do it in the name of "empowering" anyone. For that, pick the challenging, interesting tasks and delegate them.

2. *Specific Objectives.* This comes up again in a page or so; there's no need to elaborate on it here. Just remember that the more specific you can be about what you want from people (but

not how they are to accomplish it), the better the performance they will give you.

3. *Appropriate Rewards.* To a point, the freedom and responsibility that come with delegation are an incentive to many people—but only to a point. If all the rewards still go to the players who put in their time, don't make waves and never take risks, you'll have a difficult time indeed when you try to empower anyone.

4. *Competence.* Effective delegation requires players who are competent at their jobs; this should be self-evident. You should also know, from the first chapter, that it requires players who're skilled at managing themselves. Part of delegating is helping the individual acquire whatever competence he needs to succeed.

This is a good beginning, but it takes more to really empower people.

TAKE THESE POSITIVE STEPS _____

Help People Succeed

The goal of empowerment isn't tossing everybody to the sharks and seeing who successfully swims away. The goal is developing shark-killers, spending whatever time and effort are necessary to see that everyone becomes effective at managing themselves.

Another way to put this is to say that you must effectively manage each individual's learning curve. Some players will soak up their new freedom and responsibility like a cat lapping milk; these players make managing easy. But not everyone is like this; even individuals who will become effective empowered players may take considerable time learning how to do it. When you've helped an individual like this become an independent, self-managing player, you get a tremendous feeling of satisfaction.

There's a fine line between being independent and getting in over your head—and the line is different with each individual. On the one hand, you don't *ever* want to penalize the individual if she makes a mistake because she showed too much initiative. After all, you want her to develop initiative. But you don't want her to "wing it" without really knowing what she's doing. Knowing when you're into deep water and need to go for help is a crucial self-management skill. Helping every player develop this skill is one of your top priorities.

Measurable, Realistic, Challenging Objectives

Here we are at objectives again. When you're dealing with individuals instead of teams, it's no less important to set measurable, realistic, and challenging objectives. They're the only solid basis for effective empowerment. Period.

Some of these objectives will simply be standards. If your players do lots of reports, for instance, you'll want a general standard for all reports: format, language, length, type of summary, etc. If they work with customers, you'll want standards such as the number of complaints that are resolved satisfactorily on the spot. Even though these standards may be routine and may not change much from month to month, they should be measurable, realistic and challenging.

No matter the kind of work, you'll also need specific objectives. They might be "get well" objectives: "Within six months, all reports will be produced on the day due or before." They may be improvement objectives: "We will reduce the time taken on the line with customers by 10%, with no reduction in customer satisfaction." When you empower players, you'll almost always want to do it with a combination of clear, constant standards and specific objectives. They keep you and the other players focused on the goal, and keep disagreements from disintegrating into personalities and excuses.

There's one other advantage to good standards and objectives. You're probably very good at what you do. Chances are that this is one of the reasons you were selected as a manager. And I'm sure you've heard a dozen (or a thousand) times the shop-worn copout: "If you want something done right, you have to do it yourself." You may have agreed with it every time, and I sympathize with you if you did—but it's a sure loser. Believe it, and neither you nor the players around you will be very empowered. They won't have any responsibility, and you'll be so busy you won't have time for anything but the daily grind. The only way to avoid this is to develop measurable, realistic, challenging objectives and standards and use them as the basis for delegation. That's how players become empowered *and* successful.

I wish that there were more time to talk about objectives and standards here; I know it's not enough to tell you that you need them and then go on to something else. Unfortunately, that's what I have to do. I'll trust you to follow up on this one yourself.

Insist that Commitments Be Made Carefully and Kept Exactly

I hope you know this already—it's so basic. I only mention it because so few individuals practice it. It's really simple, and it goes like this:

1. Ensure that your players make commitments carefully—and exercise equal care when they accept a commitment from another. There's a tremendous temptation to make commitments simply to get rid of unpleasant pressure, or to force someone else to make an unrealistic commitment to "stretch" them. Your players should avoid all of these like the plague! They should not make, insist on, or accept unrealistic commitments—period.

2. Once a player has made a commitment, or another player has made a commitment to her, it should be followed exactly as made. Not "nearly" or "close" or "it would have been, except. . . ." *Exactly.* I'm not going to go into the research behind this, but I can assure you that nothing is more important to the credibility of empowered players than this. When you assign a project to an individual or team, negotiate realistic commitments with them and then insist that they be kept exactly.

3. And what if something happens? The commitment turns out not to be realistic? Conditions change? An unexpected problem comes up? The players involved should renegotiate the commitment, and renegotiate it immediately. If a player promised a prototype and suddenly can't get parts, he may be able to work around it—or he may not. The important point is that the moment he knows he can't make the commitment, he needs to renegotiate it.

In short, these are two mortal sins:

1. *Making a commitment that's not intended to be kept exactly as made,* and

2. *Telling another player at the last minute that a commitment can't be kept.*

(We'll look at this again, in a different context, in Chapter 9.)

EVERY PLAYER NEEDS A CUSTOMER _____

This is the last section on empowering players as individuals. From here on, we're going to look at teams. Unless and until you go to an organization made up 100% of self-managed teams, though, you'll still have players working as individuals. Let me give you one last recommendation for these individuals, based on the model of effective performance we looked at in Chapter 1:

1. Give each player a specific customer to serve. (He may have several or even dozens of customers; that's fine. If you have to assign two or more players to one customer, though, see if you can't organize them as a team.)

2. Let that player deal directly with that customer and take complete responsibility for satisfying him. (Of course, this requires that the player be completely committed and competent. If he's not competent and committed yet, you need to provide more guidance until he is.),

3. Then give that player control over everything he needs to satisfy that customer. (If he can't control it all, give him as much control as possible.)

If you're not sure how to do this, let me immodestly suggest that you read my book, *Front-line Customer Service,* which has detailed guidance on developing customer-focused, empowered players. Here are a few brief examples of some ways to do it:

1. I'm writing this book with the WordPerfect word processor on my IBM-compatible computer. If you've ever dealt with

the WordPerfect Corporation, you know what a committed, competent, customer-focused and empowered customer service representative is. These representatives are carefully selected and carefully trained. Their job—and this is clear when you talk with them—is to do whatever is necessary to solve your problem. They take it personally. When a WordPerfect customer service representative picks up your call, *you* are his or her customer until your problem is solved. SAS airways and Federal Express are even more widely known for empowered front-line people dedicated to customer satisfaction.

2. Let's look at a very different situation. You manage a group of procurement agents that buy supplies and operating equipment for the organization. Do you have a book of policies and procedures, with reviews by senior workers, supervisors, even yourself before a buy can be made? Does this focus everyone's attention on seeing that the i's are dotted and the t's crossed—with the customer coming in a distant second? Develop the competence of your procurement agents. Give them specific customers. Provide them with a few, clear policies to follow. Monitor their work until they're up to speed, but don't come between them and their customers. It will take time and effort and there'll be rough edges—but you'll be amazed at the increase in customer satisfaction, quality of procurements and (almost certainly) productivity that results.

3. This last example is simple and provides a great lead-in to the rest of the chapter. Suppose you manage the service shop of a new-car dealership. Customers leave their cars, your mechanics work on them, then the customers pick them back up—complete with bill. Suppose that clipped to each bill is a card that said: "My name is Joe Smith. I did the work on your car, and I'm proud of what I did. If you have *any* problem, call me at 123-4567." You might have problems getting support for the idea at first—but what do you think would happen to commitment and quality once your players began to work this way?

I hope that this has given you ideas on how to effectively empower your players as individuals and as members of empowered teams. From here on, we focus directly on teams, starting with quality teams.

QUALITY TEAMS REALLY WORK _____

There are many different kinds of teams that an organization can use. The first kind we're going to look at is the quality team—for six very good reasons:

1. Quality teams can be used anywhere, at any level, in any kind of organization. While these teams started on the manufacturing floor, they've been used everywhere from there to the executive suite.

2. Quality teams have a clear purpose—to improve the quality of an organization's products, services, processes and work environment. Remember that one of the requirements for a successful team is a worthwhile goal outside itself. In most organizations, improving quality is exactly such a worthwhile goal—one that players at every level can commit themselves to. And, as studies have consistently shown, if you improve quality you will improve productivity. (The reverse is definitely not true.)

3. Quality teams are traditionally trained in both group skills and problem-solving skills. *All* teams require these skills, so starting with quality teams is a good way to begin developing not only the skills themselves but the idea that both sets of skills are essential.

4. The guidelines for establishing quality teams are widely known. There are dozens of books on the topic, and even more consultants with the skills to help companies establish meaningful programs. While starting and maintaining successful quality teams is never easy, at least you don't have to reinvent the wheel.

5. Successful quality teams are empowered teams. Most of the issues that are raised by teampower are raised by using quality teams, and most of the skills that you need as a teampower manager are needed to manage quality teams.

6. Successful quality teams generate tremendous pressure to move beyond their initial form into other, more powerful kinds of teams. (This is particularly significant, and we'll revisit it in a few pages.)

There's one more reason for starting with quality teams, one that's tangential to the purposes of this book but immensely relevant to good management. Quality teams are part of a process that sees good management as "data-driven." In this environment, "decisions are based on data, not guesswork. Use of a scientific approach becomes standard procedure. The focus is on improving products and services by improving *how* work gets done (the methods) instead of simply *what* is done (the results)."[24]

By implementing quality teams, you begin to train both the teams and yourself to make decisions based on facts, not guesses or habit. That's a management curriculum in itself.

WHAT QUALITY TEAMS DO _____

Your organization may already use quality teams, or may have experimented with them and then discontinued them. If so, you already have some idea of what they are. Originally, they were called "Quality Circles." In organizations with full-fledged Total Quality programs, they're often called "Process Action Teams" or "Corrective Action Teams." Many firms have given them more unique names, attempting to reflect their own approach to quality.

Despite the variations in names, the purposes of quality teams are very similar from one firm to another. Here's a beginning definition of this purpose, taken from one of the many books on quality circles:

> [Quality teams] are organized within a department or work area for the purpose of studying and eliminating production-related problems. They are problem-solving teams which use simple statistical methods to research and decide on solutions to workshop problems.[25]

With this definition as a start, here are what I believe are the most important characteristics of quality teams:

1. They focus on *quality*, not on productivity or cost-reduction. I know that this repeats what's already been said, but it bears

repeating. In firms without quality programs based on the ideas of Deming and Juran, the cost of poor quality is normally so high that improving quality even slightly improves productivity and lowers cost. The reverse never happens; if you start out to improve productivity, quality will stay the same or decline and productivity may or may not improve. (Just in case you've forgotten how great the cost of poor quality is, here's an idea. If your firm doesn't have an effective quality program, the cost of poor quality is almost certainly between 25% and 40% of your total costs.)[26]

2. They begin *within a specific work area*. There's a good reason for this: Most front-line players only really understand what happens in their immediate area. It makes sense to begin solving problems that are most familiar, then to move on. In general, almost any work area has problems enough to occupy a team for one to two years.

3. Within this area, they are *problem-solving* teams, trained in problem-solving techniques and focused on specific problems. There's virtually no limit on the problem they can attack. Quality teams solve problems of machine malfunction, workflow, process delays, health and safety hazards, absenteeism, hospital admission procedures—you name it.

4. They solve problems by working on *specific processes*. Quality teams are not primarily motivational devices, designed to "pump up" their members or increase their commitment (though both may happen). Instead, they identify processes that are causing problems, study and analyze these processes, and find ways to improve them. This is a basic meaning of the phrase "data-driven" that we looked at just above. In an organization with a fully functioning Total Quality program, they also "own" the processes that they work with.[27]

5. They *have help* to accomplish their goals. Besides their training in group processes and problem-solving methods, most groups have a facilitator to help them.

There's one other characteristic, a critically important one. They often don't have the authority to make the changes they identify. Instead, they present their findings and recommendations to management, who decides whether to implement them or not. Doing the presentations lets team members develop additional skills and gives them a chance to show what they can do.

But that puts the burden on management to listen, respond and (whenever possible) implement the teams' recommendations promptly. Teams need to see their recommendations implemented, or they need *very* good reasons why not. A team that works hard and comes up with one or two recommendations that are vetoed will loose interest rapidly. (You have a check here. Normally, you or another supervisor will be on the team. One responsibility that player can take is to "test the water" if he thinks a recommendation might not fly. If the idea gets a cold reception, he can explain the situation to the rest of the team and guide them in a more productive direction.)

The best single motivational poster I've ever seen for quality teams was a sign, posted widely in the organization, that said simply: "We implement over 85% of the recommendations of our quality teams."

HOW QUALITY TEAMS PAY OFF

The paragraphs above covered the benefits to the organization in general. Quality teams don't work "in general," though; they work on specific problems. The question is: What can you expect from them? Many of their recommendations are small ones. For instance, a team at Cap Snap in Kingsport, Tennessee found that a poorly located wall added four minutes to the stock change time on labelling machines. Removing the wall saved some $1500 per year.[28] Don't think this happens only in industrial situations, though. At West Paces Ferry Hospital near Atlanta, Georgia, one team decreased the waste of IV medication by over 40% (saving $22,000-plus per year), while another team reduced the number of unnecessary trips to the pharmacy by almost 80%.[29] The payback may be even smaller: a team might recommend a slight change in a form, with an annual payback in time saved just barely greater than the value of the time they spent in finding and solving the problem. That may not sound like much, but it is. Small changes—if you keep building on them—turn into large, money-saving changes.

Here are two examples of how many, many changes can pyramid into tremendous results:

> In less than a year, the quality program of the Kodak copier division reduced defects from 50,000 parts per million to 950 parts per million. During the same period, the number of quality inspectors dropped from twenty-five to none.
>
> It doesn't just happen in private industry. The Internal Revenue Service decided to try quality teams. From 1986 to 1987, returns processed increased some 7%, but the number of processing errors dropped 90%.[30]

Most savings produced by quality teams are small—but not all of them. Here are two dramatic but not unique examples of what can happen:

> One of Ford Motor Company's four transmission plants is in Livonia, Michigan. There, two-person teams (one person is salaried and the other hourly) teach three-day T.E.A.M. (Targeted Employee Action Methods) classes to production workers, supervisors, and managers. One team that took the course went back to its department, identified and solved a problem with chip contamination in transmission castings, and saved the company $320,000 per year. Another team identified a modification to a transveyor line and logic system. When they presented the idea to a group of managers, the team estimated it would save $164,000 per year. The Comptroller was at the presentation and took issue with their figures. "You've left out one factor," he said; "The actual savings will be closer to $184,000 per year."[31]

Most solutions by quality teams don't come close to this magnitude, and they don't need to—but don't forget that it's always a possibility. Teampower truly is power, and the worse thing you can do is fence it in with limited expectations.

IF YOU DON'T HAVE QUALITY TEAMS—START THEM _____

I hope I've whetted your appetite for quality teams, and that you'll at least look into starting them in your organization if you don't already have them. Let me give you one strong caution, though:

> *Don't try to start quality teams just from the information given in this book—there's not enough of it.*

After all, this isn't a book on quality teams. But there are shelves full of books on the subject. Several of them are in the bibliography, and I particularly recommend *The Team Handbook* by Peter R. Scholtes. There are also dozens of consultants who have proven track records for implementing quality teams; your organization may even have internal consultants who are expert in the area. Use others' expertise here and don't waste time reinventing the wheel.

MOVING BEYOND QUALITY TEAMS

Quality Circles, the first form of quality teams, sprouted like the proverbial mushrooms in the early 1980s. If you've ever watched mushrooms in the wild, you know that shortly after they sprout they die—and quality circles have often done the same. Is this because they don't work? No. We've seen that they do. The problem is that they *grow*, and as they grow they *outgrow* what a localized quality team can do. They can do it in one or more of several ways—and here are four of the most common ones:

1. Many of the sticky, high-payoff problems are those that involve not an individual work area but the *relationships* between two or more work areas. An effective quality team very soon finds that to progress it has to deal with these problems. The other area may have no interest in dealing with the team. Management may forbid the team to deal with areas outside its own. Whatever happens, the team gets discouraged and, quite possibly, bored. It may feel that it had its wings clipped for no reason. Motivation starts to wane.

2. The standard problem-solving tools used by quality teams are helpful but limited. An energetic, effective team may find itself tackling problems that are too big for the tools. It gets frustrated when it can't get a handle on the problem and

loses confidence. It may go back to simpler problems for a time, but sooner or later it will probably lose its motivation and began to fall apart.

3. Effective quality teams may start meddling, questioning some of the sacred cows of the organization. Management suggests, tactfully or bluntly, that the team should back off, and the team begins to question management's commitment to them and their task. Once again, motivation wanes and the team loses its effectiveness.

4. In conjunction with any of these, or on its own, managers may begin to feel that the team has too much independence. This may happen openly; the team may simply be told to limit itself. Or it may be covert; management suggests that the team spend less time as a team, or the players find it harder to get cooperation of others. Once again . . . .

One or more of these or similar conditions may happen in a few weeks, or months, or not until the team has been working a year or two. But something almost certainly will happen that will make it more and more difficult for the team to function productively. This creates a crisis for the team, or even for the whole program.

Is that the end? Not necessarily. Each successful quality team is a reservoir of group and problem-solving skills. The players on these teams have experienced work that was more challenging, more under their control, more cooperative. The players have demonstrated self-management skills—and probably acquired new ones. This is a tremendous asset for the organization and for the player who established the team(s) in the first place.

What do you do? One possibility is that a quality team can become a special projects team. Or it may grow into a continuing multifunctional team. There's one other possibility:

The transition into self-managing teams is also a possibility. [Self-managing] teams are intact work groups in which the workers assume responsibility for performing many of the functions that supervisory or support groups previously carried out. They may, for instance, perform their own scheduling, assigning of workers to tasks, monitoring of work quality, and goal setting. Teams foster participation by giving employees responsibility for day-to-day decision making concerning their work. Quality circles can prepare employees for this type of structure by fostering development of skills and knowledge.[32]

In other words, you can help a successful quality team transform itself into an even more empowered team. Then the players can continue to develop their skills and make even more significant contributions to the organization.

With this in mind, let's look at some of the alternative ways you might use teampower.

THE ADVANTAGES AND PITFALLS OF PROJECT TEAMS _____

Project teams (often called "task forces") have been around for a long time; you may have been on one or several of them yourself. What distinguishes a project team is this:

It has a specific objective, and when it achieves that objective it goes out of business.

Project teams can support an incredible variety of objectives: developing McDonald's Chicken McNuggets, improving production machinery, investigating the Challenger disaster, selecting new office furniture, finding the origin of an epidemic, recommending a new organizational structure, improving workflow within or among offices—almost any purpose for which two or more people working together are more effective than individuals working alone. For instance, the project team that developed IBM's personal computer wasn't unique at the company. Much earlier, a similar team had developed the System 360 computer—one of the most revolutionary and successful computers in IBM's history. Perhaps no one has developed the art of the project team as completely, though, as Lockheed's "Skunk Works." Sherm Mullin, president of the Skunk Works, "picks small teams of highly motivated people, gives them very austere budgets, and puts them in isolation to keep senior management off their backs."[33] The system obviously works, because the Skunk Works has one of the very best track records of all the U.S.'s defense contractors.

THE ADVANTAGES _____

These are some of the advantages of these teams:

1. Perhaps the most important advantage is that project teams have a temporary life. This keeps them from getting bureaucratically clogged arteries. They have (hopefully) a clear purpose and a mandate to accomplish that purpose. They do not have to go through all the "May I?'s" and "Would you please?'s" of established organizations. They can go right to the heart of the matter, investigate it, and reach conclusions. This is why organizations (such as IBM or Ford) so often use project teams for new product development.

2. A well-designed project team combines a variety of necessary skills within a small group. Individuals can talk directly to others with a point of view and expertise they need but lack. (We'll look at this more closely when we look at multifunctional teams in a few paragraphs.)

3. Many times, a project team can look at an issue more effectively and more quickly than an established organization—because they can evade the bureaucracy. Turf doesn't have to be defended in quite the same way that it does in formal interunit meetings.

4. Project teams—when they're well run—are marvelous ways to develop their members. Individuals who have seen the organization only from one department, or even one small unit, get to see it much more broadly. A job analyst won't become an auditor just from serving on a project team, but she will understand the relevance of internal audits to what she does in a new and deeper way. An assembler may change how he does his job when he finds what a packer has to do to package the assembly.

... AND THE PITFALLS _____

As with any other management practice, project teams poorly used are simply another way to shoot yourself in the foot. Here are some of the ways you can sabotage a project team:

1. *Don't give them clear goals and objectives.* We've seen how important these are for all teams. For a team that operates only for a short time, they are absolutely essential.

2. *Have a hidden agenda.* Project teams are often formed as a cover for a higher-level player, who expects the team to come up with the recommendations she's already decided on. This is an almost certain recipe for decreased commitment and increased cynicism. If you know what you want done and still want to use a project team, make them responsible for recommending how to implement the idea.

3. *Put someone in as leader who doesn't have experience.* Nothing turns a team off faster than someone who allows it to wallow around without accomplishing its task effectively. You'll want to see the leadership rotated, so other players can develop these skills—but only after they've seen how an effective leader does her job.

4. *Make the team too big.* If you get much beyond seven or eight players, you'll have a committee—and you'll waste a great deal of time as they design you a camel or an aardvark instead of the horse you wanted from them. Some major projects may require a larger team. If this is what you have to do, be sure you select a leader who can divide the team into effective subteams and integrate their efforts. (Xerox learned the hard way to keep project teams small. Its Memorywriter typewriter was developed and brought to market by a seven-person team—while a much larger team competing with them never even finished the project.)[34]

5. *Staff the team with individuals who're not used to working in groups.* It's amazing how often managers will select members for project teams with no regard for their group skills—and then are disappointed when the team never becomes a cohesive group. This is one of the best reasons in the world for starting with quality teams that are carefully trained in both problem-solving and group processes. If you don't begin with quality teams, see that project teams members get at least as high a level of training as they would have gotten as part of a quality team.

HOW TO MAKE PROJECT TEAMS WORK _____

Even when you do everything else right, there are two ways that project teams can fail: They can do work others should have done, and they can come up with recommendations no one else is interested in.

One of the biggest mistakes an organization can make is the routine use of "Tiger Teams" that rush into crisis situations and solve them. It may be necessary at times (though I'm dubious about that), but look what happens. Someone who was responsible for a project, product, whatever, doesn't produce as expected. So, a Tiger Team goes rushing in and takes the responsibility. The team is out to prove itself, not necessarily to find what caused the situation and how the organization can prevent it in the future. In this situation, also, team members often have axes to grind, and the team provides the perfect cover for the grinding. The combination can be deadly.

Project teams should be used only to do work that cannot be done, or cannot be done in time, by the regular organization. If things really get bad in some operation, a Tiger Team may be the only way to rescue them quickly enough. Everyone should recognize, though, that this is no more a success for the Tiger Team than it is a failure for the organization. The only effective reaction to any performance failure is to analyze why it happened and prevent it from happening again.

The danger that a project team may make recommendations no one else is interested in is a very real one. The team gets heavily involved in their work; they often eat, sleep and drink the problem; their commitment to the problem and the solution is very, very high. But that commitment may not be shared by those who haven't been involved.

Successful project teams stay in close contact with the parts of the organization that must buy into their recommendations. Will it cause extra work for Shipping? Does it run counter to one of Manufacturing's established policies? Does it establish a new role for Quality Control? The team needs to be constantly aware of these problems—and staying in touch with the other affected organizations.

At times, you may want to go further and include members of other units in the team on an *ad hoc* basis. Perhaps someone from

Shipping can help the team identify how to accomplish its goal without causing the extra work. Perhaps a player from Manufacturing can suggest how to change their policy only minimally, and someone from Quality Control devise a way to meet their goals as well as the team's. Project teams that are tackling really tough problems often bring in key players from elsewhere in the organization to deal with situations such as these.

The point is that the team must stay connected to those critical to the success of its conclusions, however it chooses to do it. If it's effective at this, it will have an established constituency for its recommendations—which significantly increases the chance that they will be implemented.

Let me end by repeating that the structured, trained approach of quality teams is an excellent preparation for an effective project team—just as becoming a project team can be one development avenue for a successful quality team. It's not necessary to link the two; many organizations don't. But it can be a powerful avenue for the progress of teampower in your organization.

CONSIDER MULTIFUNCTIONAL AND MULTISKILLED TEAMS

What makes these teams distinctive is that the players on them have different skills, and/or come from different functions in the organization. One well-known example of this kind of team is "Team Taurus" that Ford Motor Company used to design the Taurus. Not everyone knows that there was actually a wide variety of teams involved in the process, reaching to the very top of the organization. For instance, top executives formed teams to identify customer wants, change product development, and change the company's reward system to support higher quality. Members of the first team, by the way, listened directly to customers. There were also design teams that even included engineers from Ford suppliers.[35]

Multifunctional/multiskilled teams can be just as much at home everywhere else in organizations. Several firms use teams of maintenance workers skilled in different crafts; each team provides complete maintenance service to one or a group of units. American Transtech, a subsidiary of AT&T, is one of dozens of firms that use teams of clerical workers to completely process customer transactions and inquiries. And in manufacturing companies, "concurrent engineering," which includes representatives from every stage in the design and manufacturing process on the same team, is a current buzzword.

I've already pointed out that project teams are often multifunctional and/or multiskilled teams. Several examples in the first paragraph of this section, such as Ford's executive teams, are project teams. In many organizations, players at all levels are first exposed to players in other functions or skills on such project teams.

Other teams, though, are continuing ones—like the customer-order teams at Litel Telecommunications, or the sales teams at Baxter Healthcare Corp. These two teams, different as they are, share one other characteristic: they were both formed specifically to increase the firm's service to its customers. They get their work done day after day by combining a variety of skills on each team, dramatically reducing the time needed to respond to customers.

ADVANTAGES AND DANGERS OF THESE TEAMS _____

Multifunctional, multiskilled teams combine the expertise needed to attack a problem or perform a series of functions at the lowest possible level. These are some of the advantages that can result:

1. *The team gets all of the players into the act from the beginning.* Traditionally, one function or skill starts the project, then passes it to another function and then another and then another. . . . Each function has a different interest, and no function knows exactly what problems their decisions may cause other functions. As the project or product moves down the line and problems begin to develop, each function tends to blame one of the functions before it, and that function blames one before them, and that function blames. . . . If all of the functions are part of the team from the beginning, these conflicts can be surfaced and dealt with by the team as a whole. Then, when the final decision has been made, everyone can buy into it.

2. *The team gets all of the skills or functions needed from the beginning.* One of the classic examples of the lack of this is the new model the engineers in Product Design come up with that

Manufacturing can't build effectively (a common problem in Detroit during the 70s). But the same thing can happen anywhere. For instance, one group in a process may design a form that meets its needs but doesn't get the information that other groups need. If all the skills are in the team from the beginning, the need for in-process changes is sharply reduced.

3. *Multifunctional or multiskilled teams are excellent developmental vehicles.* We saw above that serving on a multifunctional project team gives a player a much broader view of the organization than she could otherwise have. The same is true of continuing multifunctional/multiskilled teams, but even more so. When players with one skill or background work daily with players with different skills and backgrounds, they begin to get a real feel for each others' work. Depending on how the team is organized, they may even be able to perform some of the work of another skill or function in a pinch.

4. Perhaps most important of all, *no way of organizing has more potential for providing customer satisfaction than a multifunctional/multiskilled team.* One team can serve one or a small group of customers, and provide the complete range of services. At American Transtech, for instance, a customer inquiry used to be routed through more than a dozen functional teams; no one team was responsible for it. Now, a single team develops the response to a customer inquiry.

Multifunctional/multiskilled teams certainly aren't all sweetness and light. In fact, these teams are extremely difficult to implement effectively, and they often fail. Here are some of the dangers that multifunctional teams present:

1. Most individuals whose background is in one function or skill identify with that function or skill. Without strong leadership, this continues on the team. The result? A multifunctional or multiskilled team becomes just a collection of individuals standing up for their own specialties. As you might guess, that's no more effective than just having specialized organizations and letting them do their own thing.

2. If you're in a union shop, craft rules may make the functional rivalry problem even worse.

3. If the organization's basic career paths are within functions or skills, individuals may see a multifunctional team as a sidetrack. While they're getting the broad experience on the team, their competitors who stayed in the function are getting the specialized experience to get ahead. (Multifunctional/multiskilled project teams, because they are temporary, usually don't raise this problem to the same degree.)

4. Even when the players get past all these problems, they require extremely skillful leadership to become an integrated, effective team. Individuals in different functions may want to cooperate with each other—but each function has a different way of looking at things, even a different language to describe them. An accountant and a human resources specialists may both talk of "human assets"—but they will look at them in very different ways. The team must have leadership that can help individuals relate to each other's point of view—and deal with the frustration that this creates.

Womack, Jones and Roos provide a superb description of what happens when these dangers aren't overcome:

> The members of the team know that their career success depends on moving up through their functional specialty . . . and they work very hard in the team to advance the interests of their department. In other words, being a member of the . . . team, say, doesn't lead anywhere. The team leader will never see an employee's personnel records, and the leader's performance evaluation won't make much difference to the employee's career. Key evaluations will come from the head of the employee's functional division, who wants to know, "What did you do for my department?"[36]

Let me caution you again—if I need to—not to try to create multifunctional or multiskilled teams without expert assistance. And let me remind you that the kinds of skills that individuals learn in quality teams can help them be much more effective in multifunctional/multiskilled teams—though they're not enough by themselves.

THE STRONGEST FORM OF TEAM:
SELF-MANAGING TEAMS _____

The most effective form of teampower, when the organization can support it, is the fully self-managing or self-directing or semi-autonomous work team. These are the kinds of teams that have made the Gaines plant in Topeka, Kansas so productive for two decades; that have become the dominant form of organization at Procter and Gamble; and that have recently been publicized in GM's Saturn plant or Corning's Blacksburg, Virginia plant. Almost without exception, fully self-managing work teams produce higher quality products and services, and they generally have a much higher rate of production, than organizations with traditional work organization.

What characterizes a fully self-managing team?

It takes responsibility for its own operation and output. When such a team is fully developed, it assumes most of the tasks normally associated with supervision: setting goals, measuring output, insuring that members perform effectively—even hiring, appraising, and disciplining members, and selecting its own team leader.

As you might guess, it takes an immense amount of effort for a traditional organization to move to fully self-managing teams. To date, many of the really effective operations based on fully self-managing work teams have been "greenfields" efforts—new plants designed from the ground up to function this way. There have also been successes at converting traditional organizations, but it takes great care and patience to accomplish this. Firms that have tried to do it quickly and easily have not generally succeeded. (One of GM's first attempts at using teams wasn't as successful as the experience at Bay City. Several years before Pat Carrigan came to Bay City, GM tried to implement teams to build a new mobile home product. Unfortunately, the implementation wasn't as well thought out and managed as it might have been. Instead, GM expected players to learn team methods with little training and coordination. This didn't happen, and the teams slowly died out.)[37]

Any use of teams requires careful planning, preparation and

training; successful quality teams prove that. If you want to be successful with fully selfmanaging teams, you may want to begin with forms of teampower that are easier to implement, and then help them become fully selfmanaging teams over a period of time.

Having said that, here are some tips:

1. Start where you are, move slowly, and build on small successes. The last chapter had suggestions on where to begin, based on your current situation. Use them as a basis for your strategy.

2. Don't expect the process to go smoothly. When you begin to use teampower, you're making major changes in what people have to know and do and in their relations to one another. Be patient, but keep everyone's eye focused on the target.

3. Set specific objectives, with specific timetables, and evaluate progress by them (this should sound familiar by now). GM's inability to successfully implement teams mentioned just above resulted in part from their failure to do this. Learn from their experience. I'm not saying that you must meet all of your objectives the first time; you almost certainly won't. Understanding why you didn't meet an objective, however, can be just as useful as meeting it—and sometimes even more so.

4. Give the players who will be affected a meaningful voice in the decisions. Many failures occur because frontline players don't have this voice—and they do have it in virtually every success. This doesn't mean you won't have to push them (and yourself); you almost certainly will. Just give them a full voice in their own future.

5. Finally, celebrate and reward the successes, even the small ones. I was embarrassed a few days ago to get a note from one of my own players, pointing out that she had been on two very successful teams that had received no recognition at all for their work. That was a major failure on my part, and as I write this I'm correcting it. Learn from my experience here; recognize, celebrate, recognize!!

YOU CAN USE A MIX OF DIFFERENT TEAMS _____

There's no rule that says you can have only one type of team.

In fact, many organizations use different types of teams simultaneously. Here's a quick example:

> At Xerox headquarters in Rochester, New York, workers called "encoders" process several million dollars worth of customer payment checks each day. Encoders often got behind, so that checks were deposited a day late. When you're talking about millions of dollars a day, even a small percentage means a lot of interest that Xerox didn't earn.
>
> When a team of encoders looked into the problem, they found that the players actually did better on Saturday than during the week. What they found was that during the week, coordinators managed the workflow, while on weekends the encoders managed their own workflow. Xerox abolished the coordinator positions; now the work is divided up by the encoders themselves. The result: in addition to the savings from the abolished position, 21% fewer checks are carried over to the next day and overtime is down 70%.[38]

Note that a quality team identified the problem, and then the encoders moved a step closer to a self-managing team by organizing their own workflow. This use of mixed teams is duplicated over and over in teampower organizations. (You'll have problems, though, if you let players work on a self-managing team and then expect them to adapt to a more limited form of empowered team.)

REMEMBER THE 6C APPROACH

I haven't dwelt on the 6C approach in this chapter, but I hope you've seen how relevant it is to all of the discussion. The more an organization implements empowered teams, the more it creates jobs that are challenging, worker controlled and cooperatively performed. You may find the sledding a little tough at first, because no one is used to it. As you go along, though, that sled will start running downhill. People really do want challenge, control and cooperation, and as they begin to see that you really mean to provide it to them, they will respond more and more positively.

I know no better way to illustrate that point and end this chapter than to quote the results of a survey taken of construction workers:

> According to a study entitled "Unionized Construction Workers and Their Work Environment" . . . there is a strong agreement among union members that doing a job in craftsmanlike manner is the most important factor in the job. Intrinsic Rewards such as the opportunity for challenging work, to accomplish something worthwhile, and to learn new things are the most important indicators of job satisfaction.[39]

If that's how construction workers feel about their jobs, do you believe that your workers care less about challenge, control of their work, and cooperation?

Chapter 4

Here's Where
It Works

I've included examples of where and how teampower works throughout the first three chapters. Now it's time to take a closer look at several major success stories. You may not be familiar with many of the firms in this chapter—and that's intentional. Rather than rehash the examples everyone's heard of, I deliberately set out to find some not-quite-so-well-known cases. They're a varied bunch, as you're about to find out. And they profit from teampower in a wide variety of ways.

WORDPERFECT CORPORATION

WordPerfect Corporation is one of the legends in customer support. The company makes and distributes a variety of software for micro and mini computers. Their flagship product, Word Perfect, is the best selling word processor for personal computers. As good as their products are, it's their level of customer service that truly sets them apart.

All customer-service operators in WordPerfect are organized into teams. I asked Robert Rose, Manager of Customer Service why. "I'd probably answer that differently depending on the day of the week," he said. "Today, it's because teams really enhance communication."

Teams at WordPerfect don't really fall into a neat pigeonhole. They're not fully self-managing, nor are they quality teams or project teams. A team is up to 22 individuals, plus a team leader, whose purpose is to solve problems for WordPerfect's customers.

This very clear goal is supported by equally clear values. New customer-service people are expected to possess good interpersonal skills. They're expected to know something about Word-Perfect products. Most of all, they're expected to have an attitude that supports exemplary customer service, teamwork, and constant learning.

Each new customer-service person goes through a three-week training sequence before he or she actually deals with a customer. The individual sets preliminary learning goals during training—goals that will be refined and broadened when he or she actually joins a team. The goals focus on three areas: productivity, product knowledge, and maintaining a positive attitude.

WordPerfect understands about productivity goals—they're all based on providing quality service. If an operator sets a goal of helping more customers in a day, the emphasis is first of all on *help*, and only then on *more*.

Remember that real quality is data driven (Chapter 3). At WordPerfect, each customer-service operator keeps a log. A new operator will review this with the team leader or senior operator, so he can get help with specific problem areas. But it doesn't end there. Each team meets once a week and the players share their most troublesome problems. The team (not the team leader) selects the most critical common problems and decides how to solve them.

What do team leaders do? Well, they have the traditional supervisory duties: counseling, disciplining, appraising performance. But that's not the critical part of their jobs. In Robert Rose's words "They're expected to be leaders, not managers. Managers work with things; leaders work with and care about people—with long-range solutions in mind." In other words, leaders are expected to be resources and facilitators to their teams. They're also expected to be mediators between their team and higher management.

Even though the teams aren't fully self-managing, they've helped WordPerfect keep its organization flat. Because there aren't layers and layers of managers, communication is that much easier. And customer-service operators have that much more freedom. In fact, there are no written limitations on operators. The one unwritten principle is this: good judgment rules. What does this mean? Well, an operator wouldn't ordinarily call WordPerfect's President to solve a problem—but no one would be offended if she did.

Unfortunately, I can't tell you how much teams improved WordPerfect's customer service; they've always had teams. Their teams work. They provide legendary support to their customers. Who could want a clearer or more worthwhile goal than that?

GE SUPERABRASIVES

For this next example, we turn our attention from computers and word processors to a manufacturing plant and one of the teams within it. The plant is the GE Superabrasives plant in Worthington, Ohio—one of the world's major suppliers of man-made diamonds. Our focus here is on a specific team inside the Maintenance Division—a team called "The Fixit Four."

Here's the necessary background. In 1986, the plant implemented a "Commitment to Quality" program. Manufacturing workers were trained in quality techniques and started to use them. In 1989, though, some individuals in the Maintenance Department looked at how successfully the program was going elsewhere and asked loudly why none of them had been trained.

They got trained, and Rob Harris, Mike Mowery, Bill Slavens, and Harold Sullivan formed a team called The Fixit Four—sponsored by J. R. Widders, the Manager of Quality Services. Remember how important it is for a team to have a clear goal outside the team. They certainly did: to find and fix the worst piece of equipment in the plant.

They used standard quality techniques, particularly Pareto Charts, to identify not one but two hydraulic presses that required constant maintenance. They kept using these techniques, until they pinpointed the exact problem. They recommended a fix to management; when management bought off on it, they applied the fix.

For an upfront investment of $30,000 they expected to save $20,000 per year. It turned out that was only the tip of the iceberg. Because the machines weren't often down for repair, additional capacity worth some $665,000 in sales per year was created. For an expenditure of $30,000!

Again, it's not just the dollars they saved. It's how they feel about themselves, their jobs, their plant. It's a pride that was absent two years ago. As one of the Fixit Four said, when management empowered their first-line workers they discovered a gigantic computer that had been unplugged for years.

THE CORRUGATED CONTAINERS DIVISION OF DOMTAR

Let's stay with manufacturing for a while. Our focus changes, though, from an individual plant to a multiplant division. It's the Corrugated Containers Division of Domtar, Inc, a Canadian firm. The Division is Canada's largest supplier of corrugated cardboard boxes, with some 1600 employees from coast to coast. Domtar is a typical traditional organization, and a conservative one at that. The Division fit right in—at least until October 1984.

That was when Norm Burgess, Manager of Technical Services for the Division, went to the Deming Seminar in Minneapolis. When he finished the seminar, he would never look at running an organization in the same way again.

Norm returned to Toronto, headquarters of the Division, and sold Camelo Gentile, the Division Vice-President, on the quality management process. On August 1, 1985, Norm went from Manager of Technical Services to Manager of Operation EXACT (EXcellence in ACTion), and things began to move.

For the next year and a half, the Division used project based, management-led, interfunctional teams to solve problems. ("Interfunctional" is Domtar's name for what we've been calling multifunctional teams.) Results of these teams weren't fantastic, but they weren't bad either. Then, in 1987, George Blackmore took over as Vice-president for the Division. He knew something about Operation EXACT—and he thought it wasn't going fast enough. He appointed a four-manager task force to find out why.

They found the answer, and it's instructive: The management system hadn't changed to support the use they were making of project teams.

Norm joined the task force, and they began to look for solutions to the problem. From Tennessee Associates, Inc., they learned about the concept of natural management teams. Every manager already has a team—his or her direct reports. When an organization wants to begin using management teams, what better place to start?

I've mentioned some of the problems firms encounter in establishing and living by teampower. Here's an appropriate point to show how powerful teampower is. By 1990, the recession had impacted Domtar. To improve their competitive position, the company reduced the Division by 200 staff positions. This interrupted not only Operation EXACT but management continuity as well. It also brought fear—the enemy both of quality and of effective teampower—back into the Division. Despite all this, when a respite came, Operation EXACT was back in gear, almost as though nothing had happened. (The fact that the Vice-president in charge of the Division strongly supported EXACT was no coincidence.)

Now teams are moving downward at the Division, downward to the working level. And they're becoming process oriented instead of project oriented. This is the reverse of the kind of transition I suggested in Chapter 3, and shows the variety of ways in which teampower can grow and develop successfully in organizations.

Chapter 2 stressed that successful teampower requires a goal beyond that of implementing teams as an end in themselves. The Corrugated Container Division's goal is a typical Total Quality one: customer satisfaction by continuous improvement of their processes. How are they doing at that? I can't give you overall figures at the moment, but these three examples might suggest the answer:

1. Certain kinds of boxes have to be coated with a wax-like material to resist moisture—and the coating machine in one plant was old, decrepit and getting more and more unreliable by the day. There weren't funds for a new one, so the plant manager chartered a quality team to see what they could do. What they did was to get the machine operating so effectively that the plant avoided the purchase of a new, $80,000 machine. As a bonus, their improvements reduced material waste to the tune of $40, 000 per year.

There's a moral in this above and beyond the money saved. It's easy to assume that the only way to improve an old process is to replace the machinery. That really doesn't take account of the power in teampower. Create a quality team made up of those who run the process—the real experts. Train them in quality improvement methods. Let them go to work. They will almost certainly improve the process. Since they understand the process, they can probably get the machine working effectively. If they can't, if a new machine really is needed, the change in process will be far more effective than just replacing the machine up front would have been. (If you need more evidence, look at how Chaparral Steel makes "the lab the plant.")[40]

2. The paperboard comes in large rolls, which are stored in warehouses until needed. Storing them and getting them out for use was damaging the outside layers on the roll. Each layer is about $1.00 worth of paperboard. That doesn't sound like much, until you damage a half-dozen layers on hundreds of rolls. And that was happening. The Division formed a multilayer, interfunctional team to solve the problem—a team that included the clamptruck operator who stacked and unstacked the rolls and the individual who mounted the rolls on the boardmaking machine. It was the clamptruck operator who came up with the discovery that led to the solution: the aisles were 4 inches narrower than the rolls! Oh, how simple—but no one knew it until they used teampower on it.

There was an interesting side benefit, by the way. The individual who mounted the rolls was amazed, he said, but not because they were able to solve the problem. He was amazed because since he'd been on the team managers actually began to ask his opinion about other things—and that had never happened before.

3. Here's the clincher. Norm was asked to facilitate an interfunctional, multilevel team to solve a $4,000,000-a-year problem at one of Domtar's paper mills. The team was mostly top-level managers, with the exception of a token first-level supervisor. You guessed it: That supervisor thought of the root cause—while he was sitting at home one Saturday

eating a hamburger. How much did the solution cost? $400—plus the salaries of several top managers who would have been more productive doing other things. Once again, teampower *is* powerful, and it doesn't take top managers to make it so.

Is teampower in the Division successful? It appears so. Is it complete? Not according to Norm. "I can't tell you we've arrived," he said, "because you never do." As he sees it, process improvement teams seem to be a natural step in the evolution of self-directed work teams.

THE CITY OF ALBUQUERQUE, NEW MEXICO _____

Don't think that teampower only happens in private industry; it doesn't. Here's an example from the public sector. And this example takes us back to white-collar organizations.

Richard Quillin is the Manager of the Information Systems Division (ISD) of the Department of Finance & Management of the City of Albuquerque. When he looked at his operation in the Spring of 1987, he didn't like what he saw. It wasn't that ISD was in bad shape. It probably operated about as well as most information systems (IS) shops around the country. But he wasn't satisfied, because

1. The people in ISD were traditional, technology-oriented professionals. Instead of concentrating on the business needs of their customers, they installed products that challenged them but left their customers cold.

2. Communication didn't appear to happen, both within ISD and between it and its customers.

3. New ISD projects were all too often decided on the basis of the political clout (i.e., potential favors) of customers, rather than on any systematic evaluation of need.

4. Perhaps most damning of all, bond elections for ISD projects consistently failed to pass. It didn't seem to be a coincidence that 35-40% of the voting population for these bonds was made up of city employees.

ISD was a very traditional organization and part of a very traditional organization. It had never bothered to talk seriously with either its employees or its customers when planning changes. After a survey of a sampling of employees and discussion, Richard decided that self-managing teams (SMTs) seemed to offer the greatest promise.

Before he embarked on SMTs, though, he took a very important step. He developed a mission statement to focus everyone's attention on why they were in business. His goal was a *partnership* with ISD's clients, a partnership that would meet their needs and retain them as loyal customers.

The next step was the move to SMTs. Remember the importance of support from higher management—support that can provide a buffer for experimentation? Richard got that support. His boss, the Director of the Department of Finance & Management, wouldn't commit himself to SMTs. But he allowed Richard to try them.

Richard began by providing ISD members with training in group processes (self-disclosure, team-building, resolving inter-personal conflict, etc.) Then he asked lower-level managers to develop a plan for the implementation of self-managing teams within 90 days. Ninety days passed, and nothing happened. So he announced that the change would happen in two weeks, and again asked for their input. Again, nothing happened. When the change came, it was because he unilaterally imposed it on ISD.

(Let me pause for a moment for a comment. Richard's experience wasn't at all unique. First- and second-level managers typically oppose SMTs. At the best, they're a hard sell. But part of the reason for this is that so few higher-level managers really try to sell them on the benefits of it. That's a mistake, a serious one. We've already seen that the managing roles in a teampower organization can be much more challenging and satisfying than traditional management. Until managers see the benefits of these roles for themselves, the whole program sounds like nothing but trouble for them. So, they do what any of us would do in the same situation: Actively or passively, they oppose it.)

In February 1988, ISD changed to self-managing teams. All lower-level managerial positions were abolished. The individuals who had held them became team members. Within the first 90 days, three of the nine individuals who had been lower-level managers left (one involuntarily). Several employees also left. Within another 90 days, two more exmanagers and two more employees left. In each case, the reason was basically the same: We don't like this way of doing business. On the other hand, four of the nine original managers and some 60 employees stayed—and made the new organization work.

Over the next year, the teams began to become true SMTs. They received training in personnel processes and then began recruiting and selecting their own members. In January 1989, Richard took the then-unheard-of step of bringing all of ISD together, giving them complete information about ISD's financial situation, and asking their help to achieve a 3.5% budget cut. A committee was formed, and one of its recommendations was used to structure the budget.

By mid 1989, the SMTs were hitting their stride. Customer satisfaction rose noticeably. A bond issue for ISD passed—and not only passed but got the third highest "yes" vote of eight items on the ballot. Early in 1990, ISD absorbed management information systems employees from three other city departments. By mid 1991, ISD was able to cut 12 positions, while not only maintaining but increasing the services it provided. In a time of major budget cuts, four out of five ISD internal project funding requests were ranked "high" in the overall city budget.

I could end here, on this "and they lived happily ever after" note. Instead, let me take the time to point out two significant aspects of the ISD story.

I wrote this account based on information that Richard Quillin and consultant Suzanne Maxwell furnished me. When I read their information, it seemed that every other paragraph described training that the SMTs were getting. They were trained in group processes, then trained some more. They were trained in how to select team members. Then they got advanced training on the topics they'd learned the basics of. That's one reason teampower is working there—the players have learned what they need to know to make it work. I can't emphasize this too much—and you can't, either.

The second aspect illustrates how the success of teampower creates problems of its own. Like most operations based on SMTs, one of the first challenges to ISD was to build up the trust level in each team to the point that the team could work effectively as a unit. As each team learned to focus on the issues rather than the personalities of the individuals involved, it passed that milestone.

But that created another problem. When the relationships in an individual team became tight and close, the team turned inward looking and parochial. (Remember that really effective teams become almost arrogant about their competence.) The distrust was projected outward, to the relationships among the various teams. It took until well into 1991 for this to change, as trust *between* teams developed to the point that they began to work together for goals higher than individual team goals. In turn, that will create other problems—and ISD will become even more competent as it solves them.

The objective accomplishments of ISD are remarkable. Perhaps the best indicator of all, though, was provided by several employees eligible for retirement in late 1990. When the teams first started, these employees had been counting the hours until retirement. When they became eligible to retire, though, most of them stayed. Why? "I'm having so much fun I don't want to retire!" was the common answer. Yes, teampower is working for the City of Albuquerque.

AMERICAN TRANSTECH _____

The next example takes us back to the private sector. The story begins in 1983. In that year, Steve Jacobs dropped out of Harvard, just a few months short of his doctorate in social psychology, to become a consultant for American Transtech. Three years later, he transferred into operational management in the organization. In 1989, he became Transtech's Director of Quality Improvement. In those few facts, an incredible—and continuing—success story is hidden.

American Transtech is a subsidiary of AT&T, established in 1983 to handle the massive shareholder transactions created by the AT&T divestiture. Just getting American Transtech off the ground was a considerable achievement: In 11 months, the site went from woodlands to a staffed, operating business. In the following eight years, the organization accomplished something even more remarkable: constant improvements in performance that, in at least one case, resulted in a *500%* increase in the productivity of customer service personnel. The effective use of empowered teams certainly wasn't responsible for these achievements by itself, but it was a key factor in this remarkable performance.

There's another aspect to the American Transtech story, one that in its own way is just as significant. In the eight years from 1983 to 1991, the firm has gone through three distinct stages. Each stage has built on what went before, and at each stage Transtech's effectiveness increased significantly. And there's no reason to believe that this stage will be the last.

When Transtech began in 1983, it started with a heavy emphasis on teams, teambuilding and quality of work life. A guiding principle was that employees who are treated well will treat customers well. And it worked. Transtech accomplished what many said was impossible: they effectively managed all of the stock transactions from the AT&T divestiture. Customers were happy; employees were happy *and* productive; and the enterprise was successful.

In fact, the firm was *too* successful. There are 12 corporations in the U.S. with half a million or more stockholders. Because of its success with AT&T, Transtech was soon providing stockholder services to eight of these corporations. This made Transtech a prime target; their competitors sharpened their knives and started to move in.

To survive the onslaught, the firm had to slash its rates 50%. (In the company, this is known as the great "half-price sale.") Clearly, it couldn't go on operating as it was with only half the revenue; the company had to do something, and do it quickly. Transtech could have gotten out of the business; after all, it had been founded to take care of divestiture and it had done that. Or it could have laid off employees and cut other costs drastically. Or it could do something else.

It did something else: a dramatic redesign of the organization. When Transtech organized originally, it had expected that its teams would work together, foster good business decisions, and be committed to quality and customer needs. All of this had happened—to a meaningful extent. As a result, both customers and employees were happy, productivity was high, and there were fewer layers of management.

Unfortunately, there were also some real gaps:

- A shareholder request came into Request Processing. When it had been satisfied, it moved to Computer Operations and then to Mailing Operations (who furnished the required paperwork to the customer). Both Request Processing and Computer Operations were based on teams—but the teams were functional teams. Request Processing had a total of 30 functional teams, and Computer Operations had another 15 (five teams on each of three shifts). At least five teams in Request Processing had to work on the request, and potentially every team in Computer Operations. On the average, *25 teams* had to work the request—just to get it through to Mailing Operations.

- Because the teams were based on functions, the individuals in the teams had no reason to work together. For instance, each team in Request Processing performed only one of five functions: Telephone Response, Mail and Correspondence, Stock Transfer, Dividend Reinvestment, and Disbursements & Reconciliations. Each individual on each team essentially worked as an individual; each worker's interactions were with other teams, not with other employees on his or her team. There were teams but no teamwork—because the players didn't need each other to get the job done (remember that?).

- The organization had hoped that the teams would make sound business decisions. They didn't have any cost measures on which to base these decisions, though—so they couldn't make them.

- Finally, while the teams tried to produce quality outcomes, they were separated from their customers and had no effective way to learn what these customers needed.

Transtech's solution to these problems was to create multifunctional, customer-focused teams. Request Processing reduced from 30 functional teams to nine of the new multifunctional teams—each team with all of the functions needed to work a request. Computer Processing reduced the number of its teams from 15 to four. Now each shareholder request went through *one* team in Request Processing and *one* team in Computer Processing. Furthermore, each team had a specific group of customers. If a customer contacted Transtech in March and then again in October and November, he or she would deal with the same Request Processing team each time. (Does this make a difference? Hallways and walls at Transtech are covered with letters of appreciation from customers sent to the specific individuals who provided them service.)

The multifunctional teams created the necessary mix of skills within the teams and dramatically reduced the number of teams that had to work on the same request (from an average of 25 to two). Now each player on a team needed the other players to get the job done, so they worked together.

Then, Transtech made up-to-the minute financial data available to each team. Originally it was only the cost data, but then it was expanded to include profit and loss statements. The information is truly up to the minute; it reflects the situation at the close of business the previous day. Now each team can see the impact of its decisions—and make the sound business decisions the firm is looking for.

There was an interesting twist to this use of data. Initially, the cost and profit & loss statements were broken down only by teams. The teams are strongly self managing, though. They design their selection criteria and either select new members or recommend to the team manager whom should be selected. They choose their own team managers. And they provide performance feedback to each player on the team, including determining annual merit raises. Because the teams are responsible for themselves, they asked for profit & loss data for each individual—so they could make solid decisions about the performance of each team member. They got the data, and that's how they use it.

Individuals on the teams have the opportunity to develop a wide range of skills. They even rotate through the forecasting and scheduling jobs—which are very demanding ones—on a regular basis. The teams develop their own budgets.

What does the team manager do? He coaches and develops the teams, and coordinates their activities with other teams and higher management. (Does that sound slightly familiar?)

OK—Transtech went in solidly for empowered teams. But did it help? Remember that the firm had cut its prices to customers by 50%. (Now, please pause for a moment and think about what would happen to your firm if it cut its prices by 50% and tried to keep operating. Could it even do it? If so, how could it do it? Now you understand the situation Transtech was in.) Despite the 50% cut, the company held all of its customers, did not cut any workers—and continued to make money. In fact, it continued to expand and during the past few years has added several other lines of business. Just to put the size of their operation in perspective, they generate 50% of the inbound and outbound mail for the city of Jacksonville!

So were they successful? Yes—and no. As effective as the empowered teams were, they weren't putting the same attention on quality measures that they were on the profitability ones. The firm had no real process management, no program for constant process improvement, and no specific methods for defining customers' needs and expectations. What the firm did was effective, yes—but all too often because of heroic efforts instead of reliable processes.

So, in 1989, Transtech decided it was time to implement a Total Quality Management program. The program is just now getting up a full head of steam. (In fact, while I was interviewing Steve Jacobs he was interrupted by a call from a senior manager; she wanted him to speak to her managers about Total Quality.) It's taking time, because they're doing it right—seeing that top managers understand the process and support it, then working it down through the organization.

What will happen when Total Quality gets to the working level? The odds are that it will produce a synergistic explosion. Teams are already established and working successfully, and Total Quality gives them a whole new set of tools. The groundwork is laid for yet another dramatic increase in productivity as well as quality.

What do Steve and Transtech aim to do now? Their first goal is to completely empower their customer-service teams—giving them everything they need to completely satisfy the customer. But empowerment isn't an end in itself. The final goal is to satisfy everyone on the first call. If you're familiar with customer service, with the research and call-backs it causes, you know just how ambitious a goal it is to talk of satisfying everyone on the first call. Imagine how ambitious it is for a firm that handled 52,000,000 calls in 1990. Judging from their past record, they may just do it.

That's not all, of course, Now that Transtech has a strong customer focus, they're going through the organization to identify and cut out all nonvalue-adding activities. (You have to know who your customers are and what they want before you can determine the activities that don't add value.) In many firms, this means layoffs and reductions. That's not Transtech's goal at all. The firm is doing so well and adding new business so rapidly that they need to get everyone available performing value-adding activities—i.e., satisfying customers.

Transtech didn't do this without problems. Most of them are the ones you'd expect, the ones described in Chapter 10. One of the problems, though, deserves a comment here. Computer Operations had reduced to only four teams, but they had to modify their structure slightly. One reason was that different teams had to share printers and other equipment, and this caused a definite problem. It points out just how key an issue in team design it is for teams to share resources. Empowered teams with clear goals don't like to be held up because they can't get at a resource they need. Remember that.

NEW SOCIETY PUBLISHERS

You may think that we've looked at all of the kinds of teams there are. We haven't. Our last example is one in which an entire *firm* is the team. All members of the firm are managers. Everyone in the firm is paid the same basic rate. Decisions are made by consensus, by everyone affected by the decision. The team is held together, not by conventional controls, but by shared values. And it works.

Let me introduce you to New Society Publishers (NSP) of Philadelphia, Pennsylvania, Santa Cruz, California, and Gabriola Island, BC, Canada. NSP was founded just over ten years ago. From its beginning, it had a high sense of mission: to disseminate information about social change through nonviolent action. Its predominant value is practicing what it preaches. The firm constantly searches for ways to incorporate this nonviolent philosophy in the way it does business. That's no snap; while it's a nonprofit organization, NSP has to survive in a highly competitive environment.

That sounds idealistic, and it is. But NSP has remained in business for over a decade. There are only 11 full members of the organization, which sounds like a manageable size. These 11 members, though, are spread among the editorial, fulfillment, warehousing, marketing, finance, and production departments, and among offices in Pennsylvania, California, and British Columbia, Canada. If you think it's challenging to perform as an effective self-managing team in one location, imagine the problems when you perform as one in these circumstances. But NSP does it.

The firm makes its major decisions in an annual "face-to-face" meeting of the entire team. In the interim a general management committee (nicknamed "Pogo") coordinates and facilitates the ongoing decisions that have to be made. The committee doesn't make the decisions; the total group makes all decisions affecting the firm as a whole, and makes them by consensus. Any member of the team can block and decision. This may sound risky, but it's worked successfully for a decade—and they're not considering changing it.

Even in a company this small, though, not all decisions can be made by the consensus of the total group. Most operational decisions are delegated to the departments involved. Only the broad issues are reserved for absolute agreement among everyone. Typical of these issues are the direction of the company, what to do with the margin from sales, whether to take on projects other than books, and what if any changes to make in benefits.

Everyone in NSP has three jobs. Each individual has a primary job in one of the firm's departments. Each person also serves as an editor, acquiring and editing books. Finally, he or she has a role in the general management of the organization. (They're finding, by the way, that most people can do two of the three jobs well, but not all three. No matter how motivated, human beings do have limits.)

A new member at NSP serves nine months to a year as an Apprentice, then becomes an Associate for a year or more before becoming a full member. Apprentices and Associates are evaluated at regular intervals by their coworkers, the whole group, and (perhaps most importantly) themselves. One purpose of the probationary period is to allow individuals who don't fit to select themselves out. Even Associates, though, can veto the publication of a book—a pretty heady responsibility in a firm that exists by publishing books.

It may seem easy to dismiss New Society Publishers as a model. After all, the firm is small, it's a nonprofit operation, it serves a small niche market, and it's organized so that commitment from all members is almost automatic. And NSP has problems; running a firm by consensus is time consuming and difficult. But keep some basic facts in mind. The firm has survived for a decade—something that most small businesses can't manage. It operates effectively, performs all of the functions required by a successful business, and generates the income required to stay in business. It has all of the characteristics of a successful team, and performs the management roles required to operate as an empowered team. On top of that, this team with eleven fulltime members generated a million dollars in sales in the fiscal year ending June 30, 1991.

And that, as they say, ain't chopped liver.

Chapter 5 ═══════

Managing
Team Alignment ═══════

The first four chapters have laid the groundwork for teampower. This and the next four chapters describe the management functions required for effective teampower. When you finish these five chapters, you'll understand how to exercise these functions when you work with empowered teams—and you'll understand the skills you need to perform the functions.

The critical point in the chapters is that *management functions in teampower organizations are quite different from those in traditional organizations.* You've been a manager, and I hope a successful one, in a traditional organization. Now it's time to learn the management functions that will make you a success in an organization based on teampower.

In traditional organizations, the basic function of a manager is that of the boss: assign work, train workers, see that the work is done, deal with individuals who don't perform well. The core of these functions is simply put: As a boss, you take responsibility for the work of others. And you have the skills that go with this function: knowing how to give firm, clear direction; knowing how to be fair but strict in treating workers; knowing how to assess performance effectively; knowing how to delegate but retain control of the work; and so forth.

In a firm organized around teampower, the functions associated with the "boss" largely vanish. When Florida Power and Light first began to move toward player empowerment, they put supervisors through a special course designed to teach them their new functions. The people who went through the course got the nickname of "supertaters," combination supervisors and facilitators. This was a pretty good nickname, because individuals who exercise management functions in teampower organizations are truly facilitators, guides, coaches—even (in Tom Peters' phrase) cheerleaders. The stronger empowered teams are, the more they manage themselves. Your role is to support and guide them, and to see that they stay focused on their objectives and coordinated with what's happening elsewhere in the organization. The management functions described in these five chapters will enable you to do just that.

WHAT TEAMS MUST DO TO BE EFFECTIVE _____

In chapter 3, we took a detailed look at the eight characteristics of effective teams. Any team must have all eight of these characteristics to succeed and, at least initially, only the player who constitutes the team can bring them about. Because they're so important, I want to repeat them one more time. Here they are:

1. The players on the team share values that support teamwork among themselves, and with the player that creates the team.

2. The team has clear, worthwhile goals to accomplish.

3. Team members need each other to accomplish these goals.

4. Team members are genuinely committed to the goals.

5. The team has specific objectives by which to measure its success.

6. The team gets direct, prompt, dependable, useful feedback about its performance against these objectives.

7. There are clear rewards for team, rather than just individual success.

8. The team is competent both as a team and individually.

Once a team is functioning, there are six core processes that it must execute consistently and expertly. As the player who sets up and maintains the team, you need to know about these processes. If a team is failing at one or more of the core processes, you may need to intervene and help it come back up to speed. All of this may sound a little mysterious; as soon as we look at the six processes, though, you'll understand. Here they are:

1. The team must see that all of the players on the team get their *individual needs satisfied*. We don't need to speculate on what these needs are; the important point is that being a contributing member of the team must meet the needs of the individual. It may be that in Japan individuals subordinate their needs to those of the group. You can't count on that in the U.S. Here, if a team is to succeed, it must constantly meet the needs of each individual player. Hopefully, the team will become very proficient at this.

   • **Example:** If John is concerned to see that other people have a high opinion of his abilities and Susan needs to be recognized as a creative person, the team must find ways to satisfy these needs. It should function so that one way John gets the good opinion of others is by furthering the work of the team, and Susan's contributions are accepted and valued. Conversely, if John feels he must seek esteem by papering over honest conflicts and Susan feels she must express her creativity in irrelevant flights of fancy, the team will be seriously hampered.

2. It must have effective *interaction processes* among members. The individual players must be able to communicate with each other effectively, establish and maintain positive relationships, deal with conflict and disagreement. These are what is normally referred to as group processes, and they are essential for team success.

   • **Example:** If Maria and Roger disagree often, but express their disagreement openly and with respect for one another, they will maintain effective communication and a positive relationship. If Sarah and Michael never disagree with each openly but talk negatively above each other to other team players, the team will suffer.

3. It must have effective *managerial processes* that coordinate the activities of individuals on the team, see that the team gets resources and uses them efficiently, ensures that individuals and the team as a whole performs effectively, and mediates

conflicts of interest. This does *not* mean that someone on the team must constantly be the manager of the team. The managerial role can be performed by a team leader, rotated among individual team players, or divided among them. The point is that, however the team chooses to do it, these management functions must be performed effectively.

- If Mollie and Esteban are going to do research on the problem, either they or someone else needs to see that they don't duplicate each other's work. Eleanor, Willie and Charles may work out among themselves who will get to use the computer when, and then ask Adriene to maintain the schedule for them. Roger may be much better than anyone else at helping players resolve conflict, so he may take this role permanently.

4. It must have effective *leadership processes* that focus and maintain the purpose of the group. These processes include seeing that the group maintains its shared values and worthwhile purpose, renews itself if it begins to go stale, and relates successfully to its environment. Again, this function can be exercised by a team leader, performed at different times by different players, or divided among different players.

- **Example:** Tom may have a strong sense that the team is not living up to what it believes in and call it to the team's attention. Evan may pick up the discussion and relate the change in the team to a change in some organization policies. Then Adele may lead a discussion of just how the policy change ought to affect them, and whether they should change because of it. Each one of them is exercising part of the leadership role in that situation. Each of them might operate in the same role, a different one, or no leadership role at all the next time a problem arises.

5. It must *produce an output* effectively and efficiently. Ultimately, this is the purpose of the team, and it must do it well. When any other goal becomes superior to this one, the team is in serious trouble.

- **Example:** The team has just been compared unfavorably with a similar team in the organization. If it accepts this as a challenge to work more effectively and produce more, it may improve its performance. If it worries because it is not being given the status it deserves and begins to bad-mouth the other team, it is substituting another goal for performance.

6. Finally, it must maintain effective *interaction with its environment*. It must be able to anticipate "what's coming down the pike," as well as ensure that it has reliable supplies and is producing an output that meets its customers' needs. While you will interface with the team in various ways, one of your primary functions is to facilitate its interaction with its environment.

- **Example:** The team is making excellent progress identifying problems with the current accounting and reimbursement for expenses. At the same time, Corporate is revising the organization's accounting system and making significant changes in reimbursement procedures. The team would waste considerable time on this, except that Rosalind talks with the corporate accounting office every week or so—and finds out about the planned changes quickly. The team is able to postpone its discussion until it can get a copy of the new policy.

All of these constitute what the team as a whole and its individual players must contribute to its success. Put slightly differently, these are the basic self-management processes of the team. When they're effective, team members find their work challenging, they control it, and they work cooperatively. Their customers perceive them as committed and competent.

It's important to realize that this is just as important for short-lived project teams as for continuing teams. It doesn't have to happen to the same depth, but it has to happen much more rapidly. One of your basic roles as the player that calls the team into existence is explaining the importance of each of these processes to the team, and then ensuring that the team pays attention to all of them.[41]

THE FIVE KEY MANAGEMENT FUNCTIONS _____

Hopefully, the goal is even clearer now. You want to create and maintain one or more teams responsible for their own success. To do this, they must be as fully self managing and self leading as possible. When they do, they exercise most of the functions that a traditional supervisor performs and take most of the responsibility for the six major team processes we just examined. This brings up a question:

> *If the team takes over the responsibilities that you as a manager and supervisor have been doing—just where do you fit in? Just what do you do now?*

This chapter and the four that follow it answer this question. They describe five different functions required to support teampower and keep it working productively for the organization. They also describe the skills you need to develop—or perhaps only improve—to perform these functions effectively. Let's begin with this very brief description of each of the five functions:

Function #1: Managing Alignment

Teams need independence, but everything they do must be integrated with the needs and goals of the organization as a whole. The first function required to manage teampower does just that. The individual performing this function ensures that the goals of the teams further the goals of the organization. The other side of the function is seeing that the organization listens to its performing teams—that it solicits and uses their ideas and meets their legitimate needs.

Function #2: Managing Coordination

No team works in a vacuum, and many teams must work carefully together. A teampower manager must be able to coordinate the efforts of different teams, so that they work together effectively. She must also distribute resources where they are needed and ensure that each team operates productively and efficiently.

Function #3: Managing the Decision Process

In the past, decisions were generally made and then passed

down. In a teampower environment, this won't work. Instead, you manage a process in which teams make more and more of their own decisions. The complexity and diversity of the modern organization require the best ideas of everyone, but these ideas must be synthesized and turned into effective decisions. This means helping teams accept and use conflict productively and find ways to reach decisions that every player can support.

Function #4: Managing Continuous Learning

We often speak of constant change; in successful organizations, this is constant learning. The world is changing too fast. Not only individuals but entire organizations must become more and more effective at learning. The fourth function of a teampower manager is to facilitate constant learning by teams and by the players within them. You are cannot be just a "change agent"; you must be a "learning agent."

Function #5: Creating and Maintaining Trust

Nothing—*nothing*—a teampower manager does it more important than this. Teampower works where there is high trust, and nowhere else. Self-management exists only where there is trust. Building and maintaining trust is a high skill, and teampower managers use it constantly.

All of these functions are based on a single, simple idea. In the past, managers managed workers. Now, more and more, all of the players will manage themselves—and you'll manage the environment in which they work. Remember, the name of the game is self-management; the role of the players at higher levels in the organization is supporting and focusing this self-management. In this management role, you will do far more genuine management than you did in a traditional organization—but it will be different. Much of it will be the higher level, more creative, more demanding, more long-term managing you've always wanted to do but never found the time for.

There's one more point before we get to the first function. I want to let a secret out. The management roles in a teampower organization are immensely more satisfying and more fun—yes, more fun!—than the role of a traditional boss. Stop and think for a moment. Do you really like having to look over people's shoulders, hassle performance problems, get workers to do what they know they ought to do—and all of the other headaches that grow from taking responsibility for the productivity of others? Doesn't it sound a lot more fulfilling to work *with* individuals who are committed to the same goals and competent at achieving them? You bet!

Don't conclude from this that developing or maintaining empowered teams is easy. The truth is just the reverse. In a teampower environment *no one* has it easier—not the players who used to be just workers and not the players who used to be just managers. Everyone works hard constantly—but the work is fulfilling, not simply stressful.

THE SEVEN BASIC MANAGEMENT ROLES _____

The last chapter of this book describes how to create self-managing teams. As it will show you, there are several distinct stages that self-managing teams grow through. Every stage requires all of the management functions—but the role you play is different from one stage to another. As the team develops, you move from one role to another. You move from *supervisor* to *leader* to *teacher* to *coach* to *mentor* to *consultant* and *mediator*. Your goal is to move from role to role just far enough ahead of the team to help them grow to the next stage.

We'll look more closely at the roles in Chapter 11. It may help if you keep them in mind as you read through the functions, though, so here's a brief description of them:

1. A *supervisor* does exactly what you're doing now. He or she is responsible for the performance and behavior of the workgroup. This is the first, and shortest-lived role a manager plays in the progress of a self-managing team.

2. A *leader* sets goals for the workgroup and helps them focus on these goals. While a supervisor tells workers what to do, a leader calls out their willing support. Put slightly differently, supervisors push workers forward while leaders draw them forward. It's important for you to be a leader in the

early stages of a self-managing team. After a while, though, the team mostly becomes its own leader.

3. A critical management role for teams is that of a *teacher*. As a teacher, you don't tell people what to do. You don't necessarily even train them. You do see that they learn. And as they become better and better at learning, you play the teacher role less and less.

4. The next role is that of a *coach*, who makes sure that the team uses what it's learned. At first, you play both the teacher and coach roles at the same time. As the team becomes proficient at learning for itself, you put more of your time and effort into coaching instead of teaching.

5. From a coach, you move on to become a *mentor* for the team. A mentor shares his or her expertise with the team, intervening only when the team confronts a problem beyond their experience. The rest of the time, a mentor is in the background.

6. A *consultant* is even more in the background. When a team becomes fully self-managing, it learns when it needs to turn to someone else for assistance. That's where a consultant is different from a mentor: A consultant intervenes only when asked. When you find yourself acting continuously in the consultant role, you know that the team has fully matured. But it's not the final role.

7. That role is *mediator*. As you'll see, the team never fully assumes the first management function—managing alignment. You always perform that function, but not as someone who forces the team to stay aligned with the organization. Instead, your role is that of mediator, someone who connects the team with higher levels.

None of these roles, except perhaps the last two, should be strange to you. Even traditional managers perform in the first five roles at least some of the time. What's new (and exciting) about managing teampower is that you move from role to role. At each step, you help the team take over more and more of its management functions. By the end of the process, both you and the team have skills far above those with which you began.

But we're getting ahead of ourselves. We'll return to the roles in Chapter 11. Right now, we need to look at the management functions that effective teampower requires.

YOUR FIRST FUNCTION: MANAGING ALIGNMENT _____

In one sense, this is nothing new. It's always been a part of management. You already have basic skills at it. It works differently in a teampower organization, though, than it does in a traditional one. That means you have to hone the skills you have and develop new ones.

First, we need to look more closely at just what we mean by "managing alignment." Reduced to its essentials, this is it:

Managing alignment means seeing that the values, goals, and direction of each team remain aligned with the values, goals, and direction of the overall organization.

A quick analogy will show you how and why this is different in an organization built on empowered teams. Think back on the Gulf War. Picture an Iraqi officer responsible for several entrenched companies. The soldiers spend most of their time in the bunkers; whenever there's action, they respond in carefully defined ways. Now picture a Coalition commander responsible for a motorized infantry battalion. At any given time, the battalion may be at any point in—or spread over—hundreds of square miles. It may be dug in or moving, attacking or retreating.

The Coalition commander clearly has a more difficult job when he tries to see that his troops are meeting the strategic objectives of the army as a whole. Suppose they choose to attack opposing positions just as the Air Force is bombing them? Or withdraw from positions that the army is counting on them to hold? The mobile force has many, many more options, based on their skill and mobility—and keeping them aligned with overall goals is constantly challenging.

HOW MISALIGNMENT CAN HAPPEN _____

As a teampower player, managing alignment is very much like

working with a highly mobile military unit. This is doubly so if, as they should, everyone's responsibilities include constant improvement. Let me give you some quick ideas of how empowered teams, with the best motives in the world, can become misaligned:

- Team A has worked a particularly pesky problem in materials flow and come up with an innovative solution that increases production 20%. Just before they implement it, the organization decides to cut production of that product back by 5%.
- Team B worked out an effective way of dealing with peak workloads, but didn't tell any of the other teams.
- Team C believes they understand their job better than anyone else and are beginning to resent "interference" from higher levels in the organization. Team A shares their irritation.
- Team D is having more and more problems trying to process claims the way that the organization's processing manual requires. Productivity has already fallen off 8%.

Note that each of these problems—and thousands like them that occur constantly in the real world—happen even though the teams are working well (and sometimes *because* of it). No one has done anything wrong. But if the situation isn't detected and resolved, each team will get further and further out of alignment with the organization as a whole.

WHAT YOU DO TO MANAGE ALIGNMENT _____

If you're going to keep the values, goals and direction of your teams aligned with the values and goals of the organization, these are some of tasks you must perform.

1. *You assure that each team is clear about the goals both of the team and of the organization as a whole.* You can't integrate a team's actions with the goals of the organization unless everyone is clear about what these goals are. If you ask a worker at Ford Motor Company about the basic goal of the company, he'll point to a large, simple sign on the wall: Beat Toyota! That's

clarity! Your organization may not be able to state its basic goals quite so simply, but everyone in the organization should know what they are.

2. *You assure that each team has specific objectives that implement these goals.* Goals are meaningless unless they are embodied in specific actions to be taken, in objectives (with their associated timetables, as necessary). These objectives are the primary link between each team and the larger organization. "Beat Toyota!" may be a marvelous goal, but it doesn't make much difference unless it's expressed in objectives like "reduce number of defects per delivered car by $n\%$" or "incorporate at least n customer-suggested improvements each model year.

(The two paragraphs above should have sounded familiar to you—because they reflect the first, second, and fifth of the characteristics of a successful team. The player who establishes the team ensures that the team has these characteristics up front. Then she, or whoever manages the ongoing alignment of the team with the rest of the organization, ensures that the values and goals are clear and implemented in objectives. This is a never-ending process.)

3. *You assure that the need for change is recognized and dealt with.* Even in teampower organizations, much change originates at higher levels and passes down. Managing alignment means communicating these changes to teams and seeing that they're implemented. But that's only the beginning. It also means communicating any team's felt need for change clearly to higher levels and reporting back the response of these levels. Equally as important, it means recognizing the need for change in everyday events and surfacing it to the teams and/or higher levels. This also requires the individual managing alignment to set effective priorities, since at any time there is more potential for change than the organization can effectively assimilate.

4. *You identify and surface the need for organizational renewal.* In one sense, this is part of the task above; organizational renewal means seeing a need for change and responding to

it. But renewal is important enough to be considered on its own. All organizations stagnate. Most (such as Ford, Xerox or Harley Davidson) get shaken from their stagnation only when a crisis confronts them. Part of the function of managing alignment is staying alert to the signs of stagnation and reacting to them quickly. To anticipate a later chapter, the better that you manage team learning, the fewer the times you will have to initiate major renewal.

5. Finally, and you can see this in each of the four paragraphs above, *you assure that everyone communicates with everyone,* that information flows freely throughout the organization. The more that the players are empowered, the more information they need to perform successfully. Consider just a simple point. Workers in the Corning Plant in Blacksburg can retool a line to change the kind of filter it produces six times faster than workers in a traditional plant. This means that they will be retooling far more often than traditional plant. Think how much more information they need, and how accurate it must all be, to do this successfully.

TWO IMPORTANT POINTS

First Point

It probably sounds as though the function of managing alignment is something done by individuals responsible for teams of producers. That's true, but it's not all of it. Many teampower organizations have teams at each level in the organization, and all teams except those at the highest level must be integrated with the teams above them. For instance, individuals who in traditional organizations would be first-line managers may be responsible for five to ten teams apiece, and then these individuals form a team at the next level. The process may continue to the top of the organization, where an executive team is responsible for integrating the operations of the entire organization.

This kind of situation takes a while to achieve. Determining where the responsibilities of one level end and those of the next begin is a difficult task, one that must be learned over time. Managers used to performing independently, and often in competition with one another, need time to learn how to work as members of real teams. If the organization is changed over time into series of interlocking teams, however, it will increase the alignment throughout the organization significantly.

Second Point

The function of managing alignment and the tasks that go with it should have sounded familiar to you. The basic function didn't originate in teampower organizations. It's been around far longer—because it's the basic leadership role. Leaders integrate the various levels of the organization, seeing that values and goals remain aligned, checking objectives, finding where change needs to be made, and generating organizational renewal. This has to happen for any kind of organization to be successful.

What's different is the way the alignment is created in organizations based on empowered teams. For instance, in traditional organizations, leaders often develop values and goals in a vacuum and publish the resulting Values Statement throughout the organization. Because it is done in a vacuum, it's often difficult to implement—and often ends up as little more than a relic. If an organization genuinely bases itself on teampower, its values come from every part and every level of the organization. As a result, they are far more likely to be an accurate reflection of reality, and far more likely to mean something to the players involved.

This means that managing alignment in a teampower organization requires a very different kind of skill from the same function in a traditional organization. The same is true of each of the four functions discussed in the following four chapters. That's why each of these five chapters ends with a solid discussion of the skills required to support the functions. If you're going to be an effective player in a teampower environment, you must know not only *what* to do (the functions) but *how* to do it (the skills required by the functions). Let's turn to the skills you need to successfully manage alignment.

THE SKILLS A TRADITIONAL ORGANIZATION NEEDS _____

In a traditional organization, how does alignment usually happen? Goals and priorities are set at the top and handed down. The role of middle and firstlevel managers is to pass them on, and to see that their units fall in line. Values are a lot more "iffy." There may be formal value statements, but normally the real values of the organization are different from those in the statements. Not only that; the values in Mahogany Row are usually different—far different—from those on the working level. "Our goal is quality products and high customer satisfaction," the company proclaims. At the working level, the overriding goal is so many products an hour, no matter what. (That, by the way, is one of the primary reasons why the cost of poor quality is 25-40% of total costs.)

What kinds of skills does this take? Communicating clearly and persuasively is one. Every new manager gets at least one course in this; over her career, she'll probably get several. "Effective communication" is a frequent topic, and lack of communication is one of the most common complaints made about lower-level managers by higher-level management and employees alike.

That's not the only skill, of course. You have to have all of the supervisory skills: hiring workers, training them in the right way to perform their jobs, seeing that they perform them, then appraising performance. You also need to be able to correct performance and behavior, reward exceptionally deserving employees, and terminate those who can't or won't perform effectively. You've probably had training as well in coaching workers and other less directive ways of supervising.

Finally, you may also have had training in formal management skills: planning, organizing, directing, controlling and the like. It may not always have been clear how you exercised these functions, but you were taught that they were the management functions, and your role was to perform them.

I'm sure you've had other training, all oriented around this role of seeing that what your employees did was what the organization wanted done. And it was focused, as you'd expect in a traditional organization, on seeing that directions from higher in the organization were passed down and executed. In other words, your skills supported a one-way process.

THE SKILLS THAT TEAMPOWER REQUIRES _____

If these were the only skills you developed in a traditional organization, you'd have a long way to go to develop the skills you need to manage alignment with empowered teams. If you're really good as a manager, though, you've got some important two-way skills already: listening to what workers have to say, making accommodations to their legitimate needs and requests, helping them develop their skills, even looking the other way at times and making side arrangements that (at least in theory) were against company policy.

Well, these kinds of skills are going to stand you in excellent stead in a teampower organization. When you're responsible for empowered teams, you seldom simply tell them what to do. Managing alignment is far too interactive and dynamic a process for this to be effective. While this takes a variety of skills, it's particularly important to know and use these four:

1. How to facilitate effective goal setting.

2. How to scan the environment constantly and use the information you obtain.

3. Knowing when to give direction and when to let teams decide.

4. How to see the big picture and the details at the same time.

Let's look at each of these in more detail.

HOW TO SET EFFECTIVE GOALS _____

In Chapter 7 (Managing Continuous Learning), I'm going to suggest a process for setting goals that ensures that you and other players learn from each project you undertake. Here, I only want to cover the basics of goal-setting.

We've seen several times so far in the book how critical goals and objectives are for effective teams. In a traditional organization, different levels and functions are tied together by policies, procedures and plans. In an organization based on empowered teams, this won't work. Plans, procedures and policies from higher in the organization need to be held to a minimum. Instead, teampower organizations are linked together by goals and objectives at the various levels.

This is an area you probably know something about; hopefully, you're good at helping your players set goals. Many organizations have programs to encourage this. In a teampower organization, though, the goals that a team sets are generally more far reaching—and they must be integrated with the goals of other teams and the organization as a whole. Not only that, but teams often have significant input to higherlevel goals.

There are a number of books available on setting goals and helping other players set them; I don't plan to go into the details of it here. Instead, I want to highlight just a few important points about the use of goals to support empowered individuals and teams. No matter how good the goal-setting process is, it is likely to fail if these points are overlooked.

Joining Goals and Objectives

The words "goals" and "objectives" are used differently by different firms. So far, I haven't defined exactly how I'm using them. Let me pause quickly to do that.

- A *goal* is a statement of an outcome that an individual, team or organization intends to achieve. It is generally broad, long-term (several months or years), and very important.

- An *objective* is a very specific statement of what an individual, team, or organization will achieve. It is shorter-term and represents one step toward achieving a goal. It also identifies the period of time in which the step will be accomplished.

In other words, goals are broad, objectives are specific; goals are generally long-term, objectives are short-term; goals are important in themselves, objectives are important because they are steps to achieving goals; and goals seldom have precise time targets, while all effective objectives have specific milestones. Here are a few quick examples:

- **Goal:** I intend to get a two-year college degree. **Objective:** I will make at least a B in two night-school courses this quarter.

- **Goal:** We will become the most innovative firm in our market. **Objective:** By the end of this calendar year, we will have four new products ready to market.

- **Goal:** We will constantly improve our performance. **Objective:** By June 1, we will reduce the number of calls back to customers by 25%.

There's nothing hard and fast about this, and your firm may use the words differently. The important point to remember is that goals require objectives to achieve, and objectives exist only to move toward worthwhile goals.

Goals Need Objectives Need Goals

Goals that don't have specific objectives supporting them don't often get met; "I want to get a college degree and one of these days I'm going to start taking courses" is seldom a recipe for success. But objectives that don't support worthwhile goals don't usually work, either; Product Development will seldom bust their guts to create new products just for the fun of doing it.

It's important to keep both goals and objectives in focus all of the time. For the rest of this section, I'm simply going to refer to goal-setting, but that's always going to include objective-setting as part of the process. I'm also going to refer to team goals, since that will be your primary concern—but everything will apply to individual goals as well.

Teams Need to Own Their Goals

Goals are so much whitewash unless the individual (or individual team) is committed to them. All too many times, though, the final decision on a goal is all but forced on the individual player by his supervisor. Here's a short vignette:

Worker: I'm really concerned whether I can get a really quality product out in less than 3 months. I'm not sure that we can get everything we need any faster.

Manager: Tom, I think you're selling yourself short. I just know you could get it done in 60 days if you really worked at it.

Worker: You said you wanted it done right. If I try to do it that quickly I'm almost sure I'm going to have to cut corners.

Manager: I have confidence in you. You'll get it done. Shall we put it down for 60 days?

Worker: Well, I guess so . . . .

What's going on? The supervisor is combining a valid premise with a poor process. The valid premise is that for most of us the best goals are those that we can accomplish but that stretch us. The poor process is the manager trying to force his definition of "stretching" on the worker. And you may take it as virtual gospel that individuals resist committing themselves to goals forced on them.

There's no quick and easy solution. When teams first begin, players are used to the kinds of games traditional organizations play with goals. They may indeed try to set goals low so they won't fail to achieve them. The cure isn't to force higher goals on them. It is to build up the whole structure of challenge, control and cooperation, supported by genuine trust, that will enable the players to begin stretching themselves. If this sounds woolly or soft-headed, it isn't. There's more than enough evidence that where players are genuinely empowered they will set and meet targets everyone thought were impossible. Just give it time.

Teams Need to Own Their Measures

I shouldn't have to say much about this. Measures tell when an objective is successfully met. In the example above, if Team A reduces the number of customer callbacks by 25% by June 1, it has successfully met its objective. That was a one-time objective and a one-time measure, but a continuing objective and its measurements are no different. If Team B decides that its continuing objective is to produce at least 140% of standard, that becomes a continuing measure.

Just as a team should develop and commit to their objectives, so they need to develop and commit to the measures used to evaluate their success. This will probably be even more difficult than developing objectives; *everyone* has trouble developing solid measures. So don't be surprised if a team takes a while as they learn how to do it. Keep encouraging and supporting them, and giving them feedback when they ask for it—but leave the responsibility for developing the measures with them.

Teams Need to Learn from Their Actions

This is the last point but, to coin a phrase, it's certainly not the least. Anyone who sets ambitious objectives with solid measures will fail to meet them at times; 100% success in meeting objectives is an almost sure sign of timidity and risk avoidance. What happens when an objective isn't met is absolutely crucial to the future success of the team.

Stop and think about your experience of objectives and success for a minute. Here's mine. The actual objectives and their measures are bargained between lower-level players who want to be sure of meeting them and higher-level players who want to force them to produce. When an objective isn't met, there's an elaborate dance. The player responsible for it points out all the reasons why she's not to blame, while the higher-level player listens suspiciously. No one really learns anything—because that's not what any of the players intend to do.

If this is the way things happen in your organization, you're in trouble. This kind of slightly veiled power play is absolutely destructive of teams—in fact, of any real empowerment and commitment by anyone. Objectives only become constructive for teams when they become a way of learning to improve performance.

How do you do this? First, there has to be basic trust. The players involved must intend to set and meet meaningful objectives, and the other players must believe that this is the case. (Trust is so important that it has its own chapter, Chapter 9.) Then, when an objective isn't met, everyone concerned asks questions like

- Did something happen we didn't anticipate? If so, *should* we have anticipated it? If we should have, why didn't we?

- Did we lose control at some point? If so, why? Can we change that, or do we just have to take account of it next time?

- In practical terms, if we had it to do over again what would we do differently? Why? Would it really have made a difference? What would we have done the same, no matter what? Why?

- How do we feel about the failure to meet the objective? Does it motivate us to try even harder next time? Or does it discourage us, so we start to set our sights lower? (Watch out for that last one; it's a clear danger signal!)

These are the kind of questions that let an organization learn. When the players involved ask them honestly and answer them intelligently, there truly are no failures. Some learning experiences are more expensive than others; some are so expensive that you want to avoid them if possible. But even the most expensive learning experience has advantages over even the cheapest failure.

While I've stressed analyzing failures objectively, by the way, it's almost as important to analyze successes. We prefer to take them for granted, to prove how effective we are. When something goes really well, though, there are always reasons for it. It's worth the time to stop and look at the reasons. If you don't, you may mistake luck for wisdom—and pay for the mistake the next time, when luck doesn't come through for you.

HOW TO SCAN THE ENVIRONMENT _____

This may sound a bit strange to you. In fact, the only place I've seen the term before is in discussions of the organization as a whole. That's a mistake—because the ability to continuously scan your environment for information is a key skill for managing alignment.

The term sounds impressive, but the goal is simple: you want to know what's going on around and above you. If you're going to ensure that the goals of the organization and those of teams are integrated, you need continuing information on what's happening at every level. What kinds of problems are the teams running into (and what problems are they *not* having)? What new opportunities are there for teams to expand their abilities? How is the organization in general and your product line in particular doing in the marketplace? What directions do higher levels want to steer the organization in? If higher levels are still addicted to power, who are calling the shots and what are their objectives?

We could multiply the questions for pages. The organization is filled with information you need to manage alignment well, but you can't be confident that any of it will come to you on its own. You have to go find it. Here are some of the ways you can go about doing just that.

The Management Information System

Your firm undoubtedly has a formal management information system, one that produces a lot of reports. You may not have found the reports particularly helpful. If you want to keep up with the organization, though, you need to understand each report in detail. Somewhere in some of the reports there may be information you can use.

Some obvious candidates are reports on productivity, quality, absenteeism, overtime—the pretty standard ones. If you only look at the ones for your teams, you'll learn something. If you can see the comparative figures for a number of teams, and perhaps for other units in the organization, you'll learn a lot more.

Here's a common example. Absenteeism in two of your teams has gone up slightly. What does this mean? That's a difficult question to answer in isolation. If you see that this is a trend throughout your division, that suggests one way to approach it. If absenteeism in the rest of the division is staying level or decreasing, though, you have an entirely different picture.

MBBT

Realistically, few managers get really significant information from formal management information systems. A much more reliable way to know what's happening is Management by Walking Around (MBWA) or, as I much prefer to call it, Management by Being There (MBBT). The most reliable way to know what other people in the organization are doing is to spend time with them.

Let me give you a personal example. The organization I head is some 350 miles away from our headquarters. That puts my boss 350 miles away from me, and that has obvious advantages. But it also means that we aren't "wired in" to what's happening in headquarters.

To deal with this situation, I and several of my senior managers visit headquarters regularly. Sometimes the excuses for a trip are rather flimsy—but that doesn't stop us. We want to be seen; we want people to remember that we're part of the team. We also want to see and listen, so that we know what's happening there. This way we can perform our own aligning function more effectively and see that the goals of our organization are in sync with those of headquarters. (We also try to see that, as far as possible, headquarters' goals are in sync with our own!)

You don't have to go hundreds of miles; the person you need to stay in touch with may be two offices down. Nor does it take a lengthy visit; just a few minutes now and then may be enough.

Understand, though—this isn't cronyism. All too often, managers spend their time with other managers at the same level, and preferably managers who think like they do. That's *not* MBBT! Effective MBBT means spending time with individuals in other parts and levels of the organization, finding out what's happening there and, hopefully, influencing it. Certainly you want to spend time with your peers. Don't confuse this with MBBT, though, and certainly don't substitute it for MBBT.

Don't limit MBBT to visits; use the telephone. It's not the same thing as a personal visit, but it certainly beats any other alternative. On occasion, I and others have established regular calling schedules to stay in touch with people throughout the organization. This week I call Nancy in Los Angeles; next week Susan calls Tom in Salt Lake City. They can be short calls: "Just want to touch base—what's happening out there?"

I'm sure you have some of your own ways of MBBT. Use them. Expand them. If you intend to manage the alignment of your teams with the organization (and vice versa), you need all the information you can get. And there is absolutely no substitute for face-to-face contact (or at least mouth-to-ear contact over the phone) to provide rich, detailed, current information.

TEAMS NEED DIRECTION—BUT HOW MUCH? _____

Now here's a very practical skill: determining how much direction to give teams (to see that they follow organizational goals and priorities), and how much to let them work out their own direction. This question extends into every facet of teampower management.

You may have your own answer, and you've certainly heard others express strong opinions. They range from "Even the best teams need a strong hand to guide them" to "It works best to stand back and let them find their own way"—and every point in-between. Let me suggest that there aren't any simple answers here. You have to find how much direction your teams need and will accept from you, and how much they're able and willing to take responsibility for. And it will change from day to day, sometimes even from hour to hour.

That doesn't mean there aren't some guidelines. Here are a few of them:

1. *Who has the knowledge?* Do I know enough to make an effective decision myself? Or does the decision require the pooled knowledge of several members of teams? (This happens, for instance, when your expertise is getting more and more stale, or when things are just too complex for any one individual to know everything that's necessary.)

2. *How much will this decision affect the team?* Is it an important decision that they'll be angry they weren't consulted on, or a minor one that they'll be happy I got out of the way for them? (They may want to be heavily involved in picking the new leased space and furniture, but prefer that you take care of picking the moving date and the movers.)

3. *Can the team make the decision?* Are they mature enough to handle this kind of decision, or will it be divisive? Do they want responsibility for it, or will it help if I take the heat for it? (As when a popular player has to be disciplined, or prime office space has to be divided up and there's no agreement on criteria for who gets what.) The same logic holds whenever there are deep divisions within a team affecting the decision, and the team isn't ready to resolve them.

4. *How much time is there?* If there's little time, is the team effective enough to make critical decisions quickly, or should you do it? (If a decision has to be made within ten minutes

whether to work overtime on Saturday, you may have to make it yourself.)

5. *Does the team support the relevant organizational goals?* Even in the best team-based organizations, one or more teams may not be comfortable with some of the organization's goals. If they make the decision, they may well come up with one at odds with the direction in which they need to move. (For instance, a team may feel that its ideas for scheduling an extraordinary workload were ignored, and reject the organization's method. Given a choice, they may opt for their method, no matter what.)

Many other factors play a part. One of the critical factors is the skill and maturity of the team; the more skilled and mature it is, the greater the percentage of decisions that it can make. Another critical element is the amount of trust between you and the team. The point is that there are guidelines but no hard-and-fast rules.

Always keep in mind that the choice doesn't have to be *either* you make the decision *or* the team does. There are various levels at which the team can make an input into a decision. Here are the basic levels:

1. *The team makes the decision.* If they want input from you, they ask you for it. Once the decision is made, that's it.

2. *The team makes a tentative decision,* then discusses it with you before it becomes final. You may keep the authority to veto the decision, or just to try to persuade them to change it.

3. *You make a tentative decision,* then discuss it with the team. This is the reverse of the one just above, except that you will probably not want to give the team an outright veto on your decision.

4. *You make an almost-final decision,* but give them a review to ensure that they don't have major problems with it.

5. *You make the decision* and that's that.

This gets into the area of team decision-making, which is the subject of Chapter 7. We'll pick the topic back up there, after one final, very important point.

Many times, the critical question isn't whether you give direction or let the team decide. It's whether the direction you give *fits the values the company, you, and the team have committed to*. Here's an example. Suppose the team has a commitment to provide 100 products by a certain date. Just as the date approaches, the team finds that at least 5% of the products are defective. Let's suppose also that the official policy of the organization, and thus of the team, is that all orders will be shipped defect free. The team wants to hold up until all the defects are corrected, but you have to make a decision whether to ship on the due date or not. If you decide to ship, your decision will have almost certain negative fallout, because it violates the stated values of the company. On the other hand, if the team wants to ship and you hold it up, your decision won't have the same adverse consequences—because you're supporting a shared value.

I can't emphasize too strongly that a directive will have different long-term consequences depending on whether it furthers a shared value or not. If you intervene and overrule a team, but all of you can see that you're acting with shared values, they'll probably recover. If you act, or even permit them to act, in violation of these values, you'll almost certainly create harmful long-term consequences.

Whenever you're about to make a decision instead of letting the team make it, always ask yourself how it fits the values you and they share. If you try to impose on them a decision that violates these values, you may be setting yourself up for a double loss.

HOW TO DEVELOP THE KEY SKILL:
SEEING THE BIG PICTURE *AND* THE DETAILS _____

This is becoming a critically important skill—yet many people don't even realize that it's a skill, much less a critical one. In a typical traditional, layered organization, the division between the players who deal with the details and those who look at the big picture is pretty clear. The first two or three levels of management handle the details; the top two or three levels handle the big picture; managers between these two levels do something else.

Not so in a contemporary, flat organization—and certainly not in one that's based on empowered teams. If you're going to integrate your teams into the overall organization, you have to understand both the details of what the teams do and the broad picture of where the organization is headed. And you need to be able to go back and forth between the two quickly and easily.

Here's an example. Many organizations are grouping their customer service personnel into teams. There are a variety of reasons for this, not the least of which is that it helps prevent service "burnout." If you have responsibility for several of these teams, seeing the big picture and the details both is critical. On the one hand, you need to understand the firm's overall strategy and policies; you need a clear picture of how far service personnel can go and where to draw a line. On the other, you must understand the pressures on front-line service people and be able to give them detailed help in dealing with customers—within the organization's overall policy. This sounds simple and obvious; in all too many firms, though, the customer service manager understands only one side of the picture.[42]

Seeing both the big picture and the details is a difficult skill on its own merits, and doubly difficult because so few people have recognized the need for it. There's no easy way to develop this skill. There are some aids, though, that can help: outlining, "chunking," and practicing going from very broad to very limited issues and back. Let's look at them.

Outlining

Remember when you had to suffer through outlining in your English classes? When you finished the topic, did you breathe a sigh of relief and forget all about it? Well, dust your knowledge off. Outlining is a time-honored, effective way of combining the big picture with the details.

I admit that I'm partial to outlining. Every book or article I write begins with an outline—so I can keep both the broad flow and the details in mind. Take this chapter, for instance. Without the overall structure, I'd get into irrelevant detail and waste your time and mine. But unless the outline also has the basic details, I'm at a loss for what to write when I look at my blank computer screen.

One of the places on the job that outlining is most useful is in planning. With a good outline, you start with the overall goals and strategy, then begin to fill in more and more detail. Because you have an outline, though, you can see how each detail fits in. You may outline the plan by department (Product Development, Production, Marketing), by time (March, April, May), by individuals (John, Mary, Ernest), or by resources (Materials, Funds, Manpower).

In other words, if you're not used to using outlines, you might seriously consider starting. Remember, the point isn't to make nice, neat outlines. It's to help you develop the ability to see the big picture without losing sight of the details, and vice versa.

If you use a personal computer regularly, by the way, there are some excellent PC-based outliners available. One of my colleagues organizes meetings by developing an outline on a PC as the meeting progresses and projecting the outline. That lets everyone see exactly what they're working on and how it relates to everything else.

There's also an alternative to outlines worked out by a British writer named Tony Buzan. He's developed "mind maps," that accomplish the same goal as outlining but in a very different way. If you're interested in exploring his technique, it's explained in his book, *Use Both Sides of Your Brain* (listed in the bibliography).

Chunking

Outlining is a form of what's come to be known as "chunking." We remember information much more effectively when we can group like items together. For instance, if you want to remember an article on economic changes, you might group the items simply into "good news" and "bad news." If the article is more complex, you might try to group the information into "productivity," "interest rates," and "consumer buying,"

Chunking doesn't just apply to remembering; we also understand and use information more effectively when it's chunked. If your firm uses company-wide objectives that are broken down into department objectives and then on down to production objectives at the first line, this is a form of chunking. Having an objective to "increase sales of widgets by 10%" is much more meaningful if you know it's part of a division objective to open a new market for widgets.

Organization itself is a form of chunking. Small units, such as teams, are chunked together to form larger units, which are chunked together to form departments, which are chunked together to form . . . . Being able to understand just what each part does and how it fits with each other part is key to integrating the parts with each other and with the whole organization. And that leads naturally to the third way of seeing the big picture and the details.

Going from Overview to Details to Overview . . . .

Look at these two examples:

"Here's the latest word from corporate. First, no more overtime this month or next. Second, we have to reduce our error rate from 2% to 1% by the end of the year. Third, we expect to have a new data entry system installed by the end of next month. Any questions?"

"Here's the latest word from Corporate. The company is in the red for the last two months and has to stop the losses. They need us to cut our costs by 5% for the next couple of months. If we cut out our overtime, we can reduce our costs about 3%. We can make the rest up if reduce our error rate by half and cut out the rework costs; we were working on that already. Corporate's also just about finished a new data entry system that they plan to install next month. It's supposed to be much easier to use, and should help us cut our errors. Our part of all this is using no overtime for at least two months, cutting our error rate at least in half, and getting ready for the new data-entry system. Now, let's talk about what this really means to us."

The first example deals only with the details. It's the way that a first- or second-line manager in a traditional organization would typically approach the matter. The second example is just as clear about the details, but relates them to the overall objectives of the company. The team will have a much clearer idea of why they're doing what they're doing and what it's designed to accomplish. Since they see the broad view, they may be able to come up with other alternatives to accomplish the same goals. (And, if they were in a company that was serious about teampower, they would have had significant input to the decision in the first place.)

The ability to go from a broad view to the details and back again is neither quick nor easy to master. But you can work on it in any situation. Here are some ideas:

1. Whenever you have to pass on specific instructions, as in the examples above, make sure you know the broad background for them and pass it along, too.

2. The reverse is true, too. When you're discussing broad questions at higher levels in the organization, think about the specific impact they might have. If the situation permits, describe the impact—so that the individuals involved can see what the linkage will be between the broad issues and the specific activities in your part of the world.

3. Make a habit of going from broad to specific to broad with every issue. Try to see how each influences the other. Broad policy restricts what teams can do, but what teams can do also limits how effective broad policies can be.

There you have it. The key skill of managing alignment is the ability to see both the broad issues and the details of operations. Outlining or some other form of chunking (such as Mind Maps) may help. No matter what else, though, you can train yourself to move from the specifics to the general issues and back—in every situation.

Chapter 6 ═══════════════

Coordinating Team Performance ════════════

The second management function in a teampower environment is that of managing coordination. There are two different levels at which you do this:

1. You coordinate the actions of the teams for which you're responsible with each other.

2. You coordinate your actions and those of your teams with the other players (and their teams) at the same level as yourself.

Coordination has always been an essential management function, though it hasn't always been described very clearly. If you're above the first level of management, you've already had at least some experience of coordinating the units that report to you. But different kinds of organizations require very different amounts of coordination.

There are two kinds of situations that require only minimal coordination. In the first, all of the units perform the same function—such as independent computer programming teams. In the second, the units perform different but independent functions—such as purchasing, accounting and personnel in an administrative branch. Because the units are relatively independent of each other, coordination is minimal. And, at least in theory, it's the boss's responsibility to provide the little coordination that the units need.

There's another situation, though, that requires a great deal of coordination. In this, the units aren't independent; they depend on each other to get work done. In a personnel office, for instance, job analysis, recruiting and training must work very closely together to be effective. Even more routine functions like stock-picking, packing and shipping in a warehouse are closely related. When you manage this kind of workflow, coordination becomes much more of a challenge. What each unit does affects every other unit.

If you've been in this latter kind of situation, you know a lot about coordination already—which means that you have a lot of the skills you need. You've probably also developed skills at working with your peers to coordinate what your individual operations are doing. True, that's supposed to be your boss's responsibility. In the real world, though, a tremendous amount of it gets done by individual managers working with each other. In fact, if a manager has to force coordination on the units that report to her, she's in trouble already.

HOW ALIGNMENT AND COORDINATION RELATE _____

So your function as manager of coordination is a big one, on both of its levels. It might help put it in perspective if we diagrammed the relationship between alignment and coordination this way:

Alignment is a vertical process, ensuring that the different levels and parts of the organization line up with the organization's goals and values. Coordination is a horizontal process, ensuring that each unit produces an output that meets the need of units further along in the work flow. Both of these processes are necessary in any kind of organization, but in an organization using empowered teams managing alignment and managing coordination are both fluid, demanding functions.

WHAT YOU DO TO COORDINATE TEAMS _____

What do individuals like yourself do when they're coordinating the activities of themselves and the teams that report to them. Here are several examples:

1. You ensure that each team is meeting the needs of its customers, internal or external.

2. You distribute the available resources (manpower, supplies, equipment, etc.) among the teams to maintain the best work-flow.

3. You help each team identify and operate effectively within its proper boundaries. (Self-managing teams, especially entrepreneurial ones, have a tendency to expand. This can be healthy, but not if it comes at the expense of another team.)

4. You see that teams are performing at the levels of quality and quantity they've committed themselves to, and work with any that aren't doing so to remedy the situation.

5. You help any team that needs assistance in resolving problems with other teams.

6. You ensure that teams share their "best practices" and that they don't deviate significantly from each other in their interpretation of policy and procedure.

7. You work with your peers to see that work moves effectively among different units and to prevent or resolve problems in work flow, resources, scheduling, policy interpretation, etc.

Coordination must be actively and continually managed, or

teams get out of sync with each other. Let me give you a hypothetical example of how this can happen, based on a real success story. Shenandoah Life Insurance of Roanoke, Virginia, was an early user of self-directed teams. By creating semiautonomous teams of five to seven workers, in combination with an effective use of automation, Shenandoah Life reduced the time to process a policy conversion from 27 days to two days.[43]

Clearly, that's success. Suppose you duplicate it in your organization, with equivalent success. That's great.

If each team is empowered to process conversions without management control, though, it's easy for teams to start drifting apart in how they apply the rules. Add to this the different short cuts and workarounds the teams will develop, and you can see that there's tremendous potential for each team to start doing things a little differently. Time goes by, and the little differences turn into major inconsistencies and arguments over who's right. Seeing that this doesn't happen—without becoming a "boss" again—is one of the challenging aspects of managing coordination.

One of the ways you help a situation like the one above is to enable teams to communicate with each other regularly and effectively—just the reverse of the way a traditional organization tries to work. If the teams work in a trusting, cooperative environment, they can share their ideas and stay much more in sync with each other. Again, you can't force this—but you need to facilitate and support it constantly.

Exactly the same thing will probably be true on your level. If you're supporting empowered teams, the odds are good that other players on your level are doing the same. This means that all of you have much more autonomy than you would in a traditional organization. Here, again, there's tremendous potential for different ones of you to move in different directions and progressively do things just a bit differently from each other. Knowing how to work with other players—in your team and at your level—to see that this doesn't happen is part of the function of coordination.

That's really about the simplest case. If your teams are performing different functions that depend on one another, the complexity increases (just as it does in a traditional organization). Because each team is used to operating with great autonomy—and probably takes great pride in its skills and accomplishments—there's every opportunity for friction. It becomes immensely important to develop the same teamwork *among* the teams that there is *within* the teams. The same is true, and perhaps a bit more so, for relationships among the players at your level. This is another demanding facet of coordination.

THE SKILLS YOU NEED _____

How do you accomplish this coordination, particularly since you can't simply direct people to work together? (Which isn't that bad, because just telling people to work together never worked that well, anyway.) There are four essential skills that the coordinating function requires:

1. You must be an effective *negotiator*.
2. You must use *influence* (rather than direct authority) effectively.
3. You need to understand the various tools that help you understand, "debug," and improve *processes*.
4. And you must have the ability to *empathize* with a broad variety of other players.

Let's look at each of these in more detail.

HOW TO NEGOTIATE WIN-WIN SOLUTIONS _____

Negotiating is a critical skill at every level of a teampower organization. It's also become more and more critical in traditional organizations, as rapid change requires managers at every level to substitute negotiation for unilateral decisions. This means that you probably already have significant negotiating skills—and that puts you several steps down the road to effective coordination in a teampower environment.

I don't intend to write on negotiation at great length. There are dozens of books that will help you learn negotiating skills; several of them, very different from one another, are in the bibliography. What I want to do is hit a few critical points that you must understand if you want to be a successful negotiator. Just knowing

ʄ

these points won't make you a success—you need more training
and experience for that. However, they will help you keep out of
serious trouble while you're learning.

Negotiation and Bargaining

You may think of negotiation as the same thing as bargaining.
Many people use the words to describe the same process. I think
there's a real difference between the two, though—and understanding the difference helps you be more effective:

- *Negotiation* is what happens when you and I work together
  to find a solution that meets the needs of both of us. Each of
  us is concerned that *both* of our needs get met. How well I
  do is a factor of how skillful we are and how hard we're
  willing to work.

- *Bargaining* is what happens when I try to get as much as I
  can for *myself* and don't worry a lot about what you get out
  of it. How much each of us gets is primarily a result of the
  power I have vs. the power you have.

In other words, negotiating is a joint win-win process, while
bargaining may range anywhere from win-win to lose-lose (if each
of us is powerful enough to block the other but not to force what
he wants on the other). This section is about negotiating, but let
me say just a word about bargaining.

When the parties have to work together, even hard-nosed bargainers are careful just how strongly they push the other individ-
ual(s) concerned. John Winkler summarized the reason for being
careful this way:

> Remember that you are setting up deals for the future in the
> way you bargain now. If you are too strong, show too much
> power, and you stand firm for too long, then next time they
> will get you. They will use force to coerce you into move-
> ment. You have taught them how to deal with you.[44]

This isn't just theory. Research has shown that experienced
bargainers are much less apt to push their counterparts into a
corner or take advantage of them than inexperienced bargainers.

In this sense, bargaining is a lot like playing in a sports league. The football team you beat 50-3 this year will be back next year (and the next and the next) and they'll remember what the loss felt like. By bargaining too hard, you give your colleagues strong motivation to do the same thing to you as soon as the opportunity permits.

In other words, even if you have to bargain—and sometimes there's no other way—be careful how much you exact from the other(s). Have a clear idea of what you're after beforehand, then push hard for it and stop when you've gotten it. In a union contract negotiation years ago, I worked hard and got a provision I thought was important. Then I pushed for some more—and my counterpart on the union team brought me up sharp. "Look, you may not have everything you want here," he said, "but you have everything you need. Now let's get on to the next issue!" He understood.

Let me make one more point about bargaining. If you have to bargain, learn from successful car salespeople. When you go to buy a car, the job of the salesperson is to sell you a car at a price that will make money for the dealership. A good one will do that, but he won't stop there. He'll do his best to see that when you walk away you're convinced that *you* got a good deal. This is critical in all bargaining. Do your best to see that everyone concerned feels good about the transaction. That's almost as important as the result you get.

Regardless of how skillfully you bargain, though, bargaining is a poor substitute for negotiation. Bargaining is based on *power*, and that's incompatible with most operations in an organization that really intends to empower its players. Negotiation is based on *influence*, which gives it a completely different goal.

Negotiation is a Win-Win Process

In real negotiation, your goal isn't to get the most you can for yourself and your organization. Instead, it's to get the best possible outcome for everyone. While this may not be easy, it's the primary goal nonetheless. That may sound a little soft and squishy to you, particularly if your experience has been in a traditional organization where bargaining was the order of the day—but I assure you it's not. In their excellent book, based on the Harvard

Negotiation Project, Fisher and Ury state three standards for successful negotiation:

> Any method of negotiation may be fairly judged by three criteria: It should produce a wise agreement if agreement is possible. It should be efficient. And it should improve or at least not damage the relationship between the parties.[45]

Please note that last point. This is one of the basic differences between bargaining and negotiating—a difference that's critical for successful negotiation in a teampower organization. Effective negotiating may actually *improve* the relationship between the parties.

How does this happen? It's a product of a goal that is the best possible outcome for everyone concerned. When we realize that the person we're negotiating with cares about the outcome for us as much as for himself, our attitude changes. Here are two ways that a player named Larry might approach one of his peers. Read his two approaches carefully, and note your reaction to each one:

- "Louise, your team isn't meeting its deadlines with us, and that's got to stop. You know how important this project is to the boss."

- "Louise, we have a problem. Your team isn't meeting the deadlines we agreed on, and that's throwing us behind. I know that you don't want this any more than I do. What can the two of us to do turn it around?"

There's a tremendous difference in the tone of the two comments, and in the way each structures the situation. In the first, Larry is implying clearly that Louise and her unit are the problem; in the second, it's a joint problem. Louise is almost certainly going to be defensive in the first situation. "Well, if your team would just make up its mind about what it wants we'd give it to them!" wouldn't be a surprising answer. The same response would be completely inappropriate in the second situation, because Larry hasn't accused Louise and her team of anything.

(I do have to add one other comment to this. You may actually have reacted more strongly to the second statement than the first—because it may have sounded like the speaker was being dishonest. In many companies, there's a strong human relations veneer covering a traditional power-based approach. This is perhaps the worst possible situation, because it makes it almost impossible to get at the real issues. If this is your experience, please understand that it really is possible to say and mean the second statement. I have known and worked with very effective managers who took this basic approach to problems.)

In other words, an effective negotiator always assumes that there's a joint problem, that needs to be attacked jointly. It's entirely possible that there is a misunderstanding between Louise's team and the other one; perhaps the team isn't clear about what the other team really wants. Approached as a joint problem, it's not only solvable but easily solvable. And the players concerned can solve it far faster and more effectively than any higher level player could.

To repeat what Fisher and Ury said, the purpose of effective negotiation is to find agreement if it's possible, (and it usually is), do it efficiently, and strengthen the relationship in the process. That's a true "win-win" situation.

Negotiating from Strength

Now that I've stressed the need to work for everyone's good in negotiating, let me turn around and stress the need for you to identify what you legitimately need and hang tough until either you get it or it's plain that it cannot reasonably be gotten.

Does it sound strange for me to say this? It may—but there's a clear purpose to it. When individuals try to work together as a team and work for each others' good, there's a danger they have to watch out for. It's called by a lot of names, but mine is *overaccommodation*. It happens when everyone gets to concentrating so hard on being a good team member and being cooperative that important issues don't get raised. Harmony gets maintained by sweeping potentially troublesome issues under the rug.

Let's go back to the situation between Larry and Louise. Larry brings the matter up, tactfully, and Louise responds positively. Perhaps the conversation goes something like this:

Louise: I know how important this is to you, and we really mean to get the material to you on time. For three weeks, though, your players have changed what we thought they wanted.

Larry: Yeah, I know. They have gotten pretty picky. Are you sure your players are giving them just what they ask for each time?

Louise: Oh, yes. I know my team, and they really want to do the job well.

Larry: I tell you what. I'll talk to my folks and tell them to get what they want down right for once and for all and get it to your folks. We'll put an end to this for good.

When Larry left, he may have been feeling good about the exchange. After all, he paid attention to Louise and her team's needs in the situation, and he reached a helpful agreement with her. Right? Wrong! This was an excellent example of overaccommodation, in two ways:

1. Larry accepted Louise's account of the situation without checking with his own team. They may see the matter very differently. That doesn't mean that they're right and Louise's team is wrong—that's back to blaming and bargaining. It does mean that Larry took Louise's account as gospel. When he talks the matter over with his team, he may not hear what they need to tell him. Equally as bad, he may change his mind about what really happened and have to renege on his promise to Louise.

2. In his hurry to accommodate Louise, Larry did what his team should have done. It would have been better if his team had brought the matter up directly with hers and not involved either of them. A self-managing team would normally do just that. Perhaps these teams aren't used to working with one another, or they're relatively new and not skilled at negotiating yet. Perhaps there was some other reason that Larry brought the matter up directly with Louise. Once the matter's been surfaced, though, it needs to be returned to the teams. Larry and Louise may want to sit in, to facilitate their teams dealing with each other—but the teams should settle the matter directly between themselves.

How might this have been done? Here's a quick snapshot:

Louise: I know how important this is to you, and we really mean to get the material to you on time. For three weeks, though, your players have changed what we thought they wanted.

Larry: Yeah, they've gotten pretty picky; they're determined that they're going to get this just right. It sounds like the situation is causing a problem for both our teams, though.

Louise: Oh, yes. I know my team, and they really want to do the job well. I'm sure they're trying to give your folks exactly what they want.

Larry: Look, we need to get them together and have them work it out. I wouldn't even suggest we sit in on it except that I think both of the teams are a little uncomfortable with each other. Could you and some of your team meet with me and a couple of my team at 2:30 tomorrow afternoon?

Louise: I suppose so. We do need to get this settled as quickly as we can.

Notice that Larry wasn't judgmental; he didn't try to blame Louise or her team. But he steered the situation where it needed to be: between the two teams. This gives each team the opportunity to present the situation as it sees it and then to try to find the best solution. The teams may be able to do this on their own; if not, Larry and Louise are there to help them.

In Chapter 3, we looked at some of the reasons that quality teams often cease to function effectively. One of these reasons is that many significant problems can't be solved within one unit or team. They happen in the interaction *between* units and teams. These problems are generally harder to solve than problems within one organizational unit; they take more time and require more skill at both problem-solving and interpersonal relationships. These are the kinds of problems, at your team's level and at your own, that you handle when you manage coordination. And they won't go away or be solved just because you want to be cooperative and look out for everyone's welfare.

That's why you have to insist that your valid concerns are dealt with (and sometimes that another player's are as well—since you don't want to be overaccommodated, either). Issues and problems such as boundary conflicts don't miraculously vanish just because you're using empowered teams. The problems change somewhat and pop up in different forms, but they're there. A major part of the function of managing coordination is to see that they're identified and dealt with before they can cause serious disruption in the workflow.

The next skill you need to manage coordination in a teampower environment is the effective use of influence. Since negotiation depends so directly on influence, looking at influence will lead to an even better understanding of negotiation.

HOW TO MANAGE EFFECTIVELY WITH INFLUENCE _____

"Influence" is a much used and, in my opinion, must misunderstood idea. There are several books on influence listed in the bibliography; each of them grasps part of the overall idea. I certainly don't have space in this section to draw an elaborate picture of what I believe influence is. I'll do my best, though, to present the basics and to describe how influence differs from power.

Influence and Power

We had one example of this when we talked about the difference between bargaining and negotiation. Bargaining uses power; negotiation uses influence. This is the difference between the two:

- When I use *power*, I force you to do something you would not do if given a free choice. Part of using power is seeing that you cannot use power on me; to use power effectively, I must remain as *independent* as possible, and keep you as dependent as possible.

- When I use *influence*, I get you to want to do something you might not otherwise have done. As part of my influencing you, I allow you to influence me. Effective influence creates *interdependence*.

This sounds nice and neat, but of course it isn't. Here are some real-world examples that illustrate how one shades into another:

1. Tom, Marie's supervisor, tells her to forget about the project she's working on and put all of her time on the Acme project. When she objects, he tells her to do it or he'll write her up for insubordination.

2. Eleanor, the chief of budget, tells Tom that if he doesn't get her new personal computers for her in the next two weeks his budget is going to be the last one approved.

3. Paul, chief recruiter in the Human Resources Management Office, tells Eleanor that if she will support his request for another recruiter he will see that Eleanor's two vacancies get first priority for filling.

4. Oscar, current leader of one of the manufacturing teams, drops by and persuades Paul that if four vacancies in Manufacturing don't get filled productivity is going to drop sharply.

5. Wilhemena, the most knowledgeable technician on the staff, eats lunch with Oscar and Ralph and shows them how a small change in one of the line processes can reduce defects at least 10%.

6. Arnie, the most senior of the technicians, takes Wilhemena aside; he tells her about the feathers she ruffled at the Division level with a proposal she sent to a vice-president and then helps her develop a plan to calm the situation down.

These six examples shade from power to influence. The first is power in the form of *authority*. In every organization, individuals with authority have the "right" to use power to get others to do what they want done. This is the basis for the traditional organization. The second and third examples are also common in most organizations. Eleanor and Paul are using the power inherent in their job functions to get what they want from someone else. Eleanor is using her job power as a threat, while Paul is using his as an incentive. In both cases, the individuals are bargaining with one another on the basis of their power; influence is playing a relatively small role. These kinds of bargains are how the work of many organizations really gets done, even though it never shows up on any organization charts or in any policy and procedure manuals.

With the fourth example, the scene shifts more markedly to influence. Oscar is skilled at presenting facts so that others are persuaded of his point of view. Eleanor is going to do what he wants, but she's going to do it willingly—because he is persuasive. Wilhemena is also persuasive, but in a slightly different way. Oscar and Ralph have worked with her before, and they know that she has good, practical ideas. They don't understand exactly why this new idea will work so well, but they respect her knowledge enough to implement it. Finally, Arnie has taken Wilhemena under his wing and she knows that he sincerely cares about what happens to her. Even though she may be irritated that she has to do it, she doesn't hesitate to work out with him how to soothe the necessary feathers. This is influence based on demonstrated concern for someone else's success.

Notice that as you go down the list from 1 to 6 power becomes less and less appropriate. There's no room at all for negotiation in the first incident; it's pure power. In the sixth one, though, any attempt by Arnie to force Wilhemena to take some action would be very destructive. There is the same shading from independence to interdependence. If Marie sees that Tom is using his authority to force her to do something she doesn't want to do, she'll do what she can to get some independence. (She may complain to the union, ask for a transfer, work strictly "by the book," sabotage Tom behind his back, or take any of a wide variety of steps to make it harder for him to use power against her.) The sixth situation is just the reverse. Wilhemena welcomes Arnie's intervention and depends on it. Conversely, if she went to him with a suggestion he would almost certainly listen closely to it.

The Importance of Influence

It has always been the case that the most successful managers and executives have succeeded because of their tremendous influence rather than their power. Various writers today speak as though influence were something exercised exclusively by leaders. I think this shortchanges the thousands of managers and executives who effectively use influence every day to help the organization function effectively—and to change organizational objectives they don't concur with. In other words, for good or ill, influence is pervasive in all organizations. There are six basic reasons for this, all directly relevant to the management of coordination in a teampower organization:

1. *Power invites resistance.* There are individuals who prefer highly authoritarian situations. They want to be told what to do, when and how to do it. In the U.S. and most Western countries, though, these are generally not the people who are committed to their jobs. These individuals also tend to define competence very narrowly, as the competent performance of the narrow range of duties they've been specifically assigned. The kind of players who really produce for a company are those who value their own autonomy, and feel resentment when forced into a particular course of action. In other words, it is precisely the players capable of making the greatest contribution to the organization that most resent power (and simple authority) as a means for getting things done.

2. *Power erodes commitment.* This is a result of much the same factors. I will do something because I want to (am committed to it) or because you force me to—but almost never from a combination of both motives. In other words, commitment always requires something more from a manager than the simple use of power.

3. *Influence supports interdependence supports cooperation.* While teampower organizations support individual independence, they also depend on a high degree of cooperation and interdependence. Individual players must be willing to work together to achieve organizational goals. To the extent that they can influence one another, their willingness to cooperate is enhanced.

4. *Influence is always mutual.* True influence always works both ways; you have the maximum opportunity to influence those whom you are willing to let influence you. This is just the reverse of power, which can only be used effectively by resisting others' power. There is good research support for the mutuality of influence, and it's been borne out in my 20+ years as a manager.

5. *Influence builds relationships.* The best that power, even in the form of bargaining, can accomplish is to maintain relation-

ships. Influence, on the other hand, strengthens them. When players are confident they can influence one another, they have positive reasons to maintain and develop their relationship.

6. Finally, *influence is unlimited*. There is always a limit on power. It is what researchers call a "zero-sum game"; if I get more power, it can only be because you now have less. This isn't true of influence. In fact, just the reverse tends to be true: The more influence I have on you, the more influence you will probably have on me. Nor is it limited in the number of people who can exercise it; everyone can increase in influence at the same time. This is the whole basis of effective team performance, which is built upon the willingness of all team members to influence others and be influenced by them.[46]

Again, remember that the millennium is not at hand. Influence is hard to develop, difficult to maintain, and easy to lose. It doesn't work unless everyone believes in it; one individual who deals from a power position can seriously erode the ability of others to manage coordination with influence. And there are times that operations must be coordinated—as organizations must be aligned—by using authority and overruling what individuals and teams would otherwise have done.

Having said all that, teampower organizations function by broad use of influence, or they do not function effectively. This is even more true at your level. If you're skilled not only at using influence but at promoting it throughout all your teams, you will likely succeed. The reverse, unfortunately, is just as true.

How, then, do you develop influence? Chapter 9 deals with *trust*, and every single skill described there is fundamental for influence—because influence is utterly dependent on trust. The last section of this chapter describes the importance of *empathy*, and empathy is critical to influence. There are certain other very specific steps you can take to develop and increase your ability to influence others. Here are six basic ones:

1. *Be competent*. If you look back at the examples of influence on page 33, you'll see that one of the bases of influence is competence. In fact, if others don't believe you're competent you'll have tremendous difficulty trying to influence them.

Conversely, if you're known to be extremely competent your influence will be magnified. Competence doesn't just mean job competence; it includes understanding how the organization operates, how to get something done, who the "movers and shakers" are. The more expert you are at all of this, the more other people will be willing to rely on you.

2. *Deliver.* This gets very close to the discussion in Chapter 9, but it needs to be mentioned here as well. Nothing else matters if you can't come through for other players. This involves the expertise mentioned in the paragraph above, but knowing "who and what" is useless unless it can be turned into effective action. Others need to know that what you say you'll deliver you will deliver. We'll leave it at that until Chapter 9.

3. *Be honest.* How many times have you heard this? And how many times have you looked at the organization and how it operates and said "no way!"? Honesty is often praised but, as Hamlet said, often "more honored in the breach than the observance." Let me tell you clearly that if you intend to empower players, and particularly if you intend to empower them in teams, this has to change. Empowered organizations only work when there is full, free and *honest* communication among all of the units, teams and players. As soon as players begin playing games and shading the truth to make themselves look good, the power starts to seep out of teampower. It doesn't take much before it's gone completely.

4. *Concentrate on goals, not methods.* This isn't as important as the three before it or the next two, but it plays a part. One element of influencing effectively is letting others do things their way, as long as the outcome is what you both agree on. This was the whole point of Management by Objectives in the 70s, and it's just as important in the 90s. If you and your teams are in clear agreement on *what* they should do, let them have maximum discretion on *how* to do it. The same with relationships with your peers; establish agreement on what you want from each other, then leave each player free to provide it in his or her own way. This increases the freedom others feel, but still gets done exactly what needs to be done.

5. *Let yourself be influenced.* If you're not used to dealing through

influence, this can be scary. I remember when I first decided that this was the way I wanted to manage. For months, I wondered if I was just unsure of myself and hiding behind letting myself be influenced. I know now that this wasn't the case, that letting others influence me has had powerful results. I have had far more influence than I otherwise could have. Again, this doesn't mean being a washrag and simply accommodating other people. But it does mean staying open to their ideas and using those that you can. You're not used to doing this? Try it—you'll like it!

6. *Live and act by the shared values.* When you state your goals and values, and when you buy publicly into those of the organization, you make a commitment to live by them. The last chapter emphasized how important it is that your decisions follow these values if you want them accepted. It's equally important to follow the values if you want to influence others.

HOW TO UNDERSTAND AND IMPROVE PROCESSES _____

There are many practical skills you can use to manage coordination, but perhaps none is as important as knowing how to analyze and control the processes that connect all parts of an organization and are the means by which it produces its output. Tools for analyzing processes have been around for years, but the importance of processes has been brought into the spotlight in the last decade by the various quality programs. As we saw in Chapter 3, finding and then fixing problems with work processes is a major goal of quality teams.

Processes are the core of any organization's activities. In technical terms, processes turn inputs into more valuable outputs. These processes may be internal: By examining and validating vouchers, a voucher examining function provides the disbursing function with the input it needs to pay the vouchers. Other processes take inputs from outside the organization—for instance, the receiving and storing function of a warehouse—or provide outputs directly to customers—such as a skilled technician who repairs computers for the firm's customers.

Every activity in an organization involves processes (which is why quality techniques can be applied anywhere in an organization). Processes are nothing more or less than the series of steps that change the unit's input into its output. These steps normally involve some form of human action, such as machining a part or interviewing candidates for a job. They also involve some form of technology, whether it be actual machinery (such as a milling machine) or a body of applied knowledge (such as the technology of conducting effective interviews). These are tied together by procedures, which spell out the steps to take.

The processes within a team or unit are important. In terms of their potential impact and problems, though, the processes that happen *between* teams or units are even more important. A new product takes form as it flows from Research to Product Development to Manufacturing to Sales. A customer request flows through a series of processes, beginning with logging in and ending with the generation of a letter or phone call to the customer. Whenever a process moves an idea, product or other output from one organizational unit to another, there is the potential for a problem. One classic example is Manufacturing's complaint that Product Design gives them impossible products to build, while Product Design complains because Manufacturing refuses to make even the simplest changes once the plans are drawn.

Processes facilitate this movement, or they interfere with it. Part of your responsibility to manage coordination is seeing that the processes connecting your teams, and connecting your operation with others, do the maximum of facilitating and the minimum of interfering. Negotiating and influence help this materially. But you also need specific tools to let you and the other players involved analyze the processes, find any problems with them, and improve them.

Tools to help you analyze and improve processes are widely available and you can get information about them easily. Let me just mention a few tools you might find helpful.

Quality Tools

The problem-solving methods taught to quality teams are basic problem-solving tools. They range from freewheeling brainstorming to carefully structured cause-and-effect diagrams and Pareto charts. One of the reasons for starting with quality teams is that everyone learns these tools. They're not sufficient to solve really big problems, but they enable everyone to identify, structure and solve a wide range of basic problems. Then, when they're ready to move beyond these basic problems and basic tools, they already know the essential problem-solving process.

There is another whole group of tools used in the quality movement, known collectively as "The 7 New QC Tools." These are intended to be used with higher-level, less structured problems. They're the relations diagram, affinity diagram, systematic diagram, matrix diagram, matrix data analysis, process decision program chart and the arrow diagram. If you're not familiar with them but would like to be, they're covered in Mizuno's book, listed in the bibliography.

Work Simplification and Value Analysis

Not all process analysis tools come from the quality movement. A number of years ago, there was a program called "work simplification" that focused on administrative processes. Its goal was to train every supervisor to analyze his or her own operations and then (as the name suggests) simplify it. Some of the techniques were very effective and—under other names—are coming back into vogue. During the same time period, value analysis, a method of analyzing products to ensure that they met the customer's need, became popular. It's still around in places, and books on value analysis are available in some city and university libraries.

Process Management

A newer and proprietary form of process problem-solving tool is "process management," a method specifically designed for understanding and improving the processes that connect different units. The method is based on the premise that "the greatest opportunities for performance improvement often lie in the functional interfaces—those points at which a baton is being passed from one department to another."[47]

"Process management" uses a very specific methodology to analyze and improve the process flow from one unit to another. You can find out more about the methodology in the article from which the quote above was taken, or from Rummler and Brache's book listed in the bibliography.

There are many other ways available to analyze and improve processes. Your company may already use one or even several. The point is that you should find at least one method you're comfortable with, and then see that you and the other players concerned learn and use this method to continually improve the processes you and they are responsible for.

HOW TO DEVELOP THE KEY SKILL: EMPATHY _____

Now we get to the key skill for coordination (and for a great deal else). This is empathy—the ability to see a situation from another person's point of view. Empathy is critical to both negotiation and influence, because neither works unless you can demonstrate that you can see the situation from the point of view of the players you're working with. Empathy is a way of showing that while your goals are important they are not automatically more important than those of others.

How much empathy you've developed is at least partly a reflection of the kind of organization(s) you've worked in. Many companies are highly competitive; sometimes it's not clear whether the major competition is another firm or the organization down the hall. If you've been in this highly competitive environment, you probably haven't had a chance to develop or use strong empathy skills. The odds are, though, that you've been in a somewhat less dramatic environment, and that you already have basic skills at empathizing with others. The more successful you've been at working cooperatively with your peers, the better these skills are.

In a teampower climate, though, your skills must be even better. Like most other important skills, effective empathy can't be learned overnight, or even in a month. But it can be learned—and it can be learned and practiced as you go about your daily job. There are six aspects of empathy that you can work on; as you improve your skills on each of them, learning and using the others will become easier and easier.

As a way of approaching these six aspects, let me set up an all-too-common situation. You have several teams, each of them combining several skills and performing independently of each other. At the end of the month, you collect data from all of them, consolidate it, and send it to another branch to be summarized and published. Your teams have missed the deadline two of the past three months, though only by a couple of days. Pete Jenks, to whom you send the information, is upset that it's been late. He wants to meet with you to "straighten out" the situation. (Yes, even in a teampower organization these kinds of interface problems can persist.) We'll look at each of the six aspects of empathizing in general, but also look at how each might play out in this situation.

1. Focus on Overall Goals

This is the place to start. If you want to understand the values and goals of other players, begin by focusing your attention and theirs on the overall goals that all of you share.

This isn't always as easy as it sounds. You spend most of your workday worrying about the goals of your unit, your teams, your players. They're what you're responsible for. When you're trying to coordinate your teams with each other, each of them is used to focusing on even smaller areas—their part of the action. The same with the other players on your level. What's most real to them is the daily round of problems they confront. Pete has to get his report out on a specific schedule, and he's focusing on that.

As long as you focus only on your problems and Pete only on his, neither you nor any other players are going to have much empathy for each other. The best you'll be able to do is strike a bargain both of you will accept but neither is really happy with. So, you have to break out of this narrowly focused point of view.

The quickest way to do this is to focus on the goals the report serves or is related to. Let's assume that what Pete produces is a monthly "flash production report," used by higher levels to track productivity and estimate future workload. If you and Pete focus on that, not just on your individual pieces of the action, you'll create room for genuine negotiation.

For instance, you might see if Pete's willing to begin with his due date and work backward from that. Perhaps there's some slack time in there; perhaps he could meet his deadline if he got your information a day later than the current schedule—if he could be absolutely sure that the information was always there when promised. Perhaps you could change the format of what you submitted, so that he had less work to do on it after he got it. If you stay focused on the organizational goal you both are trying to meet, you increase the chance that you can find this kind of solution.

2. State Goals Up Front

Another way to facilitate the process is to be very clear up front what your goals are, and ask the other player(s) to do the same. Use a blackboard or a flip chart and write down each player's goals. Take as much time as you need to complete this step, so that everyone sees exactly what's at stake in the discussion.

One of your goals might be for your players to have an extra day to put their information together, so they can do their planning for the coming month before anything else. One of Pete's might well be to always have his report ready on the due date—no exceptions. On just a quick look, these aren't mutually exclusive goals. It's quite possible that you could each get what you want. There may be other goals, and some of them may conflict with one another. As you look at them and sort through them, though, you may begin to see where some areas of flexibility are. Remember that one of Fisher and Ury's three characteristics of successful negotiation is that it finds agreement if there is any agreement to be found. If everyone is clear up front about their goals, this increases the chance for that agreement.

After the players concerned have experience at this, there's a second step in stating goals that can help. You may have three or four goals you want, but they're probably not equally important. The same may be true of the goals of the other player(s). Pete may want to even out his workload, but that goal is probably not as important as his desire to get his report done on time. As you each prioritize your goals, you become clearer and clearer about what each of your bottom lines really is. Again, this helps you find how great the area of possible agreement is, and where it is.

3. Keep an Open Mind

This is the next step, and it's a harder one. We all form opinions of what other players are like, and what they *really* want. Pete is angling for a promotion; he wants to look good. Sarah wants everything neat and orderly; she hates surprises. You want flexibility; you resist getting tied down to the same routine over and over. Day by day, we each form more and more complete stereotypes of what we and others are like. These simplify our relationships.

Unfortunately, these stereotypes also confine our relationships. When Pete raises a concern, you don't hear the concern; you hear him trying to look good. When Sarah questions your need for flexibility, you hear her trying to prevent surprises. And you just know that if you have to follow someone else's procedure you'll lose the flexibility you need. So each of you works out a stock pattern of responding to the others—a pattern based not on what the other is saying but on the "real" reasons for their saying it.

If you're going to empathize with others, you have to find a way to suspend your habitual patterns, even if at first they don't suspend theirs. Starting by stating goals openly is one way of doing this; it changes the focus from the person to what he or she wants from the meeting. And as the relationship gets stronger, the stated goals can be deeper and more complete. In a really effective relationship, there's no reason why Pete couldn't say: "Hey, I really want a crack at Mary's job when she retires this summer. I'll do everything I can to cooperate but I just can't do anything that makes it look like I can't manage my own operation."

Another way of breaking stereotypes is by dealing directly with what you believe the underlying issues—the hidden agendas—are. And that takes us to the next aspect.

4. Confront Honestly

This takes some skill, but all of us are capable of doing it. Suppose you believe that Pete's fundamental motivation is to look good and get promoted. You try to believe his stated goal, but it just doesn't ring true. What then? One way people often deal with this kind of situation is with questions like: Are you sure that's all? Is that what's really important to you? Or to say nothing at all but disbelieve the other.

All of these are crooked responses. They don't build relationships—they keep them superficial and often ruin them. If you genuinely believe that Pete isn't stating his true goals then say just that. Say: "Pete, I know you want to get ahead, and that's fine with me. Isn't that one of the things you're concerned about here, about not looking bad to the Front Office?" Don't do it judgmentally, though. Don't sound like you're accusing him of something. You're not; you're simply putting in words what your honest perceptions are.

Will Pete respond? That depends on a great many factors. If the relationship is strong enough, he may own his desire for promotion as a goal. Or he may completely reject it. He may persuade you that you were wrong. Or he may persuade you that he's not being honest about it. No matter what, you no longer have a hidden agenda. You've laid your cards on the table.

A word of caution: Don't use this as a ploy to get "one-up" on Pete. Maybe you want a promotion, too. If so, put that on the table. "Pete, I think you want to get a promotion, and, frankly, so do I. Let's see if we can solve this thing so that we both look like heroes." (There'll be more about presenting yourself honestly in Chapter 9; it's absolutely critical.) It doesn't matter whether you want a promotion—the important point is that you level about your real goals. No worthwhile relationship ever got built by one person opening up and the other playing his cards close to his chest.

5. Help Everyone Succeed

This is what empathy is all about. If I genuinely intend to help you succeed, I'll adopt strategies that will do just that. If you genuinely want Pete to succeed, you'll approach dealing with him in that way.

It may not work at first, particularly if the organization has been highly competitive. Pete may see this as a golden opportunity to get just what he wants and ignore what you want. That's no better than its opposite, going for your goals without concern for his. Again, that's a good reason to be clear about what your goals are—and clear that you want to meet them.

One way to handle this is to tie the goals of the different players together. In the situation with Pete, it might be: "OK, we're going to find a way to handle this that's going to make you look good and keep the flexibility for me that my folks need—right?" Sometimes it's harder and more complex, but the principle stays the same. Make sure that every player's primary goals are on the same level, and that each player commits to achieving all of the goals.

You may have to take the lead. If you've all recently been in a traditional organization, someone will have to. And someone will probably have to keep pushing through some rocky times. Being honest about goals and caring that others succeed requires considerable openness and trust, and this takes time to develop. Which brings us to the last point.

6. Be Patient

I remember a management job I had several years ago. I went into an office that had been run by an extremely capable but very directive manager. From the beginning, I made it as clear as I could that I wanted the office to run much more as a team operation. For weeks, though, anything I said elicited a "just fine" from the managers that reported to me. Then, slowly, they began to open up. They began to feel me out, to become a little more honest about what they wanted in the situation. It took months before we reached the level of openness and empathy for each other's goals we needed to work closely together. But we did reach it. (Even then, we never reached as far as I would have liked; each of us kept part of ourselves back.)

Changes don't happen quickly and easily, even when everyone involved intends them sincerely and is willing to work for them. The change from an environment in which I compete with you to one in which I empathize with and support your goals is a major change. Even where competition hasn't been that strong, moving to real empathy isn't trivial. Pete may want to trust you and believe that you genuinely want to help him as well as yourself. But can he really trust you? Will you do what you say? Are you being honest with him, or trying to get a step up on him? These questions take time to answer.

We'll return to the basic questions about trust in Chapter 9. For now, I have one final word about empathy: It seems to have crept even into our computer games. A computer game manufacturer named Sierra has an extremely popular series called "Leisure Suit Larry," a game in which one or more individuals play roles in the story as it develops. The third installment of the series has a feature that permits players to change roles in midstory and "see the story from someone else's point of view."[48] Actually, as funny as that may sound, it may lead to management computer simulations in which you and I can switch roles in midstream and see the situation from each other's point of view.

Chapter 7 ════════════

Managing the Decision-Making Process ════════

This chapter focuses on the third management function—supporting effective decision-making by teams—and the skills you need to perform the function successfully. To understand the function, we need to look first at (1) the growing complexity of operations in firms today; (2) the increasing diversity of the American workforce; and (3) the organization of work above the first level in an organization based on teampower.

WHY YOU MUST DEAL WITH INCREASING COMPLEXITY _____

The saying, "'taint nothing simple anymore," has been around for a very long time—but it seems somehow more true today than in the past. Consider these few examples:

1. When I began writing this chapter, Operation Desert Storm was raging in the Persian Gulf. Despite the harsh environmental conditions, the efforts of the Iraqi defenders and the sheer volume of Coalition sorties, the number of lost planes was a fraction of a percent of those flying. Patriot missiles, never before fired in combat, have been almost 100% effective against the Scuds. Yet modern planes and missiles are tremendously complex systems, combining thousands of electronic and mechanical components. Manufacturing these so that they work almost perfectly is an amazing achievement.

2. One of the big buzzwords these days is "reduced cycle time." Many companies find themselves competing in markets where the life of a product is shorter than the time traditionally required to design it and get it to market. This is a sure recipe for disaster. Toyota has pioneered in reducing this time; for instance, they have shortened the time necessary to for retooling production equipment from hours to minutes— a few minutes. Corning's filter plant in Blacksburg, Virginia, has reduced the time typically necessary to retool a line for different filters by 83%. This increases the complexity of the individual production worker's job, and how!

3. Don't think that complexity occurs only at the working level. Think back to Chapter 3 and Ford's executive-level teams. Three major teams were functioning at that level, each of them dealing with one aspect of the total situation. Their efforts had to be coordinated throughout the process, and then their output integrated into one overall approach. If you've had much experience on management teams, you know that—at the very least—it's as hard to build an effective team at that level as it is at the working level.

There's every sign that, at least for firms that intend to compete globally, this complexity can only increase. Time frames are being compressed—not a little, but a lot. This requires processes and components to be simplified (as, for instance, IBM has done with its printers). Paradoxically, effective simplification itself is a complex process, particularly when it follows hard on the heels on the initial design. At the same time, many common products are becoming more and more complex; high-end Xerox copiers not only talk users through making copies but monitor their own operation and automatically phone service facilities to warn of impending breakdowns.

We've talked of teams as a response to the need for competence and commitment on the part of players. They are. They're also a response to this growing complexity. More and more, processes require "people who need each other" working together to produce a successful product or service. Shrinking cycle times require organizations that can make decisions at the lowest possible level, delegating the authority to act down and stripping away the layers that slow down response time.

In this environment, decisionmaking processes must change. No longer can staff offices at the corporate level work out detailed strategy that is passed down for execution at the operating level. Now the operating level becomes the focus of significant decision making. In a teampower organization, this means that more and more decisions are made by teams—using processes dramatically different from those of traditional organizations.

WHY YOU MUST ALSO DEAL WITH INCREASING DIVERSITY

There's always been diversity, even in the most traditional organizations. Italians, Irish, Japanese, Chinese, Hispanics, Poles and individuals from a myriad of other ethnic groups have worked together in differing mixes throughout the country. Now African-Americans are entering the mainstream of American industry, joined by refugees from Southeast Asia and the rest of the world.

In one sense, this just continues the American tradition of the "melting pot." In the current situation, though, there are some major differences:

1. Women are entering the workforce, and staying in it. Many of these women are heads of families, further complicating their work situation. And not just at lower levels; for a number of years now, there have been more women than men in American colleges.

2. The diversity of groups in the workforce is increasing. The difference between the Italians and the Irish in Boston or New York two generations ago was pronounced, but nothing compared to the difference between (say) African-Americans and Japanese. On top of that, there are now many more groups represented in organizations. Even relatively small units may contain not only individuals from a Western European background, but possibly Hispanics, African-Americans, Middle Easterners, Orientals from several different countries, and perhaps another ethnic background or two. Many of these individuals will be female.

3. Arguably the most notable development, though, is that white men of Western European descent are now in a minor-

ity in the workforce—and they will become even more of a
minority. The real significance of this isn't the numbers
themselves; it's that the basic organizational culture of the
United States was created and maintained by this group, and
reflects its values. As other groups take larger and larger part
in American business and industry, other values will be
competing for attention and adoption.

Let me give you an example of this, particularly of the last
point. Firms have traditionally been organized so that their members worked from nine to five in a specific location. The actual
hours might have been eight to four-thirty, or eight p.m. to four
a.m. The location might have been a factory, an office, or the office
of a salesman's customer. But it was contained within specific
geographic and temporal boundaries; workers performed at a
specific place, at a specific time, or else.

This has never been the work pattern of most of the world. It
has never been the work pattern of a woman who worked at home
(unless she chose to organize her life this way). It is not necessarily
the best way to organize many kinds of work, particularly the
information work and "knowledge work" that is becoming more
and more important. And the various communication media—
telecomputing, facsimile machines, massive information utilities,
etc.—make the rigid time and place restrictions of traditional
work less and less significant.

Cultural and sexual diversity also impact mightily on the way
that an organization makes decisions. When individuals share a
common ethnic background, communication is expedited (but
only relatively—a white male of Western European descent in
Marketing still has a difficult time communicating with another
white male of Western European descent in Manufacturing!).
When this common background is taken away, communication
becomes less sure, more time consuming. More and more time
must be devoted to the process of communication itself, of explaining ourselves to the others.

Now add to this the dispersion of the workforce. In my own
organization, everyone works on the "maxiflex" system. Individuals may begin work on an average day anywhere between 6:30
and 9:00 a.m. They may work four hours or ten, four or five days
a week. When a player is injured, recovering from an operation or

childbirth, or otherwise confined but not disabled, he or she often works at home. Further our 130+ players are located in five different states. This imposes severe limits on what we can accomplish by team power—limitations that will in all probability increase throughout the 90s.

WHERE MIDDLE- AND UPPER-LEVEL TEAMS FIT IN _____

Many organizations have had management teams in some form or another for years. Many of these teams have been like that at Chrysler: One member of Lee Iacocca's top management team described their decision making as a democratic process in which they each had one vote and Lee had five. Very few management teams at any level have operated as the kinds of successful teams we've been looking at in this book.

That begins to change when an organization commits itself to teampower, or else. First of all, as we've seen, the neat distinction between managers and workers vanishes. "Manager" and "worker" are two words rarely heard in the vicinity of self-managed teams —because managerial, and especially supervisory, tasks are increasingly performed by teams.

Second, there are far fewer players above the first level. Remember that the 150 workers at Corning's Blacksburg plant require only two "line leaders" and a plant manager to do their jobs (and the basic functions of the line leaders are those being discussed in this book). This is hardly unusual; as self-management increases, fewer and fewer players are needed to manage others.

Third, when teampower becomes the way of life at the first level it begins to impact how things are done higher up in the organization. Many of the first self-directed teams were at individual plants (Volvo at Kalmar and then Uddevalla, Sweden, Gaines Dog Food at Topeka, the plants of Procter and Gamble's Paper Products Division, and others). Now, though, self-directed teams are becoming a way of life in office environments (Shenandoah Life, AT&T Credit Corporation, Aid Association for Lutherans, and others). That makes them harder to isolate from the overall functioning of the firm. At some point, the self-management of the teams comes into conflict with the traditional control strategy of higher levels. Something has to give.

Procter and Gamble's Paper Products Division provides an interesting example of this. We've seen that they began using self-directed teams in plants early in the 70s and had concluded by 1975 that these were their most productive plants. Yet the teampower approach didn't spread beyond the plants until 1984, when Richard Nicolosi became the head of paper products. He created a top management team that became the paper division "Board," and then organized the division around category teams and business brand teams. While the teams were useful in themselves, they also helped the division focus on customers and on Total Quality.[49]

Where teampower becomes the rule, then, successful organizations tend to structure higher and higher levels as teams. You might be responsible for facilitating and overseeing five or ten teams, and then you and a half-dozen of your peers might form a team of your own. In turn, the player responsible for facilitating and overseeing your team might be part of a next-higher-level team herself.

The point of all this? The team decision-making process that we'll be discussing for the rest of this chapter isn't just something for the teams that you support. Increasingly, it is the process in which you and your peers will be involved—making decisions that were formerly made at higher (perhaps *much* higher) levels in the organization.

Complexity, diversity, your role as both team facilitator and team member—all of these make your function as a manager of the decision-making process a critical one. Now let's look at the function and the skills you need to perform it effectively.

WHAT YOU DO TO MANAGE THE DECISION MAKING PROCESS

In a traditional organization, managing decision making would mean implementing your boss's decisions and passing your decisions on for your workers to implement. Even this process would be limited, because the organization would have higher-level managers and powerful staff offices that limited both your boss's decision-making authority and your own. By the time decision making got to your level, there'd be room for little discretion. By the time it got to your workers' level, there'd be even less.

If you've worked in this kind of organization at the first or second level, your primary role was that of a supervisor who got the production out. You were expected to communicate clearly what was to be done, and then see that it was done. Your role included as well the responsibility to "motivate" workers to produce rapidly and not cause problems. This combination of getting production out and not causing problems for your boss was the heart of your role.

This isn't what happens in a teampower organization. Significant decisions are made at all levels in the organization. The players who do the actual production may not make the same kinds of decisions as the top-level players who set strategic directions, but they make meaningful decisions nonetheless. Self-managing teams often do their own hiring and firing, take responsibility for the quality and safety of their operations, even prepare and review their capital and operating budgets.

Sometimes it goes even further than that. In 1978, John Ludwig became general manager of the Orange, Texas plant of Polysar Gulf Coast. When Polysar's top management made the decision to close a unit of the Orange plant and lay off 100 workers, Ludwig created a team of foremen, operators, and managers to study the problem and recommend a solution. The group came up with a plan to reorganize both the production divisions and the workforce—and the plan was implemented almost exactly as recommended. From this beginning—which averted the layoff—Ludwig created quality teams that spread responsibility broadly throughout the plant.[50]

Your teams may start with more limited decision-making power. For instance, they might begin by only recommending changes in processes or whom to hire. But if all of the players involved are serious about it, they will grow into more significant responsibilities, requiring more significant decisions. As the manager of decision making for the teams, you will play a key role in this.

Just what does this function involve? These are some of the basic tasks required to manage the decision-making process:

1. As much as organizational policy and the maturity of the team permits, you facilitate decision making by your teams, not make decisions for them.

2. You help them learn effective group decision-making processes.

3. You guide their decisions as necessary to fit organizational goals, and then support the decisions.

4. You use group decision-making skills yourself as part of the team at your level.

THE SKILLS YOU NEED

To accomplish these tasks, you need to know and be able to pass on these skills:

1. How to generate a broad variety of ideas

2. How to build and maintain the team's self-confidence

3. How to deal with workplace flexibility.

4. How to face conflict and use it creatively

HOW TO GENERATE A BROAD VARIETY OF IDEAS

There's all the evidence you'd ever want that one of the most successful ways to solve problems is to begin with a broad range of alternatives. Since the purpose of decision making is to solve problems (and, less frequently, to seize opportunities), generating alternatives is at the core of effective decision making.

The need for good alternatives is a requirement of effective decision making in any environment—from the most authoritarian to the most self-managed. What makes it special in a teampower environment, though, is that the decisions made at any level are almost always more demanding and more significant than in a traditional organization. So the tools you use must be more sophisticated and effective.

One of the most widely known and used techniques for generating ideas is *brainstorming*. While the technique is widely taught and used in quality teams, it didn't originate with the Japanese or even in the quality field. It was popularized by Alex Osburn, an American advertising executive, in the 1960s.

There are dozens of books on brainstorming; any manual for

quality teams will have a section on it. Here, I only want to stress the central core of the technique: the separation of idea generation from idea evaluation. That sounds simple, perhaps a little abstract, but it's an exceptionally important idea.

Brainstorming begins with everyone contributing ideas without evaluating them in any way. If John suggests an idea, Martha doesn't criticize it—nor does she praise it. Instead, the team leader or someone else writes it down without comment. If the idea suggests a related one to Martha ("piggybacking"), she will add that idea. Because no one is criticizing or evaluating the ideas, everyone is free to use their imaginations. Many of the ideas will later be discarded, but in the beginning phase that's not important. The goal is to get as many ideas as possible on the table. Then, in the second phase, these ideas can be evaluated and the best ones selected for further study.

There's a variation on this technique, also sometimes found in manuals for quality teams, known as the *nominal group technique.* This technique has the same goal as brainstorming—the generation of a variety of ideas—but the method is different. Instead of calling out ideas, team members write down their ideas individually. The rules are much the same as those for brainstorming; ideas should be written quickly (normally on 3x5 cards) and not be censored. At the end of the idea generation period, the cards are collected. One member of the group can read them out while another writes them down on a flip chart. Alternatively, the cards may be distributed at random to all of the team members, who then read them out so they can be listed for the group to see. After that, the group discusses the alternatives and chooses the best ones (a la brainstorming).

·Why use the nominal group technique? There are at least two basic situations in which it will probably be more effective than brainstorming:

1. If the group or team members aren't used to working in teams. Individuals may be uncomfortable calling out ideas; many good ideas may never get put forward. In this circumstance, it's generally much easier for players to write down their ideas individually and perhaps even let someone else present them.

2. If several layers of players are in the group. It takes a while

for a team to get so confident of itself that it can put forth and defend its own ideas no matter who's listening to them. For a time, there's still the fear that higher levels will react to any suggestion of criticism—and so players censor their ideas. If ideas are prepared individually and presented anonymously, much of the fear is dispelled. Then the ideas can be discussed more on their own merits, without any individual having to bear the onus of putting them forward.

The nominal group technique is not so widely discussed as brainstorming, but you can find it in several books in the bibliography. Shuster's book, *Teaming for Quality Improvement*, has a short but useful description of it. Fox's *Effective Group Problem Solving*, is a whole book devoted to it.

HOW TO TAP EVERYONE'S EXPERTISE _____

There are other methods for producing a variety of alternatives to consider, but there's not space to go into them here. Remember that the goal is to get as many potentially useful ideas out on the table as possible, as quickly as possible.

Remember, too, that part of the goal is to tap everyone's expertise. As work gets more and more complex, the skills of more and more players are required to produce a successful product or service. The increasing diversity of even small workforces also requires as broad a range of ideas as possible.

Brainstorming and similar techniques are also a cure for the kind of stereotyping that we examined in the last chapter. We don't get a chance to find out how limiting these stereotypes are in the routine of daily work, because this work is organized around them. When the routine is loosened by effective group techniques, such as brainstorming, the mental pictures also began to loosen. We find that Marlene, who seemed so uncreative, is great at drawing ideas from others. We see that Oscar, who appears to oppose all change, wants to see change but is cynical about what will really happen. Suddenly, these are much more real, much more capable people than we all thought.

Don't take this as some kind of fuzzy, isn't-everybody-great kind of preaching. I can assure you that it isn't. I've experienced it time and time again for years. And the research supporting it is overwhelming. Here's one (harrowing) example. A number of years ago, at the beginning of the year, a researcher slipped the result of an IQ test into the file of each member of a class. No point was made of the scores, but the teacher saw each of them. At the end of the year, the classroom performance of each pupil was just what you would expect, given his or her IQ score. The catch? The scores were phoney, and were assigned to students on a completely random basis. So strong were the teacher's expectations, based on this single, phoney bit of information, that each member of the class ended up conforming to them.

Our stereotypes of each other can be just as confining and often just as misleading. If you give the members of your workgroup the opportunity to relax the mental pictures they have of each other (and you have of them), I can almost guarantee that you'll be amazed at the talent you discover. Since mental pictures are closely connected with ethnic and racial stereotypes, allowing everyone to contribute on an open basis also begins to dissolve these stereotypes. Individual players begin to see each other as just that: individuals. This further enhances the ability of each player to contribute, and to accept the contributions of others.

HOW TO BUILD AND MAINTAIN THE TEAM'S SELF-CONFIDENCE

You may have been expecting me to get into really sophisticated techniques for managing complex decision-making. Perhaps really detailed spreadsheet models. Or complicated statistical methods. At least some fancy computer programs. After all, if you're going to deal with complex decision-making, you certainly need these elaborate methods, don't you?

Certainly they have their place, but they aren't the key to really good decision making. We've already seen that generating a broad range of alternatives is the most important factor of all. Another critical factor has nothing to do with decision-making techniques and methods. It's this: If you want to manage decision making effectively, you must *help maintain (and if necessary, develop) the self-confidence of each player individually and of the team as a whole.*

Look back at the incident with the phony IQ scores above. You can bet that the self-confidence of those with phony high scores was gradually built up by the teacher, while the self-confidence of those with the low scores was undermined. The latter group, no matter how confident they had been to begin with, began to doubt their own abilities. This became a vicious circle, in which lowered self-confidence produced lowered performance, which produced lowered self-confidence, which produced . . . .

If you and your teams are in a situation where work and work solutions are complex, one of your great strengths is self-confidence—and one of your great dangers is the lack of it. When a team knows that it can somehow tackle and solve any problem that confronts it, it can. The reverse is also true.

How do you promote self-confidence? Dozens of ways exist to do this, and you probably know many of them. Here are a few that seem to me to be basic:

1. *Treat every situation as a learning situation.* One of the most deeply ingrained habits of traditional organizations is the tendency to find someone to blame when something goes wrong. You have a relatively clear choice here: You can have an effective team, or you can have a collection of individuals concerned, above all else, that they shouldn't do anything they can get blamed for. The next chapter looks in detail at what you must do to manage learning effectively. Here, you need to understand that learning from mistakes, rather than finding someone to blame for them, is one of the great confidence builders.

2. *Celebrate successes, both large and small.* It's a sad fact that so many of us (myself included) fail at this. Admittedly, when you have a team that's demonstrated its competence, it's easy to take it for granted. You shouldn't—and you certainly shouldn't overlook the successes of a team that's just getting its feet on the ground. Is the goal a 20% improvement in productivity, but so far they've only accomplished 3%? Celebrate that, as a step in the right direction. Did they point out a problem that's caused by one of your own sacred cows? Swallow your pride and celebrate their willingness to take the risk. And, no matter how good they get, keep celebrating. (One of the characteristics of high-performing teams, is that

they *know* they're better than anyone else. This sounds an awful lot like arrogance, but it's reality.)

3. *Be patient.* You've heard that before, but it's just as relevant here. Some people simply don't learn or change quickly. This doesn't mean they're slow, or dumb, or uncooperative. It simply means that they take time to process change. Give them the time, work with them as you need to, and celebrate their smallest successes. You'll find that often someone who starts slowly picks up steam as he goes along and begins to catch up with the others, or even pass them.

4. *Don't compete with them; discourage them from competing with each other.* I hope you've never been the kind of manager who built himself or herself up by downing others. Unfortunately, there are managers like this, and none of them belong in a teampower environment. But competition within a team is just as destructive. Many individuals don't contribute because they've learned that they can't compete with other, more aggressive players. If there's competition within the team, it reinforces both their reticence and their lack of selfconfidence. Competition can be helpful, but only if (1) it's *friendly* competition, (2) it's *between teams, not individuals,* and (3) *the teams don't depend on one another* for work.

5. Finally, *practice empathy and help other players practice it.* It will become increasingly clear as we go through this and the next two chapters that skills carry over from one function to another. Empathy is important for you to function as coordination manager; there, you empathize with other stakeholders so that you can work for the best possible outcome for everyone. Here, you empathize with the individual players on the team, so that you can understand and encourage their strengths. You also encourage empathy on the team itself, for exactly the same purpose.   •

HOW TO DEAL EFFECTIVELY WITH WORKPLACE FLEXIBILITY _____

If you're lucky, your team consists of permanent, fulltime and hopefully long-term players. It's very difficult to have any kind of team without this stability. To the extent that your firm uses the various forms of flexible work schedules, though, any team may have difficulty in working together. The difficulty is compounded if some players work at home some or all of the time.

That's just the beginning. Even though the major players are permanent and full-time, there may be individuals who support teams, administratively or technically, who don't have this same kind of stability. They may be part-time and/or temporary, perhaps furnished through one of the temporary help agencies. They may perform contract work at home, and seldom if ever be present at the work location. At times, even consultants may play key roles even though they are available only sporadically.

Managing effective decision making in this environment is truly challenging. Worst of all, the situations in which this happens are so different that it's almost impossible for me to give you general guidelines here. The best I can do is make a few suggestions that may be relevant:

1. *Use computers and communication methods as fully as possible.* With perfectly serviceable computers under $1,000 and fax machines and voice messaging systems under $500, it becomes practical to use both as an ordinary part of business in many locations. Tremendous amounts of work remain to be done, but we already have the beginning of ways to connect people in different locations and, to some extent, at different times. The greatest problem isn't the technology, but finding the right ways to combine it. The books in the bibliography by Johansen and Schrage look in depth at this problem.

2. *Give teams maximum freedom to set their own schedules.* This is where clear goals, objectives and measures are so important. If teams know just what is expected of them, they can exercise good judgment when they deal with the flexibility of the 90s workplace. The organization will have some formal requirements, and the team needs to abide by them. If teams can manage their own hiring and budgeting, though, they can certainly manage their own scheduling. In other words, the more the organization deals with its teams through goals and objectives rather than limiting policies and procedures, the more effective teams will be.

3. *Make everyone part of a team.* This may be easier said than done, particularly if the organization uses temporaries from a service and/or contracts work to be done at home. There are still practical steps you can take. First, try to get as much stability as possible. Even a temporary basic typist will perform better if she believes that she's part of a team and her performance is important to the team. Second, try to get people together face to face periodically. How often? That depends on the work situation. If you can get everyone to meet once a week for an hour, that would be worthwhile. If you can only collect them once a month, that's better than not at all. It takes time for people to become comfortable with one another, and it requires personal contact for it really to happen.

4. And that leads into the final point: *Bring players together socially whenever that's appropriate.* The crowded and varied schedules of most of us often make this difficult—but many times it's the only way the players can get together. It doesn't have to be fancy; potluck dinners, picnics, even a softball or bowling league can help. A word of caution, though. If only certain players can come, it may divide the group more than it unifies it. A lot of common sense and good judgment are the order of the day here. If possible, let the team exercise them.

HOW TO DEVELOP THE KEY SKILL: CREATIVE CONSENSUS

You may have blanched already, just from reading the word "consensus." All too often, working for a consensus has meant "groupthink" or a similar dead uniformity that's the very antithesis of what an effective team does. The whole idea of consensus decision making is associated with Japan, where the subjugation of the individual to the group is deeply ingrained (to the point, in fact, that many Japanese are beginning to decry it.) It's also true that a team doesn't have to reach a consensus at all to be effective; the players on it may decide that some other form of decision making is the best. On the other side, if the GM Saturn plant can operate effectively using consensus—well, maybe it's worth looking at.

Let me be clear, too, just what I mean by consensus, especially a creative consensus. If it isn't uniformity and the lowest common denominator, just what is it? In my own judgment, these are some of the characteristics of an effective consensus:

1. It begins by surfacing a wide variety of ideas and points of view. That's why this chapter dealt with brainstorming and other techniques for getting this variety before it got to consensus.

2. It not only tolerates but absolutely prizes disagreement. That's pretty heady stuff, but it happens. This is one of the characteristics that most separates American consensus decision making from its Japanese counterpart.

3. It protects each player's right to exercise his or her judgment. An effective team doesn't pressure one or two players who disagree with the rest. Instead, the other players listen carefully to each other's reasoning and present their reasoning in return.

4. It is based as solidly in facts as possible (and that it shares with its Japanese counterpart). Whenever feasible, data is found that will settle disagreements.

5. It rests on mutual respect and trust.

6. It doesn't require complete agreement. This varies from team to team and situation to situation, but teams often reach a working consensus even though one or two players don't fully agree with the decision. They are persuaded enough of its validity, though, to support it. This question—*can everyone support the decision?*—is the critical one.

7. Finally, the outcome of the decision is always evaluated and the lessons learned fed back into the reasoning for future decisions. When this is done genuinely and faithfully, it strengthens the judgment not only of the team as a whole but of each player on it.

WHEN TO USE CONSENSUS DECISION MAKING _____

The characteristics above are some of the most important ones you find where consensus decision making is effective. I've already hinted, though, that not all decisions can be made by consensus. There are no hard-and-fast rules for when to use it and when to use another method—but here are a few ideas:

1. Consensus decision making is easiest when the team is considering an *incremental* change—that is, when whatever will be done is only a little different from what is done now. Suppose a team must decide how to handle a sudden requirement for overtime. If the team has had considerable experience allocating overtime, and this requirement is similar to previous requirements, it can reach a workable consensus with little difficulty. When change is incremental, most of the factors involved are well known and a great deal of data is available. Individual judgments can be firmly anchored in and tested against the data.

2. The situation changes when a team must choose among courses of action that are riskier and harder to predict. Here, there is a greater strain on consensus decision making. This isn't because the team will select the most conservative course of action; in fact, there's evidence that teams often make riskier decisions than individuals. As the outcome of a decision becomes less predictable, though, the data on which to base the decision is weaker and weaker. Opinions are less subject to test. Since the decision can't be data driven, a risky solution can be chosen without realizing just how risky it is.

3. One way of dealing with this and similar circumstances is to use a resource person who has a strong background in the field of the decision. This individual can serve a leader for the decision process, insuring that the team understands the risks and payoffs involved in different options. He or she might even make the final decision, after full exploration of the situation by the team. Or the individual might simply serve as a resource person, volunteering information when asked or when the discussion was becoming divorced from reality. (A quick note: If you have an otherwise effectively functioning team, it is ordinarily *not* an effective step to simply jerk even the riskiest decision back to yourself. If you feel you must make it, make sure the team understands why—and give them the maximum opportunity to explore the issues and suggest alternative solutions.)

4. The strains on consensus decision making imposed by risky decisions can be largely offset to the extent that the team is *mature* and has the *time* to explore the alternatives carefully. By "mature," I mean not only experience in working as a team and proficiency in group methods, but the self-confidence that the team can handle difficult problems. The time available is a critical factor as well; the more difficult and risky the decision, the more time that's required to weigh all of the options carefully and select the best one.

5. Finally, there's a broad range in what can genuinely be called "consensus decision making." Different teams will interpret it in different ways; one team may well mean something different by it at one time than another. Beginning teams typically tend to avoid conflict and find consensus by selecting a safe alternative or going along with a player who presents his opinion vigorously. More mature teams develop more organic consensus processes, with the strengths and weaknesses of all players figuring in the outcome. Mature teams can also decide on ways to make decisions when time is tight. For instance, a team may delegate decision-making authority to an individual with known expertise in the area of the decision, and then back her decision fully.

HOW TO USE CONFLICT TO CREATE CONSENSUS _____

We can't talk about consensus without talking about conflict management. And this is what needs to be said:

You can't have effective team decision making unless the group can surface and resolve all of the conflict involved in making the decision.

This is one of the hardest of all team skills to master. After all, it's so much easier to avoid the conflict and work around it. Traditional organizations do it all the time. You sit in a meeting where the group moves dispassionately and professionally to a decision. After the meeting, though, the real issues begin to emerge. Members criticize the decision, question the motives of those who made it, perhaps even plan how to get it overturned. But in the meeting, where the decision is being made, none of this appears.

Teams go through a process as they learn to function effectively. They normally begin with a great deal of superficial politeness—perhaps carrying it over from their experience in meetings like the one just described. Then they gradually began to question their roles, perhaps to express doubts about what the team can accomplish. There is often a struggle between the players who want to deal with all of the negatives and others who want to "think positively" and get on with the task. Cliques or subgroups may form.

Very often, the kinds of power relationships individual players have experienced outside the team begin to show up within the team. Winning—getting *my* idea accepted—may become an issue for different players. Part of the team may attempt to control the team ("OK, we heard what you had to say—now it's time for you to quit objecting so we can get on with it!"). If the team survives through this, it can begin to function constructively, with shared leadership, consensus, concern for the value of an idea rather than who first broached it, etc. In a fully successful team, this leads on to solid trust and openness, where every player and his contributions are respected and valued.

This final stage is marvelous to see and experience—but the road to it lies through conflict. Until the team finds ways to recognize and deal creatively with their conflict, the road is closed. No team can have confidence in its ability to make decisions by consensus until it has mastered the skill of conflict management.

Since this isn't a book on team skills, I'm not going to give "five handy tips on how to manage conflict." Besides, you learn to manage conflict by experiencing it and dealing with it in the real situation, not by reading about it. This is one point at which a trained facilitator is immensely valuable.

I can give you some hints on how you can help a team manage their conflict. This is a central part of your function as manager of the decision-making process. If you perform it well, the team will learn the skills they need that much more quickly. Here are the ideas:

1. *Don't try to hide or avoid conflict.* Just the process of everyday organizational life creates plenty of conflict. As I've already mentioned, traditional organizations often try to sweep it under the table. You may be tempted to do so also. Remem-

ber, though, that if you do you will make it that much harder
for your teams to face their own conflict constructively. You
will help them immensely if you simply acknowledge conflict when it appears. You don't have to resolve it right then.
But you do have to acknowledge it.

2. The flip side of admitting conflict is to *take positive steps to
resolve the conflict*. This sounds both simple and obvious, but
often it isn't. There's always a temptation to do whatever's
quick and easy to make the conflict go away. One common
form of this happens when two players are having a "personality conflict." All too often, a manager's response is to
talk with each individual about understanding the other and
make it clear he expects the conflict to go away. The predictable outcome of this is to drive the conflict underground,
where it becomes much harder to confront. The healthier
approach is to find out how each player experiences the
situation and then, if possible, help them resolve the conflict
themselves. The "how" or "what" isn't critical—but taking
steps to resolve the conflict is.

3. *Don't try to resolve the situation by blaming someone*. Again, this
is a common way of dealing with conflict in a traditional
organization: find someone to blame for it. That approach
won't work at any point in a teampower environment; teams
work only when every player supports every other player.
This doesn't mean that you simply accept whatever anyone
does. If a player goes around her teammates and complains
to you about someone in the team, you don't blame either
that player or the person she complained about. You do
identify that the individual has a problem, the team has a
problem and (because of that) you have a problem. Then you
set the wheels in motion so the team can surface and resolve
the conflict.

4. Finally, *make it clear that you expect conflict to be used constructively*. Words help here, but they aren't enough. What
you do will be the real teacher. Every conflict is an opportunity for progress—that's not pollyanna preaching, but
solid advice. Every time the team can resolve a conflict, it
grows stronger. It builds up not only skill but self-confidence in its ability to deal with conflict constructively. Your

job is to make it clear that this is what you expect, from them and from yourself.

Well, these are the basics of your function as manager of the decision-making process. Now we turn to another function: creating an environment in which you and your teams can learn continuously. The idea of the "learning organization" is a big one these days—and if it means anything it has to mean it squarely at the working level. Let's see what it means there.

Chapter 8 ═══════════

Managing Continuous
Learning ═══════════════

WHAT IS A "LEARNING ORGANIZATION"? _____

The term "learning organization" is *hot* as I write this book.
Peter Senge popularized it, describing learning organizations as

> organizations where people continually expand their ca-
> pacity to create the results they truly desire, where new and
> expansive patterns of thinking are nurtured, where collec-
> tive aspiration is set free, and where people are continually
> learning how to learn together.[52]

On the next page, Senge quotes Arie De Geus, head of planning
for Royal Dutch/Shell: "The ability to learn faster than your
competitors . . . may be the only sustainable competitive advantage."[53] This same view is shared by Hanover Insurance, which is
consciously designed as *a system intending to learn from its environment more rapidly than its competitors.*"[54] Closely allied is the
consensus of numerous economists that *human* capital—which
depends on learning—is the critical economic factor in the 90s and
beyond.[55]

Little wonder! Just look at the rate of change in your own
organization; chances are it's been accelerating steadily. Each
chapter up to this one has described factors contributing to this
acceleration: the quality movement, shrinking cycle time, increasing workforce diversity, to name just three. The important point,

of course, isn't change. What counts is how we stay on top of it. What counts is how well and how quickly we learn.

That's your fourth function in a teampower environment: *managing continuous learning*. In a traditional organization, managers are generally seen as expert teachers and trainers. In that context, you and I are expected to know more than those who work for us—and one of our jobs is to train them to at least a minimum level of skill. We show them what to do and how to do it, and they're expected to do it just the way we taught them (though this doesn't always happen). We're expected to do some learning, too, in management development sequences and courses. This learning, however, is for our own development; we're not expected to pass it on.

Throughout all of this runs the central thread that learning means training, that the only really good learning happens in formal classes (or from sexy new techniques like computer-based training). The learning that happens on the job, on the shop floor, by the water cooler, is secondary, a pale reflection of the *real* learning. After all, one of the proudest boasts of many companies today is that they spend $x\%$ of their labor budget on training.

That's fine, and I wouldn't discourage you or anyone else from getting training. But that's the wrong focus. The question today— and even more so tomorrow—is not what you've been trained in, but what you're learning now. And this learning has to happen every day, on the job—not once or twice a year at a workshop or seminar.

The players around you will be learning at least as rapidly as you, and they will quickly go beyond your expertise. Sorry, but if your teams are really effective you will no longer be the expert. You will, in fact, have to run at top speed just to stay in the same ballpark with them. That's as it should be, because the players in the level above you are going to have to run at top speed to stay in the ballpark with you.

So your job isn't to teach or train your teams, but to manage the continual learning that you and they will be doing. Let me let you in on the key to this right now:

Really effective learning comes from taking an action, observing its outcome, and then acting again using the knowledge gained from the first attempt.

Some management thinkers have advocated a "Ready, Fire, Aim" approach—take some action, no matter how tentative, then learn from it and take a better action (then learn from it, etc.). I don't think I'm quite ready to advocate firing before aiming—but in a complex, rapidly changing world there's no way to learn effectively without acting and then assessing the results. Trying to analyze all the factors and plan for them in advance takes too long and is much too uncertain. Individuals, teams and organizations will have to find ways to take small steps, learn from the results, then take bigger steps.

WHAT YOU DO TO MANAGE CONTINUAL LEARNING _____

What do you do when you function as a manager of continual learning? Here are a few of the basic tasks:

1. You help teams identify their training needs and arrange training to meet them. Wait a minute—didn't I just say that in teampower organizations the emphasis on formal training will give way to an emphasis on learning? I did—and it's true. It's also true that in the process of learning teampower organizations will require far more training than traditional organizations. First of all, an immense amount of up-front training is required. In the Corning plant in Blacksburg, for instance, 25% of the players' time the first year was spent in training of one kind or another. After the initial training, there's continual technical training. Players are constantly learning how to use new work methods and processes, machinery, and automated systems. Formal training is only a part of total learning, but identifying and providing the right training at the right time is a major responsibility that you and your teams exercise. It is key to this function to make sure the responsibility is exercised.

2. You help your teams become better and better at on-the-job training. No matter how much formal training occurs, the training that a player gets on the job is far more significant. This is how new players learn the basics of the job and of performing as part of a team. It's also how experienced team members learn many of the new methods and processes.

3. Even more, you help your teams become better and better at *on-the-job learning*. Right now, on-the-job learning is pretty haphazard in most organizations. It's all too often something that happens by accident. You insure that it happens on purpose, constantly, effectively.

4. Finally, you help create an environment in which constant learning is the norm. That's very different from the situation in traditional organizations, where no one really thinks of learning as a vital part of the job itself. The situation changes in organizations dedicated to Total Quality and continual process improvement—and changes even more in teampower organizations. Success requires constant learning, and you're a key player in this learning.

THE SKILLS YOU NEED _____

In a traditional organization, training comes down from above. Your basic skill is making the arrangements for it and then seeing that workers attend it and put it into practice. As we've seen time and time again, this downward flow doesn't work in a teampower organization. New methods and processes may come from one of your teams, or from a team somewhere else in the organization. Many of these changes will be small, not worth a formal training course even if there is one. Many times, learning consists of finding out how to do something no one is quite sure how to do yet. Learning can occur everywhere, all the time, unpredictably.

You perform this management function to assure that the learning does occur, and to manage the environment to make it occur as effectively as possible. These are the basic skills you need to know and use:

1. How to facilitate change—because all learning requires change.

2. How to pass down to your teams more and more of the skills required by the five management functions discussed in the book.

3. How to hold effective meetings.

4. How to provide your teams the tools they need to learn effectively.

5. How to create and maintain an environment in which players can identify and take the intelligent risks necessary for effective learning.

HOW TO MANAGE CHANGE SKILLFULLY _____

If you want to manage constant learning, you must manage change. I don't intend to write at great length about change management; there are many other books to advise you on that. I have a few suggestions, though—and this is the key one:

People do not resist change; they resist <u>*being changed*</u>.

My good friend Tony Putman puts it even more succinctly: "Resistance [to change] is nothing more nor less than a reaction to being pushed around."[56]

This is where you start: When people resist change, they're telling you that you're pushing them around—that they don't have any stake in the change. How do you improve this situation? Well, people often decide to change when they believe three conditions are true:

1. *The change is worthwhile* and beneficial to them. In short, they believe they will be better off with the change that without it. What if the players don't believe they'll be better off? "Why should we take the time and effort to learn the new method you want; it's not going to help us do our job faster, easier, or more effectively—and it won't put any more money in our pockets."

2. *The change is worth the effort.* Many things in life are worthwhile in the abstract—but not worthwhile enough to justify the effort it takes to achieve them. The same is true at work. If the players don't think the change is worth the effort? "Look, this new version of the automated system may be an improvement, but it's not worth putting in. They'll have the next version out before we learn this one—and anyway learning to use it will disrupt operations too much."

3. *The change is possible.* Some changes are just too difficult. They'd be worthwhile and worth the effort, but the players

who must make them happen lack the skill, or the materials, or the machinery, or whatever. No matter how great a change may be, the individuals involved have to believe they can pull it off. If they don't? "Sure, we'd like to do a thorough-going quality program, but the Division will never give us relief from the standards long enough to get it implemented. Besides, a quality program takes training, and our training budget for the year is shot."

If you really want a player or a team to believe that these three conditions are true, there are two steps you need to take:

1. To the extent you can, let every player take part in deciding on the changes that significantly affect him or her. Let the players who must execute and live with the change be involved in deciding what it will be. When players participate in choosing the change to make, they understand its benefits, they see its feasibility, they believe they can do it.

2. Make the new condition you want to create as real as possible. Describe it in vivid terms. Draw pictures. Have someone who's experienced that situation describe it. The best approach: Take the group to an organization that operates that way and believes in it. Anything becomes more desirable when we can experience it. If this is why department stores put sampler bottles for perfume and after-shave out, can you do any less?

HOW TO PASS ON YOUR SKILLS _____

In an organization that really learns effectively, skills continually move down the organization to lower and lower levels. Just using teampower starts the process. You'll see in the final chapter that as teams pick up speed, they acquire and use more and more of the skills that supervisors use in a traditional organization. They organize and evaluate their work, do their own budgeting, hire their own members, perhaps even divide up compensation among their members. These are essential self-management skills, and ones that empowered teams need to develop and use as quickly as possible.

That doesn't end the process, though. Teams can learn to manage more and more of their alignment and coordination with other teams and other levels; they can learn to manage more and more of their decision-making process; they can learn to manage more and more of their learning process; and (to anticipate the next chapter) they can learn to create and maintain trust.

You can see how critical it is for you to be good at passing on the skills they need—but how do you do that? Here are some of the basics.

1. First, you need to be able to do them and do them well yourself. The most successful way for other players to learn anything from you is to see you doing it effectively. They learn useful negotiating skills, for example, by seeing you negotiate. If you can achieve your goals and at the same time help others achieve theirs, your players can learn that this is what to do by watching and emulating you.

2. But—and this is a big but—they can only do this if you make it clear to them what you're doing. If you've reached a mutually satisfactory agreement with another unit, for example, you need to see that your players understand what your goals were and how you achieved them.

3. The next logical step is easy: you begin to let some of your players perform this function with you. Again, take negotiation. Select a situation where the issues are clear and you believe a resolution is easy (or relatively so, at any rate). Have a player or two from your teams sit in with you. Let him or her see just what happens—and how it happens. Let the individual participate as much as possible.

4. Spread the skills around, building on the abilities and preferences of individual players. One individual may be excellent at using personal computers, while another is really good at projecting empathy. As with any other skills, you want as many members of each team to have as many of these management skills as possible—but that's the result of a long process. Begin by developing each individual where his or her talents and interests direct, then spread the skills around.

5. Here's a really useful tip: never tell someone what you can ask them. Take the negotiation example again. When you're

preparing for a session, ask them what they would do; then show them how you would do differently (if you would), and discuss your reasons with them. When the session is over, talk with them again. Ask them to describe what happened, and why they believe it did. Then give them your explanation, and discuss it. (A word of warning. *Don't* ask a question if all they can do is guess at the answer. That's frustrating and purposeless. Ask questions when you expect them to have reasonable answers—though they may be wrong or incomplete. If they'd just be guessing, tell and go on from there.)

6. Finally, learn from them. One of the key factors in exercising influence is to let yourself be influenced—and one of the key factors in helping others learn is learning yourself. No one in a teampower organization is expected to have all the answers, or even a lot of them. *Everyone* is constantly learning. When the players around you see you learning, and willing to learn from them, it helps them open up and increase their own learning. That's one of the best of all examples that you can set.

HOW TO HOLD EFFECTIVE MEETINGS _____

Have we just moved from the sublime to the ridiculous, moving from the challenge of learning to the all-too-ordinary topic of meetings? Not by a long shot. Even in a traditional organization, much of a manager's time is spent in meetings. In a teampower organization, the time is multiplied. Whatever else teams do, they meet. You need to see that they—and you—meet well and effectively.

If you've read much about meetings, or perhaps been to a training course or two, you've probably been exposed to some popular gimmicks. One of the most common is the advice to hold a meeting standing up—so everyone is motivated to make it a short as possible. You may also have read or heard advice on how to control the meeting, whether you're a participant or the leader. For instance, you might refrain from drinking anything before the meeting, and then try to hold the others (who weren't so foresighted) in the meeting until a solution—yours, of course—is agreed on.

This isn't how you conduct an effective meeting. These techniques, and dozens of others like them, are simply ways to manipulate others—who are simultaneously using their own favorite techniques to manipulate you. Fortunately, you don't have to use any of them to hold effective meetings, or to participate effectively in meetings. This is what you do instead:

1. When you call a meeting, *have a very clear idea of what its your objectives are*. This isn't the same thing as having an agenda, which we'll look at in a moment. It means that you have a specific purpose for the meeting—one that each participant can help you achieve. A meeting can have more than just one objective, of course; many meetings have several objectives to be achieved. But each objective should be clear. If it's not, take time at the beginning to clarify it and get everyone's agreement on it.

2. Then *be sure that every objective is an action outcome of some sort*. Take an objective that isn't, like "We will discuss the proposal of the capital improvements committee." This is all too common; you've probably been in dozens (hundreds?) of meetings that had this kind of objective. But how do you tell when you're through discussing something? How do you tell what's relevant and what's not? Instead, formulate objective like these:

   • "We will decide what capital improvements to propose to the Division." (It will be clear when a decision is made, and generally clear what discussion is relevant to making the decision).

   • "We will accept or reject each recommendation made by the capital improvements committee." (Same comment as the objective above.)

   • "We will give members the opportunity to request the capital improvements committee to clarify any items in their report." (This isn't quite as neat, but it's still focused. In a well-run meeting, the report would have been distributed well in advance of the meeting and members would be expected to be familiar with it.)

   You can easily add examples from your own circumstances. The point is that an effective objective is an action of some kind. Because it's an action, it provides a standard for what is relevant and what isn't in the discussion. Because it's an action, you can also tell when you've done it and achieved your objective. If you do no more than this, but do it consistently, you will improve your meetings significantly.

You can do more, of course, and here are a few pointers that will help:

3. Prepare a written agenda that specifies the objectives of the meeting, and see that everyone gets it well before the meeting. This lets everyone involved know what to expect. It has another benefit: if someone doesn't understand one or more of the agenda items, he can ask you for clarification

4. Don't depend on that, though. At the start of each meeting, go over the agenda briefly and summarize how you understand each item. Ask the others if they understand it the same way; if they don't, stop then and there to clarify the items. You should not get to the substance of any item until everyone understands each meeting objective.

5. Then insist that all members stick to the agenda and each specific objective. You know how often meetings bog down in irrelevant comments and arguments—so don't let it happen. Insist on relevance, and expect every other member of the team to do the same. By agreeing to the agenda, each individual has committed him or herself to those objectives. You don't deprive anyone of their right to speak if you insist that they live up to their commitment. By the way: it shouldn't just be you doing the insisting. The team should discipline itself to stick to the topic; your job is mainly to help it do this.

   (There's another advantage to setting objectives and sticking to them: it helps to surface hidden agendas. You can neither hold effective meetings nor make effective decisions if one or more players are trying to deal from agendas they want to keep under the table. If objectives are clear and discussion stays relevant, this gets much harder for them to do. In the next chapter we'll look in more detail at just how important it is to surface hidden agendas, and how to do it.)

6. What if someone comes up with what appears to be an irrelevant issue? First, check for relevance. Give the individ-

ual a chance to explain how it might be relevant. Perhaps it's not relevant to the current objective, but is important enough to schedule for a future meeting. It may even raise a related issue or broaden a topic in a way that the team believes might be helpful. If the team feels this way, there's nothing wrong with modifying the agenda on the spot to include the new issue.

(Here's an example. The team is deciding which of two personal computers to buy. A player mentions that she's heard that the team may be picking up a new type of claim to process. When the team asks her about the relevancy, she explains that both of the computers they are considering have very small hard disks, which might not be able to handle the additional data. Then the team can decide to stick to the original decision, include other types of computers, or suspend the item until a member can check on the possible new claims and make a recommendation for action for the agenda at the next meeting.)

This list of what to do to hold effective meetings is short. Anyone can do it. It makes sense to most people to run a meeting that way. It lets the team have maximum freedom without getting lost in irrelevancy. It gets the job done as quickly and efficiently as possible. Master it and learn to use it. Then if you want to think about gimmicks and sophisticated techniques, fine. The odds are good, though, that you'll find you don't need them.

HOW TO USE PRACTICAL LEARNING TOOLS _____

If you want to promote constant learning, by others and by yourself, you need the tools to do it with. This section covers a few of the most helpful of these tools.

The PDCA Cycle

If your organization uses Total Quality in any form, you should be familiar with the Shewhart or Plan-Do-Check-Act cycle. If you're not familiar with it, it's the basic method used for continuous process improvement. In brief, you should

1. *plan* what you intend to do,

2. *do* it,

3. *check* the outcome to see what happened, and

4. *act* to correct any problems you found when you checked the outcome, and then use these corrections when you plan to take the next action.

For an example, let's use the material in the section above on meetings. The team *plans* to use a fixed agenda and *does* it when it holds the meeting. At the end of the meeting, one of the players remarks that there was still a lot of discussion that wasn't relevant to any of the objectives. The team *checks* among itself to see if that is a consensus. If it is, the team *acts* to identify how it happened and how it can prevent it from happening again. When they *plan* the next meeting, they can use the insights from this meeting to help keep the discussion more relevant.

Alternatively, when the team checks at the end of its next meeting it may find that it stifled discussion because of its concern not to waste time on irrelevancies. It can then act on this learning when it plans the following meeting. The team thus uses the P-D-C-A cycle repeatedly to sharpen its skills in a specific area.

In my own opinion, some variation of the P-D-C-A cycle is the most important single tool for team learning—by a wide margin. If you don't use the P-D-C-A cycle or something like it already, I strongly recommend that you begin using it now—until it becomes the way you normally do business. Almost all other tools are just part of the total P-D-C-A cycle; nonetheless, some of them are worth considering independently.

"Lessons Learned" and "Postmortems"

I work for the Department of Defense, and one of the great strengths of the military is their systematic use of the "lessons learned" approach. If you remember the briefings during the War in the Gulf, you caught references to this. Casualties resulting from "friendly fire" and collateral (civilian) casualties were two of the issues which commanders reviewed constantly in lessons learned sessions. You may also remember that Coalition pilots systematically shared their views not only of what went wrong but of what went right among the different national forces.

In other circles, the same process is called a "post-mortem." Once again, the individuals involved analyze some action to see what really happened and what they can learn from it. I must confess that I prefer the term "lessons learned"; it doesn't have quite the negative connotations that "postmortem" does.

Whatever you call it, the process works best as part of the overall P-D-C-A cycle. Lessons are best learned when there is a systematic process for acting on them and incorporating them in the planning for the next cycle. If the team isn't ready to adopt the full cycle, though, this is a good place to start. At the very least, it gets everyone accustomed to thinking objectively about the outcomes of their actions. That's normally a major advance.

Setting Specific Objectives

We've already covered the importance of specific objectives several times, but this is a good place to mention them again. If specific objectives are important for the overall success of a team, they're just as important for its success at learning. After all, if you don't know what you intended to accomplish, it's very difficult to tell how well you did—and to learn from it.

Organizations can get trapped into dotting the i's and crossing the t's of objectives, so that they waste valuable time getting the objectives "just right." That's seldom necessary, at least for learning. As long as the team is clear about what it intends to accomplish, it doesn't have to be overly precise—particularly if it's a short-term objective.

Here's an example. A team may want to set a specific improvement objective, say the reduction of rejects by a certain percent. One player may feel that they should set an objective of 20%, while another thinks 10% is enough and a third wants to go for 30%. Rather than argue over the precise percentage, it's normally better to select one that seems reasonable and use it. If the team really feels free to learn, rather than live or die by the objective, it's probably going to be better off selecting a higher percentage. That's secondary, though. What's critical is selecting an objective, starting to work toward it, using feedback about your results to revise the objective as necessary, and keeping the cycle going.

Three more reminders about objectives. First, they should normally have specific time targets: "We will reduce rejects by 25%

within three months." Second, they should be measurable: "A reject is any part that requires rework in any form to meet specifications." Third, the team should decide in advance how they will get the data: "We will keep track of the parts we produce, and we will ask x department to return any rejects directly to us."

In short, you will learn the most from what you do if you know—in advance—*what* you intend to do, *when* you intend to do it by, *how* you will tell whether you have done it, and *what* data you will base your decision on.

HOW TO DEVELOP THE KEY SKILL: PROMOTING INTELLIGENT RISK-TAKING _____

Above all else, you must create an environment in which individuals are willing to take the risks necessary to learn. Just this isn't quite enough, though. These individuals must be able to identify and take *intelligent* risks.

This immediately brings up the question: What is an intelligent risk? It has three characteristics:

1. It is a risk. There is a chance that whatever is done may not succeed.

2. Despite the risk, there is a reasonable probability of success.

3. If the worst possible outcome occurs, the individual, team or organization will be able to live with it.
   Here are some examples of what is and is not an intelligent risk:

- A quality team commits itself to reduce rejects by 5% in six months. This isn't even a risk in most circumstances; a 5% reduction is virtually a sure thing. The team won't be stretched and will probably learn very little.

- An empowered team commits itself to a deadline on the assumption that it can cut process time by 50% during the three months of the job. Unless the team is very good at reducing cycle time, this is an extremely high level of risk. There's a real possibility that the team will fail to make its deadline—and fail by such a margin that the learning will be minimal.

- Another team, which has failed to meet its improvement goals for three successive months, vows to meet double the goal during the coming month. If the team has done careful lessons-learned sessions on their failures, this may be a realistic and worthwhile risk. If not, it is almost certainly a desperation move that will result neither in meeting the goal nor in significant learning.

- An experienced team with a good track record in constant improvement decides to set a formal goal of a 10% quality improvement per month for the coming quarter. The team believes it has a decent chance to make the improvement, based on what it's learned over the previous quarter. It believes that if it doesn't make the full improvement, it will have learned the limitations of some of its methods—and hopefully started to develop some new ones. The team is also sure that in the worst case it can still improve quality at least 5% per month over the period.

The last situation is an intelligent risk. It's not a sure thing, but the team may be able to do it. It will stretch the team, and if they don't achieve it no disaster will happen. Even in the worst case, the stage is set for them to learn a great deal about present and possible future methods. While some learning *may* occur in the preceding situations, much more learning can occur in this one.

This is the kind of intelligent risk that you want to help your teams identify and pursue. It should stretch them a little, but not so much that they'll probably fail. It should push them to try new methods, learn new techniques, constantly improve processes. It should encourage them to learn constantly, and provide them continuing opportunities to do so.

If you want this to happen in your teams, there's another change in language we need to make. So far in this section, I've used the word "fail" several times. Each time it was inappropriate, reflecting the view of reality of the traditional organization.

We've already seen that in many traditional organizations objectives are often ironclad, set-in-concrete means for forcing others to perform. The individual seldom plays a major role in setting her objectives; when she does, she's under tremendous pressure to make them more ambitious and accomplish them in less time.

If they're not accomplished? The player with the objective looks for excuses, while the boss decides how to deal with the failure.

Learning does occur in this environment, of course. Employees learn how to set objectives that are clearly achievable, to prevent failure. Bosses learn that employees don't want to stretch themselves, so they have to be forced to do so. Employees learn to keep a store of excuses in their desk drawer, so that any failure gets pinned on someone else. Bosses learn that employees can't be trusted, so that controls have to be screwed down even tighter. Whatever happens, it isn't constant improvement.

If you've experienced this environment, you know that it's the very antithesis of a learning environment. If you want constant learning in yourself and your teams, "failure" and "blame" go out the window. You and the rest of the players concerned must believe down to the soles of your feet that there are no failures, just more or less painful, more or less expensive learning experiences. The job of everyone is to see that there are as many learning experiences as possible, and that each one of them is as painless and inexpensive as possible. We're back again to the basic principle: taking intelligent risks.

How do you create a situation in which you and others can take these intelligent risks and learn from them? Here are some ideas:

1. The first *must* is pretty obvious: you don't "blame" players because they "failed." This doesn't mean overlooking objectives when they aren't met or ignoring problems that come up. It means identifying them as problems to be solved and to be learned from. It's just as important to extend this to your teams; they have to get over the same tendency to see what they do as a "success" or "failure" in the traditional sense— and they must give up forever blaming anyone for their unmet objectives. Again, you and they always look for the causes; you just don't look for someone to blame.

2. Blaming and the idea of success of failure have another shortcoming. We tend to look at an unmet objective as simply a "failure," and look for someone to blame. If the objective is met, though, we brand it a "success," and congratulate ourselves. (As someone has said, success has a thousand fathers, while failure is an orphan.) Reality is seldom so neat and tidy. A "failure" may have been almost a "success" (we would

have gotten the product out on time except that we hadn't planned for two machines down at the same time). The same may be true in reverse—our "success" only barely avoided being a "failure" (if the supply room hadn't discovered a box of forms they didn't know they had, we would have missed our target by a week or more).

In other words, whether the objective is met or not, look for both what went right *and* what went wrong. The objective was met? Did something happen that almost fouled it up, or someone have to handle a last-minute emergency that should have been anticipated? The objective was missed? What did we do that worked, that we can use next time? If you and your teams practice this, you'll probably discover that most situations are more complex than you realized before. More important, you'll systematically increase your ability to learn from these situations.

3. We looked at the importance of team self-confidence and how to support it in the last chapter. It's a necessity for effective decision making—and it's just as much a necessity for learning. Players who lack self-confidence can't afford to "fail" and so they try to avoid taking risks. (Or they take tremendous, unwise risks so they can "prove" themselves.) Self-confidence and effective learning go hand in hand. Use all of the methods discussed in the last chapter, and all of the other methods you can think of, to build up your teams' self-confidence.

4. The other side of the paragraph above is that success strengthens self-confidence. If success comes only from *meeting* objectives it may be infrequent. Just as bad, it may be phoney, based on objectives set low so they could be reached. When the goal is learning, success is always within a player's power. If he meets the objectives, he succeeded at that—and he can be even more successful by analyzing just why he was so successful. If he attained only part of the objective, that's still success—and if he learns from the attempt he will increase his success.

(You may be getting a little uncomfortable at this stress on learning. After all, isn't the goal not learning but production? What happens to the output if everyone is sitting around learning all the time? Don't worry, because that isn't what happens. Remember, what everyone is learning is how to produce more effectively. When objectives aren't met, it's normally because they're set higher than they would have been in a traditional organization. Constant focus on learning, in fact, is the only reliable way to produce continuous improvement.)

5. As your teams become more and more experienced and competent, expect them to identify the risks in any course of action more precisely. Here are two examples that illustrate this:

  - An inexperienced team poses an objective of 5% improvement per month. If you asked them what problems they foresee in achieving this, they might have trouble answering. You might even get an answer like, "Well, we don't know—but we think it's worth trying." Because of their inexperience, they have a difficult time spotting the problems they will have to solve.

  - Now take the same team six months or a year later, continuing its 5% per month improvement objective. Ask them what the problems are, and you may get answers such as: "We're going to have to find a way to get the mail sorted faster," or "We think we can cut the time it takes to handle the difficult requests by at least one day and perhaps two." Another response might be, "We can get it done if they don't shut the computer down for more than four hours at a time."

The moral of this is simple: don't press inexperienced teams to be specific about the risks they face, but help them become better and better at identifying the risks. When you get an experienced team, expect it to anticipate most of the problems that might keep it from achieving its objective. For a team like this, one of the most important sources of learning is identifying the problems that weren't anticipated, and trying to find ways to plan for them in the future.

6. Here's a final point. If you really do give up blaming and looking at events as simple successes or failures, you'll start to realize that this way of looking at work sneaks in despite your best efforts. Do you formally appraise performance

once or twice a year? Perhaps the standards you use are based on "success" and "failure," instead of learning. Did you deliver a product late your boss was counting on? Perhaps he expects you to have someone to blame and to "chew them out." Once begun, choosing to learn rather than blame begins to radiate out like ripples from a rock thrown into the water. As the ripples spread, they start to challenge all the fixed policies and procedures that are based on ideas of success, failure and blame. It's important that you keep the momentum up.

AND NOW, LET'S GET TO THE HEART OF THE MATTER _____

If you want to succeed in a teampower environment, you must manage alignment, coordination, decision making and continuous learning. None of this is possible, though, unless you can develop and maintain trust among all of the players involved. In other words, the next chapter is the heart of the whole endeavor.

Chapter 9

Creating and Maintaining Trust

If you've read the standard books on managing and supervising, you've probably never even seen "creating and maintaining trust" mentioned as one of the functions of a manager. Here's an example: not too many years ago, collection of articles on management from a major business journal was published. In the more than 20 articles represented, only one mentioned trust. That's typical of most writing on management. In the last few years, this has begun to change a little—but only a little.

On the one hand, there's no surprise in this. Traditional organizations, at least in theory, had no need for trust. Employees were assigned duties that they performed in return for wages. First-line managers gave orders, monitored performance, and rewarded and punished employees. Higher-level managers coordinated the efforts of their subordinate managers. Executives set the strategic direction and passed instructions down the organization for others to execute it.

It all sounds neat and orderly—but anyone who's worked for long in a traditional organization knows that the orderliness is often illusory. Some managers get superb results from their workers, while others are marginally effective. Higher-level managers and executives produce equally superb or marginal results.

Many factors other than trust are involved, of course. Intelligence, communication skills, decisiveness and a dozen other elements of management style impact a manager's effectiveness. But nothing—*nothing*—impacts it more than the ability of a manager to create and maintain trust. This is true in a traditional organization, and it's true in spades in a teampower organization. It's so true that without a high degree of trust a teampower organization simply cannot function.

Here are a few examples of the importance that some writers on management attach to trust:

- Badaracco and Ellsworth refer to trust as "the linchpin of effective management."[58]

- According to Gibb, "trust catalyzes all other processes, is contagious, softens our perceptions, breeds trust in others, *makes us less dangerous*, and is self-fulfilling . . . . *When trust is high, relative to fear, people and people systems function well. When fear is high, relative to trust, they break down.*[59]

- Robert Johansen has written a book on teleconferencing and its future. You'd expect him to emphasize the technology. Instead, he says that "the most important rules of thumb for teleconference implementers can be stated simply: seek out pain and build up trust."[60]

- When Lund and Hansen looked at the requirements that new technology places on firms, they concluded that "when individual responsibility becomes a key skill requirement for employees, managerial behavior and attitude will have to reflect a realization of this change through organizational realignment, improved communications, and, above all, trust."[61]

- In their superb study of leadership, Kouzes and Posner found that "trust...is the central issue in human relationships both within and outside the organization. Trust is an essential element of organizational effectiveness as well.... What happens when people do not trust each other? They will ignore, disguise, and distort facts, ideas, conclusions, and feelings that they believe will increase their vulnerability to others . . . . When you don't trust someone, you resist letting them influence you. You are suspicious and unreceptive to their proposals and goals.[62]

I could cover pages with equally strong quotes, most of them coming from authors writing in the mid to late 80s. Many of them (such as Kouzes and Posner) were writing about traditional organizations—but even in these organizations the need for a high level of trust was becoming all too clear. This high level of trust, as Lund and Hansen underline, is emphatically more necessary in organizations that seek to empower their players.

WHAT YOU DO TO CREATE AND MAINTAIN TRUST _____

The chapters on the other functions have spelled out some of the tasks that went with the roles, the kinds of things that players actually *do* when performing these functions. While creating and maintaining trust is somewhat different, there are still tasks or actions that further the process. Here are some examples:

1. You do away with time clocks, inspection systems and other processes designed to control other players.

2. You delegate work and give the individual or team the latitude necessary to complete the work with reasonable independence.

3. You treat other players with respect, regardless of the situation.

4. You listen and respond honestly to others.

5. You create an atmosphere in which blaming is eliminated and learning is stressed.

I hope you noticed, by the way, that this is only one of the five management functions that doesn't refer to "managing." To speak of *managing* trust is to compromise the function at the beginning. In a very real sense, no one can manage trust. You and I can act in ways that demonstrate our trust for others and call forth their trust in us—but we cannot manage this process. As soon as we look on it as something to manage, we put ourselves outside the situation and trust no longer exists.

Let me also add that the process of creating trust is neither quick nor simple. When players aren't used to high trust, they become cynical and suspicious of everyone else's actions. They may want to trust each other and you, but they won't until you've proven yourself—and created an environment in which they can prove themselves to each other. In other words, patience is absolutely crucial for creating and maintaining trust.

THE SKILLS YOU NEED

Now that we've looked at the background, what are the key skills involved in creating and maintaining trust? There are four of them:

1. How to listen actively

2. How to make commitments carefully and keep them absolutely

3. How to surface all of the issues for consideration (no hidden agendas)

4. How to walk your talk (congruence between what you say and what you do—in other words, integrity)

HOW TO LISTEN ACTIVELY

Several years ago, a large Federal agency surveyed its supervisors, managers and executives, asking them what skills they thought were critical to success. At every level, "listening" was one of the top three skills identified. There's no reason to believe that the results would have been different in other agencies or in private industries.

In fact, the question you might ask is: Why wait until so late in the book to talk about listening skills? Effective, active listening is a key skill for everything that a player does in a teampower organization. And this is true no matter the level of the player.

As important as it is in general, though, active listening is absolutely critical to creating and maintaining trust. Whatever else may be true, you and I will never trust anyone who doesn't listen to us. How could we? Someone who doesn't listen effectively doesn't know what we really want, or how we see things. We could never trust such a person to care about our interests. Effective listening—which means *active* listening—is the bedrock of trust.

Truly effective listening involves more than simply sitting quietly and listening. It is actually a group of *four* skills:

1. *Observing* people and their situations;
2. *Listening* actively to what they have to say;
3. *Asking* questions that draw them out and help them make their meaning clearer; and
4. *Feeling* (using intuition) to grasp what they mean.

Here's a closer look at each of these four skills.

Observing

Surprisingly enough, effective listening begins not with listening itself but with observing. An effective listener observes throughout the encounter to its very end.

Only a limited amount of what we communicate comes through words. A few years ago, "body language" was fashionable. Books were published to teach us how to observe and use body language. While the fad has passed, the basic point is still valid: people don't express themselves solely in words. We've been trained from infancy both to express ourselves nonverbally and to understand others' nonverbal expressions. Using these skills (and developing them further) is a necessary ingredient in effective listening.

For instance, traditional organizations don't handle anger well. Someone may "blow their top" to you, making it clear that they're angry. They may just as well try to hide the anger under a veneer of politeness or even helpfulness. If you simply listen to the words and settle for the veneer, you won't hear or respond to the anger— and the anger is at least as important as the content of what a person is saying.

Another example. You walk into one of your teams, where everything is apparently quiet and calm. As you look more closely, though, you notice that two players aren't speaking at all. In fact, they've moved away from you to make it difficult for you to address them. You may not need to do anything; a mature self-managing team will handle the problem itself. But it's good to know that there is a problem. You can make a mental note to check back a few hours or a day or so later to see if the issue has been resolved. If it hasn't, you may want to intervene.

Many times, individuals relax when they end a conversation. If you've been troubled by the conversation, that's the time to be especially observant. Did nothing happen but the individual seem immensely relieved? Or did you appear to deal with the person's issue but the person is still tense? Those last few seconds can give you invaluable information about what really happened—as long as you remain observant.

Listening

Just listening is difficult. From our first day in the first grade, we've been trained that smart people talk. They give answers. Only dummies keep quiet. They don't know anything. The points for participation all go to the kids who answer the questions, not to the ones who keep quiet and listen. This stereotype tends to get reinforced when you put on your manager hat. After all, managers are supposed to reach conclusions quickly and act decisively— right?

Hopefully you've learned by now that the real world doesn't work that way. In that world, the truth is often just the reverse. Anybody can give answers; the smart people listen carefully and long before they do. It was no less a person than Abraham Lincoln who said "It is better to keep quiet and be thought a fool than to open one's mouth and dispel all doubt."

The first obstacle to overcome is the tendency to jump to conclusions, to prove how quick and perceptive we are. The only cure for that is listening—simple listening. Don't underrate that. It takes both skill and discipline to sit and listen when your instinct is to jump in and solve the problem for the individual. Remember the lesson from Total Quality (in Chapter 3), that effective management is "data-driven." One of the basic ways you get data is by listening.

Just sitting there like the proverbial bump on the log often isn't enough, though. When we talk, we want to know that we're being *heard*, not just being endured. Real listening is *active* listening. It includes:

1. *Appropriate posture.* Sometimes leaning back in a relaxed pos-

ture communicates the right kind of listening. At other times it doesn't. If an individual is telling you about something he found traumatic, anything less than edge-of-the-seat, focused attention just doesn't fit.

2. *Appropriate shifts in posture.* Unless it's a very short conversation, maintaining one posture is neither natural nor effective. Even the most intense conversations still have an ebb and flow. Your posture should reflect the flow. This has the additional virtue that it lets you release some tension through movement. If you try to maintain one posture no matter what, you'll become more and more uncomfortable and find it harder and harder to concentrate.

3. *Verbal encouragement.* This may be so simple as an occasional "huh" when the conversation is going well to more focused comments like "would you go over that again for me." A few welltimed comments can both assure the speaker that you're listening and help her express what's concerning her.

Asking

I once knew a general who kept his staff on their toes in a most simple and effective way. He seldom threatened anyone. His pep talks to his staff and his employees were good but not brilliant. All he did was walk around the base, asking questions. He was a real expert with that skill, though. He'd start talking with a workgroup, and in 10 to 15 minutes he knew what was really happening in it, how it was functioning and what its problems were.

That's not the kind of questioning we're talking about here; I included it simply to illustrate how powerful good questions are. They're an invaluable part of listening.

When you ask relevant questions, you assure the speaker that he's being heard. If he's hesitant, good questions draw him out and make it easier for him to say what's on his mind. Questions help you get a more complete picture of the situation. They can help the individuals make transitions from one issue (or part of an issue) to another.

Questions can perform another vital function—keeping the individual on the topic. Some individuals are very clear and precise about what's bothering them. Others aren't; when they get upset they bring up irrelevancies and submerge the present problem in a sea of past and sometimes even imagined issues. A well-timed question ("Is that really what's bothering you now, or is it the incident yesterday?") can help the person focus on the immediate, solvable problem. (*Always* remember that the only solvable problems are present ones and future ones. No matter how serious it may have been, a problem that's only in the past cannot be solved.)

Finally, asking "What would you like me to do?" is an effective way to find out the answer to that important question. It's easy to assume that you know the answer—but you never know for sure until you ask.

There's one other point to keep in mind about questions: the difference between yes-no and open-ended questions. A yes-no question ("Did Tom specifically promise you the job?") permits only two answers. And it may telegraph the answer that you expect. An open-ended question ("Just what did Tom say that made you think he was giving you the job?") calls for a much more complete response. Asking open-ended questions is a definite skill, one you should work on if you don't already have.

Feeling

This is what some people call a hunch, or a gut feeling. Others refer to it as intuition. Whatever it's called, it's something that successful managers have and use. Nothing, absolutely nothing, will substitute for an accurate feel for situations. Does this sound soft and fuzzy? Isn't intuition what women use? Maybe it's okay if you're a female manager, but what if you're not?

The fact of the matter is that many really good managers of both sexes have well-developed and effective intuition. It's not something arcane and mysterious. It's based on experience, and it's simply the ability to take in a situation as a whole, to understand more than the bare facts presented to you. Intuition takes the data you're given and draws conclusions from it before the rational part of your mind can work them out.

This intuition is slippery, though. When you reason your way to a conclusion, others can look at your reasoning and evaluate it. When you say "It feels like...." or "I have a hunch that...."—what can anyone do with that? What's more, your intuition can be wrong. The solution that feels so "right" may flop completely. The facts you were sure would be there aren't. The decision you so confidently made begins to look worse and worse.

How do you develop and use intuition effectively? Here are the basics:

1. First, you constantly use the first three skills; you observe, you listen, you ask. The more facts you provide your intuition, the more accurate it becomes.

2. Then you remember that intuition—like any skill—can only be developed if it's used. So, use it! Pay attention to your hunches and gut feelings. If you have a sense that something isn't quite as it seems, follow it. Observe, listen and ask questions designed to get at what's really going on. Just do it carefully.

3. Finally, always check the results of your intuition. Was your feel for the situation more accurate than the conclusions you would have drawn otherwise? If not, what seemed to go wrong? Remember, intuition is always based on experience—so the better you understand and evaluate your experience, the better your intuition will serve you.

HOW TO MAKE COMMITMENTS
CAREFULLY AND KEEP THEM ABSOLUTELY _____

We first looked at this topic in Chapter 3, as part of effective delegation. We're looking at it here because it's even more than that. You won't trust me unless I listen to you—but neither will you trust me unless you can count on me to do just what I say.

At this point, I'd like you to try a small experiment. I want you to list, in your mind or even on a piece of paper, the half-dozen individuals in whom you have the greatest confidence. Whom do you really trust? Whom can you count on to come through for you in almost any situation? Please pause a moment and create that list.

Now, go through that list a second time. How many of these individuals can you count on to do exactly what they say? In old but very accurate terms, for how many of them is their word truly their bond?

Were there any individuals on the list that you couldn't rely completely on? Probably not. How do you trust someone whose word you can't take without question? And how can someone trust you if they can't take your word?

You may not have thought of it, but the reverse is also true: If you don't trust me, you help create a situation in which you can't take my word. You may pressure me, because you believe I won't deliver unless you do. Because you don't trust me, I may promise you anything just so I can get rid of you. To counter this, you devise ways to force me to deliver. Perhaps you even plan what to do when I don't deliver.

This is a common game in traditional organizations. Because trust is low, commitments can't be taken at face value, which further lowers trust. Everyone spends precious time and energy attempting to pressure and control everyone else. There's no way out of this vicious downward spiral until the players create a situation in which they can take each others' word. But how do you create the situation? Here are the basics.

The Three Ground Rules

This is what we covered in Chapter 3, and here they are (in summary) again:

1. Each player is careful both about the commitments he makes and the commitments he accepts.

2. Each player expects both his commitments and those of others to be followed exactly as made. In the absence of information to the contrary, everyone can count on the commitments made to be followed to the letter.

3. Sometimes conditions change or unanticipated problems arise. When that happens, the player with the commitment notifies the others quickly; if necessary, he renegotiates the commitment. The key rule is a simple one: no surprises.

Common and Clear Expectations

Neither trust nor commitment can be one sided. Everyone involved needs to know what she expects and what is expected of her. The three ground rules are useless, and perhaps even harmful, unless everyone is willing to sign up to them. Even more, every player must be willing to challenge any other player who may not be following them.

At first, even this may be risky. In traditional organizations, managers and workers alike often agree publicly with new initiatives—then hunker down, keep doing business as usual, and wait to see what happens. The attempt to create realistic, firm commitments can fall into this organizational black hole. The only solution is to keep your expectations clear and deliver on your own commitments without fail.

The Learning Curve

Conversion to honest commitments may have to start small. Traditional habits of pressure and control are hard to break. Trust makes individuals who aren't used to it feel very vulnerable. In my own experience (much successful, some not), developing significant trust is a matter at best of months. Creating an environment in which commitments can be made and accepted freely is part of this process. Everyone may have to agree to begin in a relatively "safe" area, and then slowly increase the area—like an army creating a beachhead and working out from it.

This is a testing process, but it's even more. Because commitments are so often created by pressure and counterpressure, control and evasion, many players lack the skill needed to make realistic commitments. They simply haven't had the freedom to make a reasonable estimate of what they could do. In short, they (and you) may have been devoting far more effort to bargaining the safest commitment than to developing the best one.

The last chapter made the point that effective teams can anticipate most risks involved in achieving their goals. This is part of the learning curve for commitments as well. As individuals and teams become more proficient, they can make stronger and more reliable commitments—because they can understand and thus plan for the risks more effectively.

In this as in so many other aspects of teampower, players must learn the roles they need to play and then the skills they need to play these roles. By starting with small, safe areas, everyone gets the opportunity to work their way toward the goal. Then, as each player begins to make and keep commitments intelligently, both the strength and the reliability of the commitments increase.

Commitments and Learning

This section ties in closely with the whole of the last chapter: Strong, reliable commitments are a powerful aid to learning. True learning requires that players accept the idea that if objectives aren't met they can still learn from the experience. True learning *doesn't* require, though, that missed objectives be taken lightly. No valid purpose is furthered by an individual or team that sets an objective in expectation that "well, we probably can't make it, but, what the heck, we're learning."

The cure for this isn't to retreat to ironclad objectives, pressure and control. The cure is to see objectives as commitments. Let me make a quick comparison to illustrate this. You need a prototype from my group, and you're under a lot of pressure to get it done quickly.

In a low-trust situation, you pressure me to produce it quickly. I hedge and evade, but you insist (and perhaps mention that merit increase evaluations are coming up soon). So, I agree to the date you want, knowing that I probably can't make it—and already lining up my excuses for my failure. Neither of us has much confidence in my commitment.

In a high-trust situation, you and I are under just as much pressure, but we respect each other too much to bargain with pressure and evasion. You ask for a date. I tell you what would have to happen to make that date, and the problems I anticipate. We talk those out. Perhaps the end result is that you commit to provide extra support and I commit to bust my gut to produce on time. But we also agree that in two weeks we'll get back together to see how the situation is progressing.

Notice the difference: in the second situation we both know just what the situation is and we both make appropriate commitments to each other. The reliability of my commitment increases dramatically. So does the chance that I will produce a quality prototype when I agree to do so.

(This isn't a book about customer service, but I have to put just a word in here about commitments to customers. Nothing—absolutely *nothing*—is more important where service to customers is concerned than keeping commitments. Leonard L. Berry, Valerie A. Zeithaml, and A. Parasuraman have spent a decade studying good and poor customer service. Their conclusion? "Breaking the service promise is the single most important way service companies fail their customers."[63]

Preston Trucking, a highly successful firm known for empowering its players, posts a Commitment to Excellence statement in each of its facilities—and has each player sign the statement. In part, it reads "Once I make a commitment to a customer or another associate, I promise to fulfill it on time. I will do what I say when I say I will do it."[64]

Need I say more?)

HOW TO BRING HIDDEN AGENDAS TO THE SURFACE _____

Real trust requires that all of the relevant issues be part of the discussion. This is hard, true—but there is no alternative.

That may seem not just difficult but probably impossible if you're used to the typical hidden agendas of most traditional organizations. Does this sound familiar?

Tom says to Karen, "We really need to produce for the next few months, and I want you to set yourself some really high objectives this quarter." What he says to himself, though, is "She's been goofing off, and I'm going to make her produce"—and that's what he acts on.

"Sure," Karen replies to Tom. To herself, though, she says: "Is he trying to set me up for a poor efficiency report? I'd really better be careful what I agree to"—and that's what she acts on.

The basic problem with hidden agendas is that they prevent people from dealing with their real issues. Is Karen goofing off? That's an issue, and it needs to be addressed. Does Tom want to give her a low rating? That's also an issue; it also needs to be faced. (The truth of the matter may be that because Karen thinks she's going to get a low rating anyway, she's decided that it's not worth the effort to do better.)

It takes commitment to put all the issues on the table—the same commitment from everyone involved. All the guidelines we looked at for effective commitments apply. Here are a few additional ones:

1. *Everyone* must commit to putting their agendas on the table. Nowhere in the whole trust equation are players more vulnerable than here. One individual who keeps an agenda hidden can spoil the whole process for everyone. An experienced team will teach any new members how important this is. A newer team may need help from you. Your first step, of course, is to see that your own agendas are always visible. Nothing leads like example, and that's especially true in this situation. Then you follow up by making it clear that this openness is a requirement, that there are no exceptions. Being a member of an effective team is an exciting and satisfying experience. Being willing to play with all your cards on the table is one of the entry requirements for this experience.

2. Everyone must also insist that others make their agendas clear—and must be willing to challenge anyone who appears not to be doing so. It can be hard to challenge another on this point. You may be wrong. Even if you're not, many of us have learned in traditional organizations never to challenge another directly. It doesn't matter; this is too important a point to let reasons like this prevent the challenge. Again, you should take the lead by challenging anyone who appears to be dealing from a hidden agenda. Far more important, you should take the lead by making it clear that anyone is free to challenge you—and then responding honestly to the challenge.

3. Neither of the above can happen unless everyone also commits themselves to dealing honestly with whatever agendas are presented. The basic reason we keep agendas hidden is that we're afraid they won't be accepted by others. For instance, most of us would have a hard time admitting: "Hey, I want this project because it's a chance to really look good," or "I don't agree with your proposal because I think your department will get 'one up' on mine if we do it that way."

If you want a high-trust environment, though, such agendas must not only be admitted but accepted and dealt with responsibly.

Let me emphasize this just a bit more. One of the problems with calls for honesty in human relations is that they are all too often one-sided. I want you to be honest with me—but we leave open what happens when you do. The commitment, and the risk, are all yours. For reasons that should be clear, this doesn't often work. I can reasonably expect you to level with me only if I'm willing to take what you say seriously. In other words, to ask another for honesty is at the same time to make a commitment to her to deal honestly with whatever her agenda is. Like a coin, you cannot have one side without the other.

All this may sound terribly risky, and indeed it is. As I've already noted, though, it's essential to authentic trust. I can't trust you until I know what you really want from me, and until I know you will respond to what I really want from you.

This openness has another advantage, one you may not anticipate. When I begin to really level with you and you with me, we suddenly begin to find out we have more in common that we thought. Your hidden agendas often look surprisingly like mine, and mine like yours. And then I find you suspected me of this all along, as I did you. Suddenly we share a bond impossible before. Suddenly, what we used to do begins to look a bit ludicrous, the thought of doing it again completely laughable. And when a whole team works through a moment like this, it makes a quantum leap to a higher level of functioning.

THE CORE OF THE PROCESS:
WHY YOU MUST HAVE INTEGRITY _____

Listening, making and keeping commitments, putting all of the agendas on the table—each of these is an important part of trust. Now we move beyond them to the last and most basic characteristic of an individual who can be trusted. There are various ways to put this characteristic. In current jargon, someone who has it *"walks his talk."* Another way to put it is to say that there is *congruence* between what he says and what he does. In simple, traditional terms, she is a person with *integrity*.

The basic meaning of all of these is a simple one: an individual who can be trusted is just what he or she seems to be. This person listens, makes and keeps intelligent commitments, puts agendas on the table. Moreover, all of this is natural, simply the person's way of being just who he or she is.

Need I say that this isn't easy? Unlike most of the characteristics we've covered so far, integrity isn't made up of a set of skills that can be listed and learned. Nonetheless, there are some helpful points that can be made about it. Here are a few of them.

It Is Intentional

Unlike Topsy, integrity does not just grow. Perhaps some people are born with it; I don't know. I do know that many others learn it at home, as the natural way of being of one or both parents. Others find it first in a teacher, spouse, coworker, or mentor. Even when this happens integrity, unlike the mumps, isn't catching. We may want to emulate the individual, we may find ourselves being changed by a relationship with her. Whatever happens, though, each of us develops integrity only when he or she *intends* to do so, not before.

It's easier to do this when you have a clear example to follow, and easiest to do it on the job if that example is your boss or mentor. Most of us can't count on that, nor can we afford to wait for it. Each day an individual fails to choose to walk his talk is a day spent doing something other than building trust in those around him. If you and I want others to trust us, we must choose for our words, our thoughts, our actions, and our motives all to convey the same message.

It Is Based on Self-trust

There are myriad reasons why individuals fail to choose integrity. One of these reasons is lack of trust in ourselves. We can become so accustomed to playing a role that we cannot trust ourselves outside the role. I am the self-confident, decisive manager; you are the farsighted, clearheaded strategist; she is the poised, self-confident leader. None of us is fully the role we play, but it is so comfortable, so familiar, so *safe*, that we continue to play it.

It takes a lot of trust in oneself to begin to step outside this role. It takes self-trust for me to say—even to myself—"I really don't know what to do in this situation." (Clearly, it also takes a lot of trust in you for me to say it out loud, where you can hear it.) To admit that I can be indecisive, that you can be confused, that she can be afraid—this takes trust that even though this is true I am strong and competent enough to work through it to success. This is quite a commitment to make!

It Involves Risk

As the paragraph above suggests, there's a risk to deciding that I will be simply who I am, that I will walk my talk. Like any expression of trust, it makes me vulnerable. You may take advantage of me—and you really may. This is not an idle fear. If I opt to be simply myself and you brand it weakness or indecisiveness, you may "win" and I will "lose."

I have deliberately avoided giving advice through the book, and I will avoid it after this. I am not wise or experienced enough to do so. The best I can do is share my thinking and let you choose any of it that seems useful. On one point, though, I am willing to stick my neck out and make a suggestion. You may have blanched as you read the paragraphs on building trust, and particularly the ones just above on walking your talk. You may be in an environment in which integrity is a joke and a hindrance. The skills you need to survive in this environment are those that let you successfully manipulate yourself and others—that permit you (in the modern version of the Golden rule) to do unto them before they do unto you.

If this is the case, I have a single suggestion: *Leave!!* Life is too short for this. Whatever you gain in income, in status, in power, you more than forfeit in the quality of your life. Your environment is sick, and there is little chance you can heal it. Just find another, healthier environment—now! End of suggestion.

If your organization is a "typical" one, integrity is scattered here and there—and perhaps prized in some areas. Here, the risk is a tolerable one. As you develop and display integrity, you'll probably draw like-minded players to you. That's the best possible outcome—one well worth working for.

It Can Lead to Self-deception

As I write this, I can see a note taped to my TV monitor. It's a note from me to me for a book I planned to write several years ago but didn't. The note says, "If you're known to have integrity, people will tend to keep the dirty work from you." I knew I was keeping that note for a purpose, and this is it. If you don't develop the mutual trust we've been talking about in this chapter, the players around you may deal with your integrity by taking care of the problems they believe require underhanded tactics—and seeing that you never find out. You have your integrity; they see to it that it doesn't interfere.

I certainly don't have a quick fix for this. In part, it's solved by developing mutual trust. In part, it requires that you combine integrity with realism. And in part it means having integrity without being rigid or—perhaps the worst sin of all—judgmental.

Integrity Is Its Own Reward

I suspect this may sound Pollyanna to you. Perhaps it is, though I don't think so. I once worked for a boss who would lie to key players—myself included—without the blink of an eye. The rest of his management style was as unscrupulous as you would expect. He was an excellent manager, but his lack of integrity held him far below where he might have been. More than that, he made life miserable for himself and those around him. Moving to another position was like breathing fresh air after months in a closed, dark room.

I can't tell you that he was more miserable than he would have been if he had integrity. I can tell you that he lived in a hostile, uncaring world—one very different from that of the individuals I have known with integrity. We all slant the world so that the people we meet in it are like ourselves. Distrustful individuals without integrity live in a world full of their fellows. That's not a very pleasant world.

ONCE AGAIN, TRUST IS THE KEY _____

As I read back on the last few pages, I realize that I need once again to stress the context. You cannot simply develop mutual trust, supported by integrity, in any old organization at any old time. But we're not talking about any old organization; we're talking about an organization that, at the minimum, is willing to let you commit yourself to teampower. And we're not talking about any old time; we're talking of the time when you must effectively perform the functions required to support this teampower.

In this organization, at this time, developing mutual trust based on integrity is not an option. It is a requirement. To end by repeating a sentence from the first of this chapter,

without a high degree of trust a teampower organization simply cannot function.

That's the unavoidable bottom line!

Chapter 10 ═══════

How to Prepare for Teampower ═══════════

All right, you want to make a major move toward empowering your players. Perhaps you're just beginning, with quality teams or project teams. Perhaps you want to move on to high-performance, self-managing teams. Just how do you go about creating them? The next chapter answers that question in detail. This chapter discussed some of the broad issues you want to answer before you actually begin.

ARE YOU READY? _____

This is the first question you need to ask and answer: Are you ready to put forth the effort to create teampower in your organization? You know what you must do for teams to succeed, what the different forms are that teampower can take, and the basic management functions required to create and encourage teampower. Are you ready to put all of this into practice?

Don't be too quick to say "yes." Implementing teampower is challenging, even in the best of circumstances. If you want to meet the challenge, you need to be prepared for it. Here are some of the forms the challenge will take:

1. If you're used to managing in a traditional organization, the change in the functions you perform will be only a few degrees short of traumatic. As I've said earlier, managing in a teampower environment is much more interesting and

even fun than managing in a traditional environment—but getting there from here requires a major change in what you do and how you do it. I hope you realize that now; if not, you might want to skim through chapters 5 through 9 again.

2. No matter how enthusiastic you and everyone else are about the change, it will be long, hard, and exhausting. Everything starts off with a bang. It's exciting. And stimulating. And it opens doors to great new possibilities. After the first flush of excitement, though, the real work begins. Disappointments will occur—boy, will they occur! There'll be plenty of disagreements, and some of those that you settle will come back again in a slightly different form. This doesn't mean you won't succeed. Not at all. It just means that everyone involved needs to be prepared to work hard for this success.

3. It will take time, in a double sense. First, it will time away from current production. This shouldn't surprise you; any real change takes a great deal of time to prepare for and execute. Any significant form of teampower requires immense amounts of planning—up front. You will already have made a major investment of time, taken from current activities, before you take the first concrete step. The change will also take time in a second sense: it will take time to complete. At the most optimistic, you're talking about several months. If the changes are extensive, they will take well over a year—perhaps several years. Implementing a new way of working is one thing; sticking with it until it's successful and institutionalized and simply the way people do business is quite another. You must be prepared to go all the way, or else.

4. Finally, all this will show up in increased stress on everyone. Many players will get caught up in mood swings, from wild enthusiasm to frustrated despair. Tempers will fray. Some people will want to give up. Others will want to ram the change down the throat of those who're resisting. All of this is perfectly normal and natural; change is stressful, and we deal with it by expressing that stress in a myriad different forms. If you want to help your organization change successfully, you must be able to accept and deal with the stress—which means letting it out in the open, rather than bottling

it up. In other words, you'll need to develop a very high tolerance for stress and help others do the same.

WHERE TO GET HELP _____

You've looked over the paragraphs just above and decided that you're ready to make the commitment to more significant teampower. Your next step is to get help. This book emphasizes one aspect of empowered teams: what you must do as a manager if they are to be successful. That's just the beginning. You can take three more specific steps to prepare to implement teampower. Here they are.

1. Learn More about Teampower

No matter what your situation is, you can read about empowering teams and you can attend courses in it. There are dozens of books on using teams; the bibliography of this book lists many of them. They're available in your public library (through interlibrary loan, if necessary). Your local public library may also have audio and video tapes on this and related subjects. Some organizations maintain management libraries; if yours does, this is another source of good books. As you find out more about teams, you can get a clearer idea of just what needs to be done to make yours successful.

The number of courses and conferences being offered on teamwork and related topics is increasing even as you read this. Some of these are commercial workshops and training courses, lasting several days to a week or two. Others are given by junior colleges, colleges and universities. Hopefully, your firm is committed enough to the idea of empowered teams that they'll send you to one or more of the courses. If not, you can probably afford to attend a night class given by a local college. Like reading, courses expand your knowledge of what the alternatives are. They do more than this, though; they give you the chance to talk with other individuals in your situation. You may even get to discuss teampower with individuals already using it. And that brings us to the second avenue for help.

2. Visit Organizations That Use Empowered Teams

Whatever else you do, visit one or (preferably) several organizations similar to your own that have successful teampower programs. While teampower isn't as widespread as it needs to be or will be, it's making definite inroads in organizations throughout the country. There are probably one or two firms near you that are at least experimenting with empowered teams. If you haven't heard about any, ask your Personnel Office or Human Resources Management Office for information. If you attend courses or conferences on teamwork, use the leaders and the attendees both as resources. Conferences and workshops are often led by individuals who are consultants in the field, and they're normally only too glad to show you where to find successful teampower operations.

Once you find organizations that are trying teampower, spend time with them. Talk with your counterparts to see what they think of it. Visit with the teams. See how enthusiastic they are and what challenges they're facing. Pay particular attention to the ways that their situation is like yours and the ways that it differs from yours. Take notes. If the organization is clearly in transition, visit it again after several months to see if the new ways are working. Above all, ask questions, questions, questions. (Here's a good chance to practice your active listening skills!)

Remember, there is *no* source of information on teams so useful to you as actually seeing people who work that way and talking with them. And this is doubly true if the organization is similar to your own, so you can see what benefits and problems to expect when you begin. When you embark on teampower, you'll want to keep all of these contacts and expand them.

3. Use a Consultant

You can learn a lot from books and courses. You can learn a lot from talking with others in teampower organizations. When the time comes to implement serious teampower in your organization, though, I recommend strongly that you get a consultant to help you. It doesn't have to be an external consultant; your firm may have an organizational design staff or some other staff experienced in implementing teams. If so, use them.

Let me add a quick word of caution. Many companies have highly talented and experienced internal consultants, with strong experience. If your firm has the caliber of consultant, by all means use them. Beware, though, of staff specialists whose experience is a few books and a training course or two. All too often, what passes for expertise is really infatuation with the latest fad—and teampower is certainly a current fad. If that's the kind of expertise your organization offers, it's all right to use it. Just don't use it as your primary source of expertise. Reserve that for someone, in the company or outside it, who has actual, hands-on experience with effective teams. (This same caution applies to outside consultants. Make sure you're dealing with one that has a solid background working with empowered teams.)

There are several reasons for using a skilled consultant. First, there's no glory in reinventing the wheel and making avoidable mistakes. There will be work enough and mistakes enough even with the best of guidance. Find someone with a good track record who can help you avoid some of the pitfalls and smooth the way as much as possible.

Needless to say, someone who knows the ropes will also save you a great deal of time and trouble. If you don't make some of the common mistakes, if you avoid some of the dead ends, you'll get to your goal more quickly and with less wasted effort. Converting to teampower the best way possible will still take significant time and effort. Don't add to it unnecessarily.

There's a third reason that's even more important than the other two. Teampower can't just be tacked onto a traditional organization. If you're serious about quality teams, the whole way you do business in a production environment has to change. If you want to use multiskilled/multifunctional teams, it takes even broader changes in the organization's culture to make them work. And if you intend to develop fully self-managing teams, you need to have the technology to support them properly.

Let me dwell on the technology aspect briefly. Self-managing work teams have a long history, springing from something called sociotechnical systems design. This is an approach that began in England more than 30 years ago and has spread throughout the world from there. Not all self-managing teams have been created using a sociotechnical systems approach, but virtually all successful ones have used some of the key ideas from this approach.[65]

One of these ideas, as the name suggests, is that the technical and the human system must fit each other. A few chapters back, we talked about Shenandoah Life Insurance Company and the dramatic improvement that resulted from their use of teampower in the form of semiautonomous work groups. The improvement happened because the company combined teampower with effective automation. They tried automation by itself first, and got a frustratingly small payback from it. When they combined automation with teampower, though, productivity and quality took off. At the GM Saturn plant, not only are the teams adapted to the technology but the technology is adapted to the teams.

It's very difficult to find the right balance between people and equipment without help from someone experienced in the field. There are just too many alternatives, and it's too easy to overlook many of them. A good consultant will have an established way of analyzing and organizing the situation, so that none of the promising alternatives get lost.

For all these reasons, you want to get help from an experienced consultant. A good one won't substitute his or her ideas for yours—but will help you find the most fruitful ways to achieve your goals. In other words, when you look for a consultant you're really looking for a partner who can work closely with you. Because of this, you want to choose a consultant carefully. Find out where else he or she has worked with teampower, and talk with them. Make sure the person (or at least the firm) has experience, too, in organizations like yours. The fact that a consultant is great at blue-collar teams doesn't create proficiency at building white-collar teams. Remember, this is *your* project. You want someone working with you that you can trust to support *your* goals.

HOW TO CHOOSE BETWEEN
MULTISKILLED AND MULTIFUNCTIONAL TEAMS _____

I have to put this section in, to help you be as realistic as possible about some limitations of teampower. When we looked at the different kinds of teams in Chapter 3, one of these kinds was the multiskilled or multifunctional team. These are actually two very different kinds of teams, and if you fail to understand the difference you could create serious problems for yourself.

In a nutshell, here are the differences:

- *Multiskilled* teams are made up of players most or all of whom can perform most or all of the tasks performed by the teams.

- *Multifunctional* teams are composed of players with different skills. The team combines all of the skills, but most players have only one major skill.

The most important point to understand is this: multiskilled teams work when individual tasks are relatively simple and can be learned in a few weeks or months. Most semi-skilled blue-collar and clerical teams can be multiskilled. This makes the job of each player more interesting by letting the individual perform a variety of tasks.

Multiskilled teams are extremely difficult to implement if the individual tasks or jobs are complex and demanding. Let me give you an example of this from personal experience. I spent a number of years as a director of human resource management in several organizations. At one time, there was a major push to create "generalists"—personnel specialists who were actually proficient in several different specialties. With no exceptions that I know of, all of these attempts failed. Under the best of conditions, it probably takes five years or more to create a personnelist who is just barely competent in even three different specialties. Nothing stays stable for that long.

Where do you draw the line? That's not an easy question, and I don't know a clear answer to it.

There's a problem with multifunctional teams as well. Individuals from different occupational backgrounds develop their own vocabularies, their own way of looking at the world, their own standards for what to do and how to do it. Just putting players from different backgrounds together on a multifunctional team doesn't overcome any of these differences. In fact, unless the organization carefully supports them and the teams are ready for hard work, multifunctional teams probably fall apart faster than any other type of team.

One answer to this problem, of course, is to begin with just a few different specialties. The Receivable Management Services of Dun and Bradstreet established five-person teams: an account manager, three sales people and a support person. For them, this was a major change in operations, and it paid major dividends: their initial team produced business volume, revenues and sales of other products above initial objectives within four months.[66] Perhaps your organization has the opportunity to make similar gains by combining just two or three normally separate functions on one team.

It certainly helps to have help from a skilled consultant, even when few different functions are involved. Getting players from different functions to work together continually is a significant change for any firm, and you want someone experienced to help you make the change successfully.

There's a final lesson I'd take from this and the previous section: the kind of teampower you use must be carefully chosen to fit your organization. Many firms have gotten into serious trouble and had to abandon promising teampower experiments because they decided on the type of empowered teams to implement without looking carefully at their workforce, technology, organization and mission. Remember, you're not implementing teampower just to have teams. You're implementing it to increase quality and productivity, reduce cycle time, and promote worker commitment and competence. Keep your eye clearly on your goals and choose the form of teampower that best supports them.

WHAT IF YOU'RE UNIONIZED? _____

There's no question that implementing teams in a unionized environment is different from creating them in a nonunion organization. On first blush, it seems to make the problem significantly more difficult. Sometimes it can. Some union leaders want nothing to do with empowerment and worker responsibility. One union leader described teampower this way: "You work as a team, rat on each other, and lose control of your destiny." Another said simply, "We don't think there's any benefit to cooperation. No way will we ever take part."[67]

Even when unions are willing to consider supporting teampower, though, established craft practices may pose significant problems. When Globe Metallurgical, Inc., wanted to move toward flexible, multiskilled workers, they ran into rigid work rules that posed a serious problem. "Under the union contract, the supplier down the road couldn't unload a delivery of wood chips directly into the bucket elevator that fed the furnace. Only a union member could do so. That meant Globe needed to have a front-end loader and someone to man it, and someone else to maintain it.

The person who operated the front-end loader couldn't drive a fork truck. A foreman couldn't help out a furnace tapper. And so on. As a result, often people sat around with nothing to do."[68]

If you're facing this kind of situation, it may make converting to teampower an even longer and more demanding process—but it won't make it impossible. Many of the firms that have used teampower successfully are highly unionized. Not all of them enjoyed good work relationships with their unions when they began, either. But both management and union saw the benefits in teampower, and they found ways of working together.

We saw just above how restrictive the union rules were at one of the Globe Metallurgical plants. What happened when the company set out to change the situation? It was tough for a while, with a lot of conflict. But the situation did change. Now, Vice-President Kenneth E. Leach of Globe is often asked whether there's a difference between two of the company's plants in Ohio—one that had been unionized but is now nonunion and a second that is still unionized. If anything, he says, the work force that is still unionized is the more involved of the two.[69]

The key here, as in so much else, is integrity and honesty on both sides. Chapter 9 stressed the necessity of trust, and certainly this is true in spades when we're talking of union-management relations. If these relations have been adversarial, building the necessary trust takes time and good will on both sides. But, as firm after firm has proven, it can be done. Some of the strongest supporters of effective teampower in the U.S. today are unions—such as the UAW, which has participated with both Ford and GM in major teampower initiatives.

HOW DO YOU REWARD THE PLAYERS? _____

If you look back at Chapter 2, you'll see that one of the characteristics of a successful team is that rewards are provided for team—and not just individual—accomplishment. Stated that way, the problem sounds simple. It is not. Many organizations that have been using teampower effectively for several years haven't yet found a full answer to the problem.

The problem is most serious in the area of selfmanaging teams, but it's not limited to them. Here's a quick sample of how the problem arises on other types of teams:

1. *Quality teams* are generally part-time assignments for workers, often no more than an hour or two a week—yet they produce valuable solutions to quality and productivity problems. How do you reward what the team does? In many firms, their contributions are recognized through the suggestion system (which appears to be the way that most Japanese firms handle the problem). That's a good approach, particularly at the beginning, but only if you have an effective suggestion system. If you don't, you'll need to develop a substitute for it quickly.

2. *Task forces* can present even more serious problems for recognition—especially if they're short-lived. If your organization uses bonuses or similar money rewards for one-time performance achievements, they can be used for the task force. There's an even more effective form of reward, though: making service on effective task forces a definite career-enhancing step. Please note that what you want to reward is not *individual* success on the task force; that's part of the individually oriented reward system that handicaps effective team performance. Everyone should understand that what counts is being part of a successful *team*. Once this is clear, the organization can make service on effective task forces or project teams part of the career ladder at a variety of levels.

3. *Multiskilled teams* have perhaps the clearest integration of individual and team rewards, at least on one level. Many firms that use multiskilled teams also use "skills-based pay." In this system, a player starts at an entry rate and then receives a pay raise for each team skill he or she masters. If each member of the team can learn three to five skills (not unusual), that makes for a significant difference between the pay of an entry-level player and a fully qualified one. While this is an individual pay system, the person's income increases as his or her value to the team increases. There is a clear tie-in between individual and team performance. Skills-based pay, however, doesn't solve the question of how to reward the performance of the team as a whole. (More on that in just a bit.)

4. *Multifunctional teams* span a wide variety of levels and occu-

pations, so it's hard to say much about them in general. If you want a multifunctional team to be more than a gaggle of functional specialists each doing their own thing, you have to find a way to reward them for working together. At the same time, you have to see that each player speaks up for his or her function's legitimate concerns. Need I mention that this isn't easy? In fact, this may be the form of teampower for which it's most difficult to work out a reward system. Most individuals on these teams actually have a divided loyalty. On the one hand, they have to participate as effective members of the team—which means they have to do more than just act like a functional specialist. On the other hand, they usually report to supervisors in their function—who generally care very much that they "stand up" for the function. If you want to make significant use of multifunctional teams, you need to work this problem early and often.

HOW TO REWARD EMPOWERED TEAMS AS TEAMS _____

Empowered teams are a major departure in the way most firms do business—and this is most true of self-managing teams. It shouldn't be surprising, then, that the pay systems for these teams are also very different from traditional pay. One researcher has summarized the characteristics of team-based pay this way:

> All systems designed to deliver team-based pay incentives are built on the same premises. First, they always have one or more explicitly stated unit- or firm-level performance goals that can be achieved only through teamwork. Second, a team-based incentive system always contains a reward component that is contingent on the successful achievement of these goals. Third, the reward must be perceived by the employee as resulting from contributions that he or she has made. Fourth, the reward must be perceived as a *fair* reward. And fifth, the behaviors promoted and the rewards offered must clearly signal what is meant by "good performance." This last premise is the most important one.[70]

A number of thorny choices are hiding within these five points. Here are a just three of them:

1. How much is pay fixed and how much does it depend on performance? In most organizations, team-based pay includes a set component and another component based on the team's performance. In du Pont's Achievement Sharing Program, for instance, an individual's pay can vary by as much as 20%, depending on the performance of the department.[71] At GM's Saturn plant, the same 20% of pay depends on a combination of quality, productivity and company profits (with quality the most important during the first year).[72]

2. Does the pay of each player on the team depend simply on the team's success, or also on his or her contribution to the team? If the latter, who decides? Many of the more advanced self-managing teams hire, rate and even fire members on their own; clearly, they have the savvy to pay their members differently for different performance if they choose to do so. Less experienced teams may not want to make these kinds of decisions.

3. How much of pay depends on the team's achievements and how much on the overall profitability of a higher-level of the organization or the firm itself? In du Pont, pay of team members varies with the overall profit performance of the department—but no team can influence more than a small part of this overall performance. Alternatively, do you pay the team on the basis of achieving its objectives, even if the higher-level organization does poorly?

Here's one final point—and it's at least as important as those above. Remember the fundamental premise in Chapter 1: teampower increases players' competence and commitment to customer satisfaction by increasing the challenge of their jobs, giving them more control over the jobs, and letting them work in a cooperative environment. None of these are money goals, and the pay system by itself can't produce them. However, if the pay system doesn't support them it will probably kill them.

In other words, the pay system must be *completely congruent* with these intrinsic motivations. If a player sees that he's doing more complex work with more control and more commitment, he expects the pay system to reward him accordingly. If this isn't the case, conflict is created. The individual may work harder and more skillfully for the same pay; he may simply drop back to is previous level of performance; or he may decide to go somewhere else— where they're willing to offer him challenging work *and* reward him for it.

This doesn't solve the problem of how to pay for teamwork. It does point out how critical it is that the pay system support the total 6C philosophy if teampower is to succeed.

HOW TO GET AND USE THE
INFORMATION YOU NEED

This is short, very general, and very important. Most organizations have information systems that collect basic performance data. Traditionally, these systems are oriented toward individual and/or department performance, and generally emphasize quantity rather than quality. This simply doesn't fit a teampower operation. If you want teampower to succeed, you need an information system that supports it. You have to have data that's usable by each team, and the data has to support quality as well as quantity.

The process of changing an established system is difficult at best. It's even more difficult when you're trying to implement empowered teams in a relatively small part of the organization. Most information systems are fixed at the corporate or, at a minimum, the department level. These higher levels may have no interest at all in changing their system for your convenience—at least not initially.

Here's where the ability of you and your teams to use personal computers may come in very handy. You can collect and analyze data manually, of course. It's much better, though, if you can put the data into a personal computer—probably into a spreadsheet— and have the computer do the analyzing and summarizing. However you do it, and even whether you use a computer, isn't the critical point. What you must do is find a way to collect and interpret the data in a way that your teams can use.

No matter how you get and use the data, one point is critical: The first players to see any report should be the ones responsible for the work reported on. In traditional organizations, reports are typically given to higher managers, to help them control the workers at lower levels. The production report on a unit, for example, is normally given not to the unit but to a manager one or two levels up. The unit finds out what its production has been only when the word on it comes done the line from above.

This won't work with empowered teams. The teams need to get the data on what they produce directly and as quickly as possible. There needs to be some way that this data gets to you and to higher levels, of course—but not before the team has seen it. The basic rule is that the data goes to the players responsible for using it; if you use empowered teams, they're responsible, and they get the data. Then, through formal briefings or some other device, they can present the data to you. If the data reveals problems, they can explain how they plan to solve them. If all this sounds too risky, at least see that they get the original of the data and you get a copy.

HOW TO DEAL WITH PLAYERS THAT
DON'T WANT TO BE TEAM PLAYERS _____

When you convert from work organized traditionally to work based on teampower, the change for you is no greater than that for the players on the team. Most of the well-known organizations that use fully self-managing teams started them from scratch. And they were very, very selective about whom they chose for their teams. GM recruited from 38 states to staff their Saturn plant. Corning interviewed 8,000 applicants in order to select 150 for their Blacksburg plant. Workers selected for Mazda's Flat Rock, Michigan plant—which uses the much more limited form of teampower the Japanese are used to—spend about 15 hours of their time in interviews and tests before the final hiring decision is made. Then Mazda hires only 4% of those initially interviewed.[73]

This kind of selectivity helps immensely. What happens, though, if you already have a workforce—and have to implement teampower with it? It doesn't make the task impossible, but it does make it more difficult. According to Randy Darcy, director of manufacturing for General Mills (which is investing heavily in teams), transforming an old plant can take several years vs. only a year to 18 months for a new plant.[74]

I'm not saying this to slow you down, just to help you be realistic. It's a good argument for starting slow, with quality teams and project teams. But it doesn't mean that you can't move directly to self-managing teams if the conditions are right for it.

You do need to accept that not everyone will make the transition from the traditional organization to a teampower organization. There will be both workers and managers who simply won't like the new arrangements. But there are steps you can take to ease the transition:

1. Don't start with the assumption that all the jobs need to be on teams. Remember, the reason for starting teams is to improve the productivity and quality of operations as well as the quality of work life for the players involved. This doesn't mean that everyone has to be a team player. There will still be jobs best performed by individuals, and nothing is gained by trying to force them into teams.

2. If possible, arrange things so that anyone who decides not to participate in teams can move to another, meaningful job. The job may be in a different part of the organization, where teampower isn't used or where there are many individual jobs left. There's another alternative, too. During the early stages of teampower, organizations need support positions to handle administration, supplies, and similar functions for the teams. As teams progress, more and more of these functions can be absorbed by them. Initially, though, it's a valid job for individuals who don't want to be on teams. After a while, some of these individuals will probably decide that teams aren't so bad—and want to join the movement.

3. Don't force players to become team members if they really don't want to. Perhaps more importantly, don't force them to become team players before they're ready. You want everyone to give it a try, but do that by encouraging them. Provide plenty of training, coaching and other support. Create situations where individuals succeed, not where they fail. Go slowly and deliberately, giving everyone concerned as much of a voice as practical. Keep a steady pressure on—but not to the point that people feel forced to become team members. Some will jump on the teampower bandwagon at first; they'll be your strongest resource. But many of those who hang back initially will also climb on board once they see that the system works.

4. When the process is going well, give those who're resisting a choice. You cannot carry them past a point. If they genuinely don't want to function on a team, and there's no appropriate support position for them, help them to move on. Some may be eligible to retire and want to do that. Others may have many good years left ahead of them; you can help them find jobs where they can continue to be productive and satisfied. But you do neither yourself nor them a favor by keeping them in makebelieve jobs where they're not producing.

5. Finally, you will get the greatest possible support for the new way of doing things if you include everyone as much as you can in the planning and execution. Try to give everyone his say, no matter how strongly opposed he may seem to the program. You need their input, even though you may not want to hear it just then. Listen to the critics; respond responsibly to them. Many of their arguments will be good ones; see that they're considered and, where appropriate, implemented. This takes time and patience, but you'll end up with the broadest possible support for the changes.

HOW TO DEAL WITH ILLITERACY AND INNUMERACY _____

Motorola is one of the pioneers in employee involvement and empowerment. When they started the process, a decade ago, they encountered some surprises. This is how William Wiggenhorn, Motorola's vice president for training and education, described what happened:

> Ten years ago, we hired people to perform set tasks and didn't ask them to do a lot of thinking. If a machine went down, workers raised their hands, and a troubleshooter came to fix it. . . . Ten years ago, most workers and some managers learned their jobs by observation, experience, and trial and error. When we did train people, we simply taught them new techniques on top of the basic math and communication skills we supposed they brought with them from school or college.

Then all the rules of manufacturing and competition

changed, and in our drive to change with them, we found we had to rewrite the rules of corporate training and education. We learned that line workers had to actually understand their work and their equipment, that senior management had to exemplify and reinforce new methods and skills if they were going to stick, that change had to be continuous and participative. . . .

Finally, just as we began to capitalize on the change we thought we were achieving, we discovered to our utter astonishment that much of our work force was illiterate. They couldn't read. They couldn't do simple arithmetic like percentages and fractions. At one plant, a supplier changed its packaging, and we found in the nick of time that our people were working by the color of the package, not by what it said.[75]

Motorola's experience is far from unique. When Ingersoll-Rand set out to modernize its Athens, Pennsylvania plant—creating the same kind of increased demands on workers as Motorola's changes did—they found that much of the training they had to provide was in basic reading, writing and arithmetic skills.[76] In *America's Choice: high skills or low wages*, the National Center on Education and the Economy reached this conclusion:

If this Commission is right, we are embarking on a third industrial revolution. This revolution will usher in new high performance work organizations that have higher skill requirements than exist today.

Our current adult training policies are illequipped to meet this challenge.[77]

Now you see one reason why Corning and GM and Mazda and the others are so selective in hiring: they have to be. Not all job applicants, whether experienced or inexperienced, have the reading, writing and arithmetic skills needed to support an effective teampower organization. These problems may be most pronounced in blue-collar work, but many lower-level white collar workers suffer from the same lack of skills and education.

You don't need to worry about Motorola's or Ingersoll-Rand's or the nation's problem with illiteracy and innumeracy. You do need to worry about the problem in your own organization. When workers are assigned routine work, told what to do in great detail, and then repeat the same steps day after day, education is largely irrelevant. Individuals with poor reading, writing and arithmetic skills can perform perfectly satisfactorily. But when work becomes challenging and under worker control, this is no longer true. Education—the education of the players in your organization—begins to matter very, very much.

I mention this so strongly to help you prepare yourself for what may be as much of a shock as Motorola experienced. The time to start working the problem is now, not when you're well into building teampower and are brought up short by the educational shortcomings of some key players. I have no solution to the problem, but I do have three suggestions:

1. Approach the problem very, very carefully. Most individuals with deficient reading, writing and math skills are very sensitive about their limitations. Launching a highly publicized literacy campaign may well alienate just the people you need to reach; after all, who but "boneheads" would need to learn to read or divide? Exercise great tact. One organization that has had reasonable success with a literacy program bills it as a "reading improvement" program and accepts individuals at any reading level. This presents some problems, but it also removes the stigma for those who participate.

2. Relate the skills specifically to the work to be done. You're not out to raise the reading level people as a good work, a contribution to the community (though it certainly is that). You're out to help players acquire *all* of the skills they need. Ingersoll-Rand combined basic literacy skills training with training in specific skills workers needed to operate the equipment on the floor. You'll probably be most successful if you do the same, as a single, overall approach to training players for the new organization.

3. Finally, get expert assistance in this. Your local high school and junior college systems probably have solid experience

in literacy and numeracy programs. Consult them. Talk to other companies who have implemented programs, so you can learn from their successes and failures. Contact your firm's training department, too, to see if they have experience with these programs. Even if they don't, they'll probably be willing to help you develop a program.

THE IMPORTANT POINT—TEAMPOWER WORKS

After a chapter stressing the challenges of teampower, you may be having second thoughts. In one sense, that's good. You want to go into a major change like this with both eyes open. But you don't want to let the challenges keep you from making a move that can increase quality, productivity, competence and commitment in your organization so dramatically.

The next chapter shows you how to make that move.

Chapter 11

How to Develop Self-Managing Teams

IT'S TIME TO USE WHAT YOU'VE LEARNED

In Chapter 10, I recommended strongly that you get help from an experienced consultant, internal or external, when you develop self-managing teams. I certainly mean that recommendation—but what do you do if you can't get a consultant, or you want to begin before one is available? This chapter will show you how to use the material in the first ten chapters to create self-managing teams. Even if you find a consultant, it will help you focus on the important steps at each stage.

Specifically, it will show you what you need to do to

1. prepare for a self-managing team, which involves choosing the goal to build the team around,

2. move to the first stage, a limited self-managing team,

3. move on to the next stage, a fully self-managing team,

4. and then determine whether to move to the final stage, a truly entrepreneurial team.

Let me add a word of caution before we begin. Chapter 2 listed the eight characteristics of a successful team. The first of these characteristics is this: All members of the team and the player who forms the team share values that support effective teamwork. Without this, any team will ultimately fail. To avoid this, make sure that the individuals you want on the team are at least open to this way of doing business. (It's even better, of course, if they're enthusiastic about it.)

When you're talking about self-managed teams, though, the shared values have to go higher than you and the team. Self-managed teams are a major change for any organization; you must have support if you're to succeed with them. If you have even minimal support from your boss, you can create a limited self-managing team. To move to a fully self-managing team, you need very strong support from your boss *and* probably from the next level up as well. If you want to go for broke and establish an entrepreneurial team, you'll need *strong* support from your boss and his or her boss, and at least agreement from the organization as a whole. No matter how enthusiastic you and your team members are, it's critically important not to outrun your support.

The players must also understand that becoming a self-managing team will be challenging. No matter how enthusiastic everyone is, there will be painfully discouraging times. You can't be sure that the players really share the values a team requires until everyone knows that it will be difficult and signs up with their eyes open.

(A quick note. This chapter talks about developing a single team. If you're a first-level manager, that's probably what you'll do. If you're at the second or third level, you may create several teams. The process is exactly the same; just put a mental "s" on the end of "team" as you read through the chapter.)

REMEMBER—LEADERS LEAD! _____

Let's go back to the basic purpose of this book for a moment. It's not about what team members need to do to create effective teams. It's not about changing the behavior of workers so they become effective team members. It's not about how to reorganize the entire firm around teams. All of these are important, but this book is about something else. It's about what *you* need to do to make empowered teams successful in your part of the world.

Please take this to heart. If you want to create winning teams, you must begin by changing how you see your role and how you act toward the players around you. There's a chart in a few pages that shows how your role changes as your workgroup becomes a more and more empowered team. This is the basic meaning in the chart for you:

> *Your role does not change after the change in the team occurs. Your role changes first—and that's what makes it possible for the team to form and grow.*

Back in Chapter 5, we looked very briefly at the seven roles a manager can play in a teampower environment. If you want to create an effective team, you do so by using these roles. And, as you'll see, you move from one role to another in a progression. You're a *supervisor* now. Creating teams means becoming a *leader*, a *teacher*, a *coach*—perhaps even a *mentor*, a *consultant*, and a *mediator*. If the role you play gets out of sync with the progress of the team, you'll become an obstacle to what you and the team want to accomplish. (If you don't remember just how the roles differ from one another, I'll summarize them for you a few pages from now.)

Remember, you start changing first; this is the way you lead the team effectively. As we go through the stages of team development, you'll see exactly what this means. First, though, we need to look at a very practical question: Just what is the basic purpose of the team?

WHAT GOAL DO YOU BUILD YOUR TEAM AROUND? _____

The first characteristic of a successful team is shared values. Characteristic #2 is that the members of the team have a common goal. This goal must also be worthwhile, something outside the team that the members can commit themselves to. The first action in creating a successful team is to find the goal to create the team around.

What is an appropriate goal? In general, people work together effectively as a team when they are united by a common *process*, *product* (or service), or *customer*. Let's take a quick look at each of these.

Processes

Individuals may share a common goal of operating and improving a process. Litel is an excellent example. When an order was received, it went into mailing and sorting, then into a group that screened it for proper information, then to another group that screened it for credit information, then to another group that keyed the orders into the computer system, and finally to a group that set the new customers up in the billing system. That was a very complex operation, with five different functions.

Litel discovered, however, that this was a single *process*. It took a customer order and turned it into customer service. The goal wasn't to get information about the customer, or to put him into the billing system. The goal was to get a customer on line, using Litel's services and satisfied with them. That's why teams were so successful there: Each team was responsible for the entire process for a group of customers. American Transtech also improved productivity dramatically when they focused on the customer-response process instead of its individual functions.

Every product or service is produced by a series of steps. It doesn't matter whether the work is "blue collar," "white collar," "pink collar," or "gold collar"—that series of steps is a *process*. Ordering, receiving and sending products to customers is a single process. So is picking, packing and shipping products from a warehouse shelf (which may be a process *within* the first process). So is creating, analyzing and filling a job and seeing that the incumbent receives initial training. Look for the processes in your organization. Wherever you have a complete process that (roughly) four to 15 players can manage, you have the potential for a self-managing team.

Products and Services

Instead of concentrating on the process, you might look at a product or service. American Transtech organized their teams around process, but they also organized them around a specific service: providing quick, accurate responses to customer requests. IBM and Sony organized project teams around specific products: computers. The products don't have to be final products; the gear assembly for a washing machine is a product, as is one of four sections of an annual report. The same with services. Paying bills promptly and accurately is a service.

Like a process, a product or service gives the team something to focus on. It feels a sense of completion: "We built another thirty quality widgets today." This lets it take ownership: "*We* built the widgets!" And it gives the team a customer they can produce for, talk with, get feedback from. That leads us naturally to the third way that teams can be focused.

Customers

Serving a real, live customer is a powerful motivator for many people. It's one thing if a customer comes to you this time but to someone else the next time. It's very different if you know that person or firm will be back to talk to you the next time they have a problem or want to purchase something. All of the team members, regardless of their specific duties, can focus on satisfying the customer.

Processes, products and services, and customers certainly aren't mutually exclusive. American Transtech is simultaneously organized around the process of producing a service for their customers. So is Litel. That's the ideal situation. If you have even one of the three focuses, though, you have the potential for an effective team.

This team doesn't have to be a self-managing team. Processes, products and services, and customers can be the focus of other types of teams. We'll return to this theme in a moment, after we look at the next requirement for a successful team.

HOW TO TELL IF YOU REALLY NEED A TEAM _____

Remember the third characteristic of a successful team: the members need each other to accomplish their goal. If individuals can do the job by themselves, without help from one another, they won't make an effective team.

American Transtech began with functional teams. Everyone on a team did the same job. Each individual in the telephone response function did just that. If he or she worked with anyone, it was someone on another team. The teams didn't really function as teams—and they didn't start doing so until Transtech reorganized into multifunctional teams. Once this happened, the individuals on each team realized they needed each other—and they began to function together as a true team.

WordPerfect's customer service people deal with customers individually, as do SAS's front-line service people. Federal Express uses teams, but they also use workers who perform individually with great initiative. Some work is simply performed better individually, or by a combination 'of individual workers and teams.

So don't make the fundamental mistake of deciding to use teams and then imposing them where individuals don't need each other to succeed. Look for a process, product or service, or customer that requires several individuals to work together to succeed. Then create the team.

Suppose you don't really have this situation? Then you probably can't create a true self-managing team. But you can create effective teams, in either of two ways:

1. *Project teams* are focused around products or services, and sometimes customers. Individuals who may not need each other to accomplish their daily tasks can still work together to accomplish a special project. They can plan a company picnic. Design a new office layout and select the best building to lease. Work out a new procedure for quick processing of capital expenditure requests. Develop a new sales or advertising campaign. The list is virtually endless.

2. *Quality teams* focus on processes. The Fixit Four at General Electric and the customer service people at WordPerfect all perform their daily work individually. But the Fixit Four formed a quality team to attack a common problem—excessive maintenance. And WordPerfect's teams work together to solve thorny customer-service problems. Though they're not formal quality teams, they perform essentially the same function.

Either on project teams or quality teams, individuals who otherwise work independently can work together to accomplish specific goals. These teams are valid, because they draw on the talents of all the team members. Though they're not fully self-managing, they allow individuals to develop solid team skills. Then, if the situation permits full-time teams, they already possess much of the competence they need.

(Those aren't just words, by the way. In my current organization, we can't use continuing teams on a day-in, day-out basis. Instead, we use highly self-managing project teams as often as we can. We also use very independent quality teams. How independent? I established a Quality Steering Committee of players at all levels except management. At their first meeting, I explained to them I'd help them as long as they wanted. After 20 minutes—literally—they told me they could go from there on their own. And they have! We also manage the organization with a management team that's rapidly becoming fully self-managing.)

In short, there is almost surely some way in which your workgroup can perform effectively as a team.

SHOULD THE TEAM BE MULTISKILLED OR MULTIFUNCTIONAL? _____

We looked at this choice in the last chapter. I don't want to repeat any of that material, except to remind you that's important to decide carefully whether to set up a multifunctional or a multiskilled team.

You have the greatest flexibility if the team is multiskilled, but this approach works well only when the skills required by each job are relatively limited. Most production jobs—both blue and white collar—can be organized into multiskilled teams. This is what happened, for instance, at both Litel Telecommunications and GM Saturn.

When individual jobs are more highly skilled to begin with, it's much easier and safer to let each member of the team perform what he or she knows best. The synergy comes from having players working with others who have different skills.

If you have any doubt what kind of team to create, start with a multifunctional team. If it turns out later that individuals can learn several skills, so much the better. But they won't have to deal with the problem of learning these extra skills at the same time they're learning how to function as a team.

THE THREE STAGES OF SELF-MANAGING TEAMS _____

"Self-managing" isn't an all-or-nothing situation. We've already seen that teams manage themselves to various degrees.

We've looked at teams called everything from "jointly managed teams" to "self-directing work teams." Now it's time to put that knowledge to work.

Firms don't jump from traditional work organization to fully self-managing teams overnight. In fact, they don't do it in one step. Instead, they make transitions from the existing situation to self-management. Think back to the 6C model in the front of the book. The goal of the whole movement toward self-managing teams is Competence and Commitment, focused on the Customer. We get it by increasing the Challenge, worker Control and Cooperation of the work. And all of this rests on the ability of each player to manage himself or herself.

If we put this into action, the task of setting up a self-managing team looks like this:

LOW   HIGH

————— Challenge of the Work   ——→
————— Player Control of Work   ——→
————— Player Cooperation   ——→
————— Self-Managing Ability   ——→

You successfully create self-managing teams by identifying progressive stages that can serve as targets. You don't try to move all of the way to a fully entrepreneurial team in one step. That's like trying to score a touchdown from your own one-yard-line in one play. Besides, neither you nor the team may want to move that far. Instead, you move one step at a time until you reach the level everyone (including your boss and the firm, remember) is comfortable with.

Fortunately, it's not too difficult to identify these stages. There are three basic stages of self-managing teams, plus a fourth, preparatory stage. Get a good grasp of these stages, communicate it to the other players, and make each stage the goal for the one before it. When you reach each goal, you and the team can evaluate your progress and decide whether to go on to the next stage. Here's a brief chart describing the four stages; then we'll look at them in detail.

STAGE	YOUR ROLE	TEAM RESPONSIBILITIES	TEAM SKILLS
Preparation	Supervisor & Leader	Normal work Help Identify goal Help plan transition	Basic team skills Basic problem-solving If a multiskilled team, learning each other's skills.
Limited SMT	Leader, Teacher & Coach	As above, plus Form team around process/product/customer Work process & product Customer satisfaction	As above, plus Advanced team skills Advanced problem-solving If a multifunctional team, learning about each other's skills
Fully SMT	Coach, Mentor & Consultant	As above, plus Personnel processes Customer & supplier relations Process coordination	As above, plus Traditional supervisory skills Administrative skills Some traditional management skills
True Entrepreneurial Team	Consultant & Mediator	As above, plus Strategic planning Full resource control	As above, plus More strategic management skills

HOW YOU FUNCTION AT EACH STAGE

It's not obvious from the chart, but there's a direct relationship between the way you exercise your managing functions and roles and the stage of team development:

- In the *preparation* stage, your ability to create and maintain trust (Managing Function #5) and create a learning environment (Function #4) are crucial. If you don't exercise these functions successfully, the team won't be able to get off the ground. You're also beginning to develop the team's problem-solving ability (Function #3), but you retain full responsibility for alignment and coordination (Functions #1 and #2).

At this stage you're still a *supervisor*, responsible for production, discipline, and personnel management. You begin to use another role, though—that of *leader*. Leaders provide a focus and vision for others, and move them toward that vision because that's where they want to go (not because they're forced). In other words, leaders lead by influence, not power.

- In the *limited self-managing* stage, the team begins to pick up some of the responsibility for maintaining trust and a learning environment. Now you focus on helping them develop their decision-making skills (Function #3). You still manage most of the alignment and coordination (Functions #1 and #2).

  You act occasionally as a supervisor at this level; the team isn't fully developed enough to take over all of that role. However, you're much more a leader and a *teacher*. As a teacher, you're responsible for helping players learn what they need to know to be self-managing. Some of this may happen in formal training classes—but even more will happen on the job. The more completely you help the team create a continuous learning environment, the more successful you'll be as a teacher. At this stage, you're also becoming something of a coach.

- In the *fully self-managing* stage, the team takes almost complete responsibility for maintaining trust and a learning environment, and for making almost all of its internal decisions. You're helping it learn how to create trust with other teams (Function #5) and how to make decisions jointly with them (Function #3). This means that they're beginning to pick up the management function of coordinating (Function #2).

  Now you almost never act as a supervisor, and the team takes over more and more of its own leadership. You're becoming a *coach*, working with them to pick up new skills and exercise the ones they have (i.e., managing continual learning). This is more of a background role than either leader or teacher; the focus is on the team itself, and you're in a helping and facilitating role. You're also beginning to become something of their mentor, using your experience to suggest to them how to handle difficult situations. Occasionally you function only as a consultant, providing suggestions only when they ask for them.

• If it reaches the *truly entrepreneurial* stage, the team now has complete responsibility for both its internal processes and its relationships with other teams. You're serving as a consultant to them, providing suggestions only at their request. Because you still retain most of the alignment responsibility, you're also a mediator between them and higher levels in the organization.

At this level, the team has no need for a supervisor or external leader. It has also become its own teacher, and seldom needs coaching. It does need an experienced consultant to whom it can go for advice and assistance in new and thorny areas. And it never outgrows its need for a *Mediator*, someone who insures that the team keeps itself in alignment with the overall goals of the organization.

We can put this into a simple chart that you and the other players can use to plan the team's development:

FUNCTION	WHO's RESPONSIBLE			
	PREPARA-TION	LIMITED SMT	FULLY SMT	ENTRE-PRENEUR-IAL
TRUST	Manager	Joint	Joint*	Team
LEARNING	Manager	Joint	Joint*	Team
DECISION-MAKING	Manager	Joint	Joint*	Team
COORDINATION	Manager	Manager	Joint	Team
ALIGNMENT	Manager	Manager	Manager	Joint

(*NOTE: In a limited SMT, you and the team jointly take responsibility for trust, continuous learning, and decision-making within the team. A fully SMT takes over responsibility for these internally. However, you and they jointly perform the functions where *relations with other teams or units are concerned*. In other words, you perform them jointly on a higher and more demanding level.)

Look at this chart and think about it carefully. It reemphasizes how important it is for your role and functions to fit the team's development. Think for a moment how much disruption could occur if this fit doesn't occur. If you hold on to all of the responsibilities yourself (i.e., remain a supervisor), the team can't assume them and grow. On the other hand, if you try to push responsibility for coordination off on the team while it's just learning to be self managing, you'll overwhelm it. Moving from one role to another is challenging, and often fun. Even more important, the success of the team depends on your ability to do so.

HOW TO EMPOWER YOURSELF AS
YOU EMPOWER YOUR TEAM

There's a final point I want to emphasize before we take up the nitty-gritty of team development. Think back to the Information Services Division of the City of Albuquerque. The division successfully created teams—but they did it at the expense of their first-level managers. I don't want to be critical of what they did; after all, I wasn't there. I do know that the manager of the division gave the managers reporting to him the chance to take the lead in implementing teams. My guess is that these managers saw teams as something threatening, something they wanted to avoid as long as possible.

Many organizations have gotten caught in this conflict. They've approached self-managing teams believing that first and second level managers were the problem. Their managers at these levels responded just as you would have expected—by fighting the change. This was a fatal and unnecessary mistake on everyone's part.

One of my basic reasons for writing this book is to help you *not* make that mistake. If you take the lead in creating self-managing teams, your organization will see clearly that you're *not* the problem. You'll have far more influence on what happens and how it happens. In fact, you may have the opportunity create your own place in the new organization. Whatever happens, you'll end up with responsibilities that will be more challenging and rewarding than your old management job. That's a perfectly legitimate goal for you. It's entirely proper for you want to empower yourself at the same time that you're empowering the other players concerned.

What if you're a second or third level manager with managers reporting to you? Take each word in the paragraphs above to heart. I don't think you want to alienate your managers and turn them into part of the problem. Start your team building with them. Be completely clear that you'll move to self-managing teams—and be equally clear about how they can fit into the new organization. Some may not be interested; find them jobs elsewhere in the organization if you can (look back at Chapter 10 for more on this). For the rest, put as much effort into empowering them as their workers.

Now, let's get down to where the rubber meets the road.

HOW TO PREPARE FOR SELF-MANAGING TEAMS _____

This and each of the next three sections is divided into three parts: *Where You Are*, *Where You Want to Be*, and *How to Get There*.

Where You Are

You're clearly the supervisor of your work unit (or units, if you're above the first level). If you're effective, you've delegated a great deal of responsibility to workers and lower-level managers. You may involve other individuals in joint decision-making. Most of your relationships with the people who report to you, though, are one-on-one. Some of your people may work together, but there's no strong sense of teamwork and most work is done individually. You have complete responsibility for work assignment and review, performance, discipline, and hiring. Workers are expected to perform their jobs and perhaps to suggest some improvements. You do most of the dealing with other workgroups and with higher levels of management.

Where You Want to Be

You're still the supervisor, but now you're also a leader—helping the work unit become a team by helping them focus and work together. Now they're used to cooperating with each other in a variety of projects. The trust level is higher; workers have less hesitation about asking each other for help. You're also creating a learning environment. Players use their new trust to surface and identify problems—to each other and to you. You're taking less responsibility for *making* your people perform and more for *helping* them perform. They're contributing more suggestions for improvement, and you're finding ways to implement most of them. You and your unit(s) have identified the processes, products or services, or customers that the team(s) will be formed around.

How to Get There

1. You begin the change by changing your role. You're still the supervisor, but now you change your emphasis; you start to become a leader. Your job here is to provide focus to the group and help it chart its new direction. You use your leadership role to help individual players begin to work together.

2. Leadership requires a growing level of trust. Read the material on creating and maintaining trust in Chapter 9 again carefully. Start immediately to build a workgroup in which everyone makes commitments carefully and then keeps them. (Note: introduce this as an improvement that will make work more successful for everyone—*not* as another boss-imposed requirement on them.)

3. At the same time, begin to build openness into the workgroup. Chapter 9 explains ways to do this; follow them. I also suggest that you try to find a training course for yourself in this, or at least find someone who's good at promoting openness to help you. (Again, don't impose a *requirement* for openness. As a leader, you take the initiative to be open yourself, and then encourage others to respond.)

4. Begin to develop continuous learning, as explained in Chapter 8. Continuous learning is directly related to openness— since openness thrives in an environment in which everyone is oriented toward learning rather than blaming (and vice versa). Master the techniques required to hold effective meetings. If you're developing a multiskilled team, having individuals learn each other's jobs is an excellent way to institute the continuous learning process.

(Let me add a parenthetical note. Introducing trust and continuous learning is no trivial matter. If you learn and use these two functions, you'll begin to change the reactions of your workgroup significantly. If you never go any further, you'll produce a significant improvement in your workgroup's performance and in your relations with them. Of all the managing functions, these two are the most powerful.)

5. At the same time, get your workgroup trained in group processes and group problem-solving methods. There may be training available in your organizations that was designed for quality teams. If there is, use it. If not, try to find another source. You also need to have these skills, if you don't already.

6. As soon as possible after everyone is trained, form a team with yourself as leader to explore how the workgroup can use teams. If there are several alternatives, you might want to set up several subteams—one to investigate each alternative. (This is another point at which you might want outside help. An experienced consultant can help you understand the different alternatives and select the best one.)

7. During this phase, start using project teams. One might plan the transition to a limited self-managing team. Another might work on an ongoing problem, such as the group's relationship with another unit. These teams might also work as quality teams, finding ways to improve their processes or safety or working conditions. Be careful, though, and don't try to create a limited self-managing team piecemeal. You're preparing to move toward teams, not trying to actually become one. Becoming one is the next step.

8. Recognize every success, small or large. You may still need to recognize individuals for individual accomplishments—but concentrate on recognizing teams and recognizing individuals for their contributions on teams. Help the players understand that effective teamwork is wanted and will be rewarded.

HOW TO MOVE TO A LIMITED SELF-MANAGING TEAM

At some point, you'll be satisfied that your workgroup has begun to learn the skills needed to work together. You and they will also have found how teams might be used to focus on processes, products or services, or customers. Everyone (or at least almost everyone) is ready to take the jump to a limited self-managing team.

At the end of the last section, I cautioned against trying to move gradually into a limited self-managing team. It's possible to do so, but it's not usually the most effective way. You're more apt to succeed if you pick a date (with the help of your workgroup) and begin operating as a limited self-managing team on that date.

Where You Are

You're still clearly the supervisor, but the organization is beginning to change. Individual players are working more closely together, on the job and in project or quality teams. Everyone, yourself included, has become more skillful at teamwork. There's a higher degree of trust, in part because individuals know they won't be criticized for honest mistakes. The tension level has dropped and the excitement level has risen. Most of the group is looking forward to taking the next step. You notice that productivity and quality have already begun to rise, and the morale of the workgroup is higher. Surprisingly, you find not only that you're listening more closely to other players but that they're listening more closely to you.

Where You Want to Be

Your workgroup has now moved beyond occasionally using teams and teamwork to becoming a team (though there may be some jobs still performed individually). The team is focused on a process, product or service, or customer—or a combination of them. The team takes responsibility for its processes, its products or services, and its customers. It's learning how to make the decisions necessary to do this. You function much more as an overall leader and a teacher than a supervisor. The team understands what it means to be constantly learning and how to maintain trust among the players. You still help with this, but they share more and more of the responsibility with you.

How to Get There

1. Again, start the process by changing your role. It's time to shed your role as supervisor almost completely. You're still

a leader—but now you're more a teacher and sometimes a coach. As a leader, you're still helping them see and move toward new goals. As a teacher, you're seeing that they develop the skills they need. And as a coach you're helping them put these skills to use.

2. Chapter 2 described the eight characteristics of a successful team. Go over them carefully, and go over them with the team. Work closely with the team to set goals (see Chapter 5) and decide how to measure your progress. Whenever you meet or exceed a goal, celebrate!

3. Here is where you really develop and use the skills of managing function #3—creating and supporting group decision-making processes. The function and the skills supporting it are described in Chapter 7. Part of this function is ensuring that the goals are challenging but attainable. Remember that teams develop decision-making skills best when they have self-confidence. They get self-confidence from setting and achieving worthwhile goals. (And then celebrating their achievement!)

4. Brainstorming or some other method for generating a variety of ideas will be important from now on. Help the team practice it (after getting training in it).

5. Use brainstorming and other idea-generating techniques to get everyone involved—and to see that the team begins to value everyone's ideas. You may have some natural leaders, or some individuals who are quicker or more creative than others. That's great, but don't let them monopolize the process.

6. One way to get everyone involved is to let the natural leaders and creative players share your leadership role. Explain that part of being a leader is getting and using everyone's ideas, and let them help you get each member contributing fully.

7. Teams don't learn to make decisions by consensus rapidly, but now is the time for them to start. As Chapter 7 explains, using conflict to achieve full consensus is the key team decision-making skill. Begin using some of the suggestions from this chapter now to help move the group toward consensus decision-making.

8. Be sure you're staying out in front of the group. This requires

skill; you need to have a real "feel" for where the team is and what it needs. While you may clearly lead at times, at other times you may turn this role over to someone else and serve for a while as a facilitator.

9. Here is where you begin to reach a real payoff for yourself. As you spend less and less time supervising the team, you're freeing yourself for higher-level work. You're still the one who coordinates your team with other teams or units (Function #2). This aspect of your job here is probably more challenging than it's ever been before—both because you have more time for it and because managing the boundaries with other teams is more demanding now than ever before. You'll also spend more time seeing that your team is aligned with higher-level goals (Function #1). Now you're really being a manager!

HOW TO MOVE ON TO A FULLY SELF-MANAGING TEAM

You may not want to move to this stage. The organization may not give you the freedom to do it. You may have too much turnover on the team, or you and the team may be comfortable with it operating in a limited self-managing mode. That's fine. Many organizations use teams that manage themselves only in limited ways; Litel Telecommunications is a good example of this. Just having made it to this stage is an achievement for you and the other players.

On the other hand, now that you and they have tasted what can be done with empowered teams, you may want to move on. The next stage is a fully self-managing team.

Where You Are

The team is functioning as a team. It's taken responsibility for managing and improving its processes. It deals directly with its customers, making sure that its products or services meet the quality, quantity and time standards agreed on. It may be dealing with suppliers as well, to be sure that it gets the agreed-on inputs from them. While you occasionally serve as leader, you share that role with other members of the team. Both you and the team see you as a teacher and a coach. The players are very open with one another and with you; problems and conflicts are surfaced and dealt with quickly. The team is now skillful enough to work through most of these without your direct intervention. You're spending more of your time in handling relations with other units and doing longer-range planning. While the team helps you, you're still responsible for hiring new players, evaluating individuals and the team, and resolving the most serious problems.

Where You Want to Be

Now the team has taken complete responsibility for itself. It hires new members. It appraises both its own performance and that of each individual. If performance or disciplinary situations arise, it takes care of them. With rare exceptions, and always at the request of the team, you help with the most difficult problems; you're not involved in the team's day-to-day operations. With your general guidance, the team does its own operational planning and manages its own budget. You're still involved in coordination with other units or teams, but other team members share this responsibility with you. You almost never give direct instructions to the team; you and the other players see your role much more as a coach, a mentor, and even as a consultant.

How to Get There

1. Once again, you help move the team by changing your roles to fit the new situation. Since the team will largely provide its own leadership, you leave the role of leader behind you. You still serve occasionally as a teacher, but the team is largely capable of learning on its own. You're still a coach, helping the team learn the skills they need. More and more, though, you're a mentor—intervening only when your skills and knowledge are directly relevant to a problem. And you're becoming a consultant to them, volunteering suggestions only when they ask.

2. A team becomes fully self-managing by taking over the responsibilities that supervisors perform in traditional organizations. They manage their own behavior and performance.

In part, this is an extension of the problem-solving skills they already have. They need additional training, though, in areas like performance assessment, budgeting and planning. They also need to actually perform these functions with you to coach them and help them through the tricky spots.

3. A fully self-managing team also takes over most of the responsibility for its relationships with other teams or units. Up to this point, you've exercised Function #2, coordinating, for the team. Now, you use the skills described in Chapter 6 to begin passing the function over to it. In particular, it takes custody of its suppliers and customers. This now goes beyond just providing customers an agreed-on product or service. Instead, the team works with customers to develop a continually better and more useful product. As a customer, it also works with suppliers to continually improve the usefulness of the product or service it receives from them.

4. As the team takes on responsibility for coordinating with other teams, it must develop its decision-making ability even further. And as it takes on responsibility for more and more of its internal operations, it needs to learn how to surface and resolve conflict in a greater variety of situations (i.e., over the performance of an individual player). Your role is that of coach, helping the team past the rough spots. You also help them become more and more proficient at learning on their own, so that even your role as a coach becomes less and less necessary.

5. The team is learning to celebrate its successes. As a coach and mentor, though, you ensure that they identify and use each occasion for celebration. It's still critical that they maintain their self-confidence in their abilities. Celebrating their successes is an important way that they do this.

6. Once again, you're staying out in front of the team, remaining as much as possible in your roles as coach, mentor (most of all), and consultant. Now you're becoming even more skillful at seeing where the team is and what you need to do to support it. Just as important, the team is becoming very skillful at this. More and more, they can tell you when they need assistance (and when they don't!)

7. As the team assumes more responsibility for itself, it's most important that you find a new role for yourself with your boss and your peers. It takes even less time now to manage your team. After all, that's what "self-managing" is designed to do. This frees you to pick up more challenging and rewarding duties for yourself. Hopefully you're a member of one or more higher-level teams. Perhaps you've taken on responsibility for a much larger number of teams. Whatever you're doing, it should give you the opportunity to manage alignment and coordination at a much higher level. Remember—and make sure your boss remembers—that in a truly empowering organization *everyone* is empowered. That includes you!

THE SKY'S THE LIMIT—
BUT DO YOU WANT ENTREPRENEURIAL TEAMS? _____

At this point in time, most organizations appear to stop with limited or fully self-managing teams. For instance, American Transtech's teams largely manage themselves but aren't currently moving beyond that. (As committed to constant evolution as Transtech is, though, this may no longer be true when the book is published.) When you reach this stage, you and the other players have accomplished much. The challenge, control and cooperation involved in the team's work has increased tremendously. So has its productivity and quality—and the satisfaction of its customers.

Something else has happened. The team is now responsible for a broader range of management duties than *you* began with. This means that, if the organization has been using you effectively, the challenge in your job has significantly increased. Your control of what you do and how you do should also have increased. And you should be working more cooperatively than ever before with your own peers. Not bad!

This doesn't have to be the end, though. There is yet another stage, one that's less clearly defined because fewer organizations use it. In this stage, the team becomes entrepreneurial. It operates as an internal contractor to the organization. It manages virtually every aspect of its operations. And it takes on much of the strategic responsibility for its future directions. While New Society Publishers isn't part of any larger organization, it's this kind of entrepreneurial team. That one reason why I included it in the examples.

Let's see how you get to this level. Be prepared, though. Because this is a very new level, it's much harder to spell out just what to do. I can only suggest the basic outlines. Besides, by the time you get ready to move to this level you and your team will have so much experience that you'll know more about how to get there than I do.

Where You Are

The team now manages itself. You coach them some as they coordinate with other teams and units, but they've largely taken over the responsibility for Function #2. Because the team is so competent, it often doesn't like to set boundaries on itself. They have to be set, though, and this is particularly where you serve as a coach for them. You've helped them build up trust with other units, and this makes managing the boundaries much easier. Now they've taken responsibility for maintaining this trust, just as they've taken responsibility for their own continual learning. They do their own operational planning and budgeting, and they handle all of the personnel responsibilities that managers like yourself used to perform. You're free to perform a much broader and more challenging set of management duties.

Where You Want to Be

Now the team is a fully entrepreneurial one. Having reached this stage, it becomes in reality an internal contractor to the rest of the firm. It negotiates what it will produce and what this will cost. It negotiates for its own supplies. It may even negotiate for "venture capital" from the rest of the firm so it can take on a new function. It still occasionally uses you as a mentor or consultant for the most difficult problems. For the most part, though, you serve as a mediator between the team and higher levels in the organization. Because the team is so independent, maintaining this alignment (Function #1) is critically important. You don't do it for the team; they don't *want* someone else to do it for them. But you work with the team and higher levels to see that alignment occurs. If the organization is heavily into entrepreneurial teams, you may be performing these duties for a number of teams.

How to Get There

1. If you want to help your team move to a fully entrepreneurial one, begin by making sure the organization is ready for it. An entrepreneurial team doesn't fit anywhere in the structure of a traditional organization. The organization might tolerate limited self-managing teams, and perhaps even fully self-managing ones. Making the final jump to entrepreneurial teams—well, that's a higher hurdle. You need really strong support all of the way up the line. Make sure you have it before you move out.

2. As always, you change your role to help lead the team to where it needs to go. If the team is truly entrepreneurial, managing the alignment between it and the rest of the organization (Function #1) may get tricky. Since you can't *tell* any of the parties what to do, you become expert at mediating between them. You're also available as a consultant to the team, offering advice only when it requests your assistance.

3. The team has learned the first three managing functions: how to create and maintain trust, how to operate in a continuous learning environment, and how to make effective team decisions. It has also developed skills at coordination. Now it must learn the basics of the remaining function, managing alignment (Function #1). If the team is going to share this managing function, it must learn to think strategically. You should have learned and must now pass on to them the skills at scanning the environment and seeing both the big picture and the details described in Chapter 5.

4. Remember that your team is already operating with a degree of competence well above that which they began. Even the most highly motivated team can only learn so much so fast. A team must maintain its self-confidence to make effective decisions. It must also be realistic about how much new responsibility it can take on in a given period of time. At some point, you may have run into problems from over self-confidence on the team's part. Be especially watchful for the problem at this level.

5. When the team became fully self-managing, the amount of time you devoted to it dropped sharply. When it becomes truly entrepreneurial, the amount of time you spend drops

sharply again. You'll mediate between it and higher levels, and perhaps consult with it on occasional problems. That's it. About the worst thing that can happen is for you to have nothing else to do, so that you start trying to find ways to "help" the team. At this level, the team needs help like a trumpet player needs hiccups. Moral: make sure you've been developing a role for yourself that provides you a challenging, rewarding job that doesn't involve spending a lot of time with any individual team.

SOME FINAL THOUGHTS

Keep in mind that every form of teampower is useful and worthwhile. A team doesn't have to become entrepreneurial or even fully self-managing to be effective. If you develop and use quality teams and project teams, you'll have done well for the team, the organization, and yourself. Don't let your workgroup get the idea that if they don't become fully self-managing or entrepreneurial they've somehow failed. (One way to keep them from getting this idea is to celebrate their successes regularly.)

Different teams progress at different rates. A highly motivated and skilled team in a supportive environment may move from conventional organization to a fully self-managing team in a matter of months. Others may take longer than that to learn limited self-management. It's important not to push or hold back a team's progress because of a fixed idea of the time frames. Again, celebrate the successes and build on them.

The distinction between limited and fully self-managing and entrepreneurial teams is useful, but arbitrary. The mix of responsibilities will vary, depending on you, the other players, and the organization. For instance, a team might start selecting its new members soon after it becomes a limited self-managing team— even though this is characteristic of a fully self-managing team. On the other hand, a team that's fully self-managing may be hesitant to appraise the performance of individuals. All of this is fine. Let the team grow at its own rate and in its own directions. One of your functions is to provide feedback to it when it seems to be overemphasizing one direction or underemphasizing another.

I mentioned in Chapter 10 that determining compensation for teams is almost always a thorny problem. Normally, this problem won't block the team's progress. But it may be a continuing annoyance. As the team moves from limited self managing to fully self managing to entrepreneurial, the problem may get more acute. The team's productivity has increased markedly from its level in the old organization—and it will want to be compensated for this productivity. If its members are paid for performance, they can easily earn more than other workers with supposedly much higher skill levels. I know of at least one very successful teambased project that was shut down a number of years ago specifically for this reason. Keep a weather eye out for this conflict and help the organization deal with it.

This is it; the book is done. I hope you're excited about empowered teams and ready to use them. If you are and you do, I can promise that there'll be problems and discouraging times. But they're nothing when compared to the rewards you, the team(s), and the organization will reap. There is currently no other form of organization that so effectively combines Challenge, worker Control and Cooperation to focus Competence and Commitment on the Customer.

Go for it!

Bibliography ==========

Baird, John E., Jr. and David R. Rittof. *Quality Circles Facilitator's Manual*. Prospect Heights, IL: Waveland Press, 1983.

Beatty, Richard W., H. John Bernardin, and James E. Nickel, eds. *The Productivity Sourcebook*. Amherst, Mass: Human Resources Development Press, 1987.

Blake, Robert R., Jane Srygley Mouton and Robert L. Allen. *Spectacular Teamwork: How to Develop the Leadership Skills for Team Success*. New York, NY: John Wiley, 1987.

Block, Peter. *The Empowered Manager: Positive Political Skills at Work*. San Francisco, CA: Jossey-Bass, 1988.

Boyett, Joseph H., and Henry P. Conn. *Workplace 2000: The Revolution Reshaping American Business*. New York, NY: E. P. Dutton, 1991.

Brewer, James H. J. Michael Ainsworth & George E. Wynne. *Power Management*. Englewood Cliffs, NJ: Prentice Hall, 1984).

Brightman, Harvey J. *Group Problem Solving: An Improved Managerial Approach*. Atlanta, GA: Georgia State University, 1988.

Buchholz, Steve and Thomas Roth. *Creating the High-Performance Team*. New York, NY: John Wiley & Sons, 1987.

Buzan, Tony. *Use Both Sides of Your Brain* (revised edition). New York, NY: E. P. Dutton, 1983.

Carr, Clay. *Front-Line Customer Service: 15 Keys to Customer Satisfaction*. New York, NY: John Wiley & Sons, 1990.

———. *The New Manager's Survival Manual: All the Skills You Need for Success*. New York, NY: John Wiley & Sons, 1989.

Chposky, James and Ted Leonsis. *Blue Magic: The People, Power and*

Politics Behind the IBM Personal Computer. New York, NY: Facts on File, 1988.

Cleland, David I., ed. *Matrix Management Systems Handbook.* New York, NY: Van Nostrand Reinhold, 1984.

Cohen, Allan R. and David L. Bradford, *Influence Without Authority,* New York, NY: John Wiley & Sons, 1990.

Cook, William J. "Ringing in Saturn," *U. S. News & World Report,* October 22, 1990, pp. 51-54.

Covey, Stephen R. *The Seven Habits of Highly Effective People.* New York, NY: Simon and Schuster, 1989.

Crocker, Olga, Cyril Chamey and Johnny Sik Leung Chiu. *Quality Circles: A guide to Participation and Productivity.* New York, NY: Facts on File, 1984.

Dickson, Paul. *The Future of the Workplace: The Coming Revolution in Jobs.* New York, NY: Weybright and Talley, 1975.

Dilenschneider, Robert L. *Power and Influence: Mastering the Art of Persuasion.* New York, NY: Prentice Hall Press, 1990.

Doody, Alton F. and Ron Bingaman. *Reinventing the Wheels: Ford's Spectacular Comeback.* Cambridge, Mass: Ballinger, 1988.

Family, V. 3, I. 3. Published by Mazda Motor of America.

Fisher, Roger and William Ury. *Getting to Yes: Negotiating Agreement Without Giving In.* Boston, Mass: Houghton Mifflin, 1981.

Fiske, Alan Page. *Structures of Social Life: The Four Elementary Forms of Human Relations.* New York, NY: The Free Press, 1991.

Fox, William M. *Effective Group Problem Solving: How to Broaden Participation, Improve Decision Making, and Increase Commitment to Action.* San Francisco, CA: Jossey-Bass, 1988.

Gabor, Andrea. *The Man Who Discovered Quality: How W. Edwards Deming Brought the Quality Revolution to America—the Stories of Ford, Xerox, and GM.* New York, NY: Times Books, 1990.

Gwynne, S. C. "The Right Stuff," *Time,* October 29, 1990, pp. 74-84.

Hackman, J. Richard, ed., *Groups That Work (and Those That Don't): Creating Conditions for Effective Teamwork.* San Francisco, CA: Jossey-Bass, 1990

Hampden-Turner, Charles. *Charting the Corporate Mind: Graphic Solutions to Business Conflicts.* New York, NY: The Free Press, 1990.

Hanna, David P. *Designing Organizations for High Performance.* Reading, Mass: Addison-Wesley, 1988.

Hasegawa, Keitaro, *Japanese Style Management: An Insider's Analysis.* Tokyo: Kodansha International, 1986.

Hersey, Paul and Kenneth H. Blanchard. *Management of Organizational Behavior: Utilizing Human Resources* (5th ed). Englewood Cliffs, NJ: Prentice Hall, 1988.

Hoerr, John. "Sharpening Minds for a Competitive Edge," *Business Week,* December 17, 1990, pp. 72-78

Jacobson, Gary and John Hillkirk. *Xerox: American Samurai.* New York, NY: Macmillan, 1986.

Johansen, Robert. *Groupware: Computer Support for Business Teams.* New York, NY: Free Press, 1988.

Karasek, Robert and Tores Theorell. *Healthy Work: Stress, Productivity, and the Reconstruction of Working Life.* New York, NY: Basic Books, 1990.

Keidel, Robert W. *Corporate Players: Designs for Working and Winning Together.* New York, NY: John Wiley & Sons, 1988.

Kelly, Mark. *The Adventures of a Self-Managing Team.* Raleigh, NC: Mark Kelly Books, 1990.

Kiechel, Walter, III. "The Art of the Corporate Task Force," in *Fortune* Magazine, January 28, 1991, pp. 104-105.

Kilman, Ralph H., Teresa Joyce Covin, and Associates. *Corporate Transformation: Revitalizing Organizations for a Competitive World.* San Francisco, CA: Jossey-Bass, 1989.

Kohn, Alfie. No Contest: *The Case Against Competition (Why We Lose in Our Race to Win).* Boston, Mass: Houghton Mifflin, 1986.

Kotter, John P. *A Force for Change: How Leadership Differs from Management.* New York, NY: The Free Press, 1990.

———. *The Leadership Factor.* New York, NY: The Free Press, 1988.

Kouzes, James M. and Barry Z. Posner. *The Leadership Challenge: How to Get Extraordinary Things done in Organizations.* San Francisco, CA: Jossey-Bass, 1987.

Larson, Carl E., and Frank M. J. LaFasto. *TeamWork: What Must Go Right/What Can Go Wrong.* Newbury Park, CA: Sage Books, 1989.

Lickert, Rensis. *New Patterns of Management*. New York, NY: McGraw-Hill, 1961.

McGregor, Douglas. *The Human Side of Enterprise*. New York, NY: McGraw-Hill, 1960.

Miller, William C. *The Creative Edge: Fostering Innovation Where You Work*. Reading, Mass: Addison-Wesley, 1987.

Mills, D. Quinn. *Rebirth of the Corporation*. New York, NY: John Wiley & Sons, 1991.

Mintzberg, Henry. *Structure in Fives: Designing Effective Organizations*. Englewood Cliffs, NJ: Prentice Hall, 1983.

Mizuno, Shigeru, editor. *Management for Quality Improvement: The 7 New QC Tools*. Cambridge, Mass: Productivity Press, 1988.

Morgan, Gareth. *Riding the Waves of Change: Developing Managerial Competencies for a Turbulent World*. San Francisco, CA: Jossey-Bass, 1988.

National Center on Education and the Economy *America's Choice: high skills or low wages!* Rochester, NY: 1990.

Nirenberg, Jesse S. *How to Sell Your Ideas*. New York, NY: McGraw-Hill, 1984.

Ohmae, Kenichi. *The Mind of the Strategist: Business Planning for Competitive Advantage*. New York: Viking Penguin, 1983.

Oncken, William. *Managing Management Time*. Englewood Cliffs, NJ: Prentice Hall, 1986.

Ost, Edward J. "Team-Based Pay: New Wave Strategic Incentives, *Sloan Management Review*, Spring 1990, pp. 19-27.

Parker, Glenn M. *Team Players and Teamwork: The New Competitive Business Strategy*. San Francisco, CA: Jossey-Bass, 1990.

Peters, Tom and Robert H. Waterman, Jr. *In Search of Excellence: Lessons from America's Best-run Companies*. New York, NY: Warner, 1983 (paperback).

Peters, Tom and Nancy Austin. *A Passion for Excellence: The Leadership Difference*. New York, NY: Random House, 1985.

Peters, Tom. *Thriving on Chaos: Handbook for a Management Revolution*. New York, NY: Alfred A. Knopf, 1987.

Reid, Peter C. *Well Made in America: Lessons from Harley-Davidson on Being the Best*. New York, NY: McGraw-Hill, 1990.

Rettig, Marc. "Software Teams," in *Communications of the ACM,* October 1990, pp. 23-27

Schatz, Kenntth and Linda Schatz. *Managing by Influence.* Englewood Cliffs, NJ: Prentice Hall, 1986.

Scholtes, Peter R., and other contributors. *The Team Handbook.* Madison, WI: Joiner Associates, 1988

Schonberger, Richard J. *Building a Chain of Customers: Linking Business Functions to Create the World Class Company.* New York, NY: Free Press, 1990.

Schrage, Michael. *Shared Minds: The New Technologies of Collaboration.* New York, NY: Random House, 1990.

Senge, Peter M. *The Fifth Discipline: The Art & Practice of the Learning Organization.* New York, NY: Doubleday, 1990.

Shuster, H. David. *Teaming for Quality Improvement: A Process for Innovation and Consensus.* Englewood Cliffs, NJ: Prentice Hall, 1990.

Taylor, Frederick W. *The Principles of Scientific Management* (New York, NY: 1967—originally published in 1911).

Thompson, Philip C. *Quality Circles: How to Make Them Work in America.* New York, NY: AMACOM, 1982.

Townsend, Patrick L., *Commit to Quality (updated).* New York, NY: John Wiley & Sons, 1990.

Walton, Mary. *The Deming Management Method.* New York, NY: Dodd, Mead, 1986.

Walton, Mary. *Deming Management at Work.* New York, NY: Putnam's, 1990.

Walton, Richard E. "From Control to Commitment in the Workplace," *Harvard Business Review,* March-April, 1985, pp. 77-84

Waterman, Robert H. *The Renewal Factor: How the Best Get and Keep the Competitive Edge.* Toronto, Ont., CAN: Bantam, 1987.

Weisbord, Marvin R. *Productive Workplaces: Organizing and Managing for Dignity, Meaning, and Community.* San Francisco, Jossey-Bass, 1987.

Winkler, John. *"Bargaining" for Results.* New York, NY: Facts on File Publications, 1984.

Womack, James P., Daniel T. Jones and Daniel Roos, *The Machine*

That Changed the World. New York, NY: Rawson Associates, 1990.

Zuboff, Shoshana. *In the Age of the Smart Machine: the Future of Work and Power.* New York, NY: Basic Books: 1988.

Notes

1. Based on Gareth Morgan, *Creative Organization Theory* (Newbury, CA: Sage Publications, 1989), p. 129.

2. Drawn from John Hoerr, "Sharpening Minds for a Competitive Edge," *Business Week*, December 17, 1990, pp. 72–78. The other examples given at the beginning to this chapter (Xerox, Harley-Davidson, Gaines Dog Food, Proctor & Gamble, Saturn) are based on multiple sources—including conversations with individuals familiar with the operations.

3. The National Center on Education and the Economy, *America's Choice: High Skills or Low Wages!*, page 3.

4. *Family*, V. 3, I. 3. Published by Mazda Motors of America, page 6.

5. Walton, *Deming Management at Work*, p. 138. Worthington Industries (Worthington, OH) is another firm that expects its workers to meet regularly with their customers. (And note that it's *their*, not just Worthington's customers.)

6. Rosabeth Kanter, "Even Closer to the Customer," *Harvard Business Review*, January-February, 1991 pp. 9–10.

7. From a talk by David A. Nadler.

8. Which is why, as this book mentions several times, moving from work organized by simplification and routinization to self-managed teams *always* results in higher quality. (Shortly after I wrote those words, by the way, I read Womack, Jones & Roos *The Machine That Changed the World* (see bibliography). After five years and five million dollars, they also concluded that high quality and customer satisfaction just can't be achieved by traditional job fragmentation and routinization.)

9. Richard E. Walton, "From Control to Commitment in the Workplace," *Harvard Business Review*, Mar-Apr 1985.

10. Much of the material in this section has been adapted from or heavily influenced by Karasek and Theorell's excellent book *Healthy Work: Stress, Productivity, and the Reconstruction of Working Life*. I recommend this very strongly if you would like to follow up on my brief presentation of these ideas.

11. James Chposky and Ted Leonsis, *Blue Magic*, pp. 62–63.

12. Psychologists have found that control of one's life is critical for mental (and even physical) health. Two readable books that discuss this are Ellen J. Langer, *MindFullness* (Reading, MA: Addison-Wesley, 1989) and Shelley E. Taylor, *Positive Illusions* (New York, NY: Basic Books, 1989).

13. The effect of conditioning workers to accept passive jobs may be even scarier. In *Healthy Work,* pp. 54ff., Karasek and Theorell describe a study of workers in Sweden. The more passive their jobs were, the more passive the workers were in civic participation, recreation and other aspects of their life. This suggests that at least some workers may adapt to the passivity of their jobs by becoming more passive in everything. As the authors point out, the implications of this for a democracy are frightening.

14. John Seely Brown, "Research That Reinvents the Corporation," in the *Harvard Business Review*, January-February 1991, pp. 102–111.

15. See Karasek and Theorell, p. 9ff.

16. Quoted in Peter M. Senge, *The Fifth Discipline*, p. 236.

17. S. C. Gwynne, "The Right Stuff," *Time* Magazine, October 29, 1990, pp. 76–77. In their coverage of the Saturn plant, *U.S. News and World Report* described it as a "jointly managed operation" in which "nearly 3,000 union members and GM managers fully share decision making on every issue" (October 22, 1990, p. 51).

18. The accounts of Pat Carrigan's accomplishments are taken from Peters, *Thriving on Chaos*, p. 325, and D. Quinn Mills, *Rebirth of the Corporation*, pp. 73–75.

19. If you're familiar with the work of Kurt Lewin, the great social psychologist of the 30s, 40s, and 50s, you know that I'm using a minor variation of his force-field analysis here.

20. Many American firms have made the change under pressure from Japanese competitors, when the issue was clearly change or perish. Read *Well Made in America,* for instance, to see how Harley-Davidson changed, or any of the articles on the Saturn to see GM's dramatic change.

21. Carl E. Larson and Frank M. J. LaFasto, *TeamWork: What Must Go Right/What Can Go Wrong,* p. 27.

22. Marc Rettig, "Software Teams," in *Communications of the ACM,* October 1990 (V33N10), p. 23

23. Larson and LaFasto, pp. 33–34.

24. Peter R. Scholtes *et al, The Team Handbook,* p. 1–2.

25. Olga Crocker, Cyril Charney and Johnny Sik Leung Chiu, *Quality Circles: A Guide to Participation and Productivity,* p. 5.

26. You can find these estimates in a number of different sources. An excellent place to start is Tom Peters, *Thriving on Chaos,* Chapter C-2 (pp. 65ff).

27. See Womack, Jones & Roos, *The Machine That Changed the World,* p. 56 "[At Toyota City] the teams were given a set of assembly steps, their piece of the line, and told to work together on how best to perform the necessary operations."

28. Mary Walton, *Deming Management at Work,* p. 145.

29. Walton, *Deming Management at Work,* p. 100.

30. Richard J. Schonberger, *Building a Chain of Customers,* p. 3.

31. From information furnished in an interview with members of the team.

32. Edward E. Lawler, III and Susan Mohrman, "Quality Circles After the Fad," in Beatty, Bernardin and Nickel, *The Productivity Sourcebook,* pp. 197–202.

33. Louis Kraar, "25 Who Help the U.S. Win," in *Fortune* magazine, special issue *The New American Century,* Spring/Summer 1991, p. 35.

34. See Jacobson and Hillkirk, *American Samurai,* pp. 185–187.

35. See Andrea Gabor, *The Man Who Discovered Quality,* pp. 125ff.

36. *The Machine That Changed the World,* p. 114.

37. Described in William M. Fox, *Effective Group Problem Solving,* p. 109.

38. Quoted in Glenn M. Parker, *Team Players and Teamwork*. The original account was in "Copy Cats Worth Copying," *Management Solutions*, Jan. 1988, p. 28.

39. Quoted in Kelsey Menehan, "Excellence at Work: The Success Story of Fifty United States," a special advertising section in *Business Week*, January 28, 1991, pp. 77–91. The referenced study was conducted by William Maloney of The University of Michigan and James McFillen of Bowling Green State University.

40. Peters, *Thriving on Chaos*, pp. 167–170.

41. These six factors are very slightly adapted from the "High Performing System Workshop" originally designed by Herb Stokes. This is an exceptionally intense and effective workshop designed to introduce participants to effective team performance.

42. For a more detailed discussion of customer service teams, see Leonard L. Berry, Valerie A. Zeithaml and A. Prasuraman, "Five Imperatives for Improving Service Quality," in the *Sloan Management Review*, Summer 1990, pp. 29–38.

43. Taken from John Hoerr and Michael A. Pollock (with David E. Whiteside), "Management Discovers the Human Side of Automation," in *Business Week*, September 29, 1986, pp. 70–75.

44. Winkler, *"Bargaining" for Results*, p. 10.

45. Fisher and Ury, *Getting to Yes*, p. 4.

46. Although the word "influence" never appears in the title, and the authors tend to use "power" where I use "influence," one of the best analyses of influence, and particularly its unlimited nature, appears in Kouzes & Posner's book, *The Leadership Challenge*.

47. Geary A. Rummler and Alan P. Brache, "Managing the White Space," in *Training* Magazine, January 1991, p. 58.

48. *CompuServe* Magazine, February, 1991, p. 53.

49. See John P. Kotter, *A Force for Change*, pp. 92ff.

50. See Joseph H. Boyett and Henry P. Conn, *Workplace 2000*, pp. 185–186.

51. The material in these two paragraphs is adapted from a model of group development by George Charrier. This mod-

el is referenced in the first section of the Participant's Workbook for the HPS Workshop presented by Herb Stokes and his associates.

52. Peter J. Senge, *The Fifth Discipline*, p. 3.

53. Senge, p. 4.

54. Charles Hampden-Turner, *Charting the Corporate Mind*, p. 59. (The emphasis is in the original.)

55. See, for instance, Robert B. Reich, "Who Is Us?", in the *Harvard Business Review*, January-February 1990, pp. 53–64—and his further development of these themes in *The Work of Nations* (New York, NY: Alfred A. Knopf, 1991).

56. Anthony O. Putnam, "Managing Resistance," in Chip R. Bell and Leonard Nadler, *Clients & Consultants: Meeting and Exceeding Expectations*, 2nd edition (Houston, TX: Gulf, 1985), p. 191–199.

57. I'm indebted to Jeff Nelson of Jeffrey Nelson Associates for the stress on asking instead of telling whenever possible. As he puts it: If they can see what you're doing, ask them to describe it; if they can't see it, tell them.

58. Joseph Badaracco, Jr. and Richard R. Ellsworth, *Leadership and the Quest for Integrity* (Boston, MA: Harvard Business School Press, 1989), p. 88.

59. Jack R. Gibb, *Trust: A New View of Personal and Organizational Development* (Los Angeles: Guild of Tutors Press, 1978), p. 16.

60. Johansen, Robert. *Teleconferencing and Beyond: Communications in the Office of the Future* (New York, NY: McGraw-Hill, 1984), p. 71.

61. Robert T. Lund and John A. Hansen, *Keeping America at Work: Strategies for Employing the New Technologies* (New York, NY: John Wiley & Sons, 1986), p. 173.

62. James M. Kouzes and Barry Z. Posner. *The Leadership Challenge*, p. 147.

63. Berry, Zeithaml, and Parasuraman, "Five Imperatives for Improving Service Quality," in the *Sloan Management Review*, Summer 1990, p. 34.

64. Gloria Pearlstein, "Preston Trucking Shifts to Performance Management," *Performance and Instruction*, August 1989, p. 3.

65. An excellent book that uses sociotechnical system concepts is David P. Hanna's *Designing Organizations for High Performance*, which is listed in the bibliography.

66. As described in *Commitment Plus*, Vol. 4, No. 1, October 1988, p. 2.

67. The first statement is by John Brodie, President, United Paperworkers Local 448. The second is from Mike Mezo, president of USW Local 1010. Both were quoted in John Hoerr, "The Payoff from Teamwork," in *Business Week*, July 10, 1989, pp. 56–62. Union objections to teams are more generally summarized in Edward J. Ost, "Team-Based Pay: New Wave Strategic Incentives," *Sloan Management Review*, Spring 1990, pp. 19–27.

68. Walton, *Deming Management at Work*, p. 210.

69. Walton, *Deming Management at Work*, p. 211.

70. Ost, p. 19.

71. Ost, p. 22.

72. S. C. Gwynne, "The Right Stuff," p. 77.

73. *Family*, p. 6.

74. In Brian Dumaine, "Who Needs a Boss?," *Fortune* Magazine, May 7, 1990, p. 55.

75. William Wiggenhorn, "Motorola U: When Training Becomes an Education," in *Harvard Business Review*, July-August 1990.

76. James L. Sheedy, "Retooling Your Workers Along with Your Machines," in David Asman, editor, *The Wall Street Journal on Managing* (New York, NY: Doubleday, 1990), pp. 76–79.

77. *America's Choice: High Skills or Low Wages!*, p. 56.

Index ═══════════════════════════